Watersheds

Watersheds

Classic Cases in Environmental Ethics

LISA H. NEWTON
Fairfield University

CATHERINE K. DILLINGHAM

Wadsworth Publishing Company
A Division of Wadsworth, Inc.
Belmont, California

Philosophy Editor: Kenneth King
Editorial Assistant: Kristina Pappas
Production Editor: Karen Garrison
Print Buyer: Barbara Britton
Designer: Kaelin Chappell
Compositor: Brandon Carson
Cover Design: Kaelin Chappell
Cover Image: ©1993 The Metropolitan Museum of Art, Gift of Robert
W. de Forest, 1925. (25.173), Glass-Stained, American, AUTUMN
LANDSCAPE, Louis Comfort Tiffany
Printer: STC

*This book is printed on
acid-free recycled paper.*

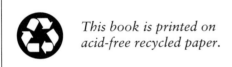

International Thomson Publishing
The trademark ITP is used under license.

Printed in the United States of America

1 2 3 4 5 6 7 8 9 10—98 97 96 95 94

Library of Congress Cataloging-in-Publication Data

Newton, Lisa H.,
    Watersheds: classic cases in environmental ethics / Lisa Newton, Catherine Dillingham.
    p.   cm.
    Includes bibliographical references.
    ISBN 0-534-21180-1
    1. Environmental ethics.   2. Environmental ethics—Case studies.
    I. Dillingham, Catherine.   II. Title.
GE42.N48   1993
179' .1—dc20   93-5619

To the land,
and to our grandchildren's future

Contents

Foreword   *xiii*

INTRODUCTION   *I*

The Nature of the Problem 1

CHAPTER 1   *TOXIN'S HALLOWEEN*   7
              The Story of Love Canal

Preface: Questions to Keep in Mind 7
Introduction 10
Background 11
The Event: The Site 13
Trouble Materializes 15
The Chemicals, the Illnesses, and the Tests 16
Legislation 18
Liability 20
Resettlement 22
Concluding Reflections 23
Questions for Discussion and Reflection 25

CHAPTER 2   *A CLOUD OF POISON*   29
              The Disaster at Bhopal

Preface: Questions to Keep in Mind 29
Bhopal and the Environment 30
The Story of a Disaster 30
The Incident: Union Carbide in India 31
The Chemistry of Disaster 32
A Factory in a Foreign Land 33
In Search of Safety 34

The Victims: Workers and Squatters 35
The Sequel: The Corporation's Response 37
Response and Frustration: Dealing with Indian
    Authorities 38
The Investigation, Within and Without 41
Accident or Sabotage? 42
Sorting Out the Demands for Compensation 44
The Incident Continues 46
The Poisons: Insects and People 48
Questions for Discussion and Reflection 51

CHAPTER 3   *CHERNOBYL*   *55*
             The Blast Heard 'Round the World

Preface: Questions to Keep in Mind 55
Chernobyl: The Event 56
The Experiment 59
The Causes and the Blame 61
Afterward: The Radioactive Aftermath 63
The Continuing Struggle 65
The Political Fallout 66
The Debate Proceeds 67
The Faustian Bargain 68
Hope for the Future 70
Since Chernobyl 71
Questions for Discussion and Reflection 72

CHAPTER 4   *OIL IN TROUBLED WATERS*   *77*
             The Wreck of the Exxon Valdez

Preface: Questions to Keep in Mind 77
Introductory Note on Responsibility 78
The Event: Ship Meets Reef 78
Prince William Sound: The End of Innocence 81
The Deadly Invasion of Oil 83
The Response: A Study in Dysfunction 84
Unpreparedness 85
The Phantom Consortium 86
The Awkwardness of Size 88
How Bureaucracy Affected the Animals 90
Systemic Disincentives 92
Appearance and Reality 93
The Effect of the Law 94

The Blame 95
Lessons About Oil 96
So That It Will Never Happen Again 100
Preservation of the Land 101
Energy 101
Questions for Discussion and Reflection 102
Appendix: The Valdez (Ceres) Principles 106

CHAPTER 5   *FORESTS OF THE NORTH COAST*   *107*
            The Owls, the Trees, and the Conflicts

Preface: Questions to Keep in Mind 107
Background: The Tragedy of Trees 108
The Owl and Its Trees 109
Endangerment and Obligations 111
Acting to Preserve the Species 112
The Tallest Trees on Earth 113
Pacific Lumber and the Logging Business 115
The Hostile Takeover 116
Trees, the Environment, and the Law 118
Government and the National Forests 120
Creative Alternatives 122
Summary 123
The Current State of the Controversy 124
Questions for Discussion and Reflection 126
Appendix and Apology: An Alphabet Soup
   for Our Time 129

CHAPTER 6   *THE DIVERSITY OF LIFE*   *135*
            Chico Mendes and the Amazonian Rainforest

Preface: Questions to Keep in Mind 135
Chico Mendes: The Man and His Heritage 136
Some Background on Brazil 137
Tropical Rainforests 139
The Threat to the Forest 140
The Role of International Agencies 142
A Global Recapitulation 143
Alternatives 144
The People and the Forest 145
A Worldwide Cause 146
Death Sentences 147
Preserving Biodiversity 149
Questions for Discussion and Reflection 150

CHAPTER 7   *THE HOLE IN THE MIDDLE*
OF THE AIR   *155*
The Depletion of the Ozone Layer

Preface: Questions to Keep in Mind 155
Background 156
Chlorofluorocarbons (CFCs) 156
History and Discovery of the Hole in
   the Ozone Layer 157
The Hole in the Ozone Layer 159
The Uncertain Chemistry of Ozone Depletion 161
Ozone Loss Since the First Hole 162
The Political Response 163
The Known, the Unknown, and the
   Meaning of It All 164
The Unknowns 166
Considerations of Justice 167
Questions for Discussion and Reflection 169

CHAPTER 8   *LIFE IN THE GREENHOUSE*   *173*
Scientists Confront a Changing Climate

Preface: Questions to Keep in Mind 173
On Not Really Knowing 173
Jim Hansen Blows the Whistle 174
The Greenhouse Effect 175
A Brief History of Our Climate 176
The Past as a Cracked Mirror 177
The Background of a Whistle-blower 177
Cassandra's Trail 179
The Scientists Call for Action 180
Complicating the Climate 181
Trying to Do Something About Global Warming 183
The Search for Solutions 184
The Politics and Progress of Global Warming 185
Continuing the Story 186
Questions for Discussion and Reflection 187

CHAPTER 9   *NORTH AGAINST SOUTH*   *191*
The UNCED Summit at Rio de Janeiro

Preface: Questions to Keep in Mind 191
Justice 192
Conferences 192

Goals 194
Warming Up: The "Prep Coms" 195
Sustainability: The Battle Is Joined 196
The Greenhouse Issue 198
The Biodiversity Issue 200
The Confrontation Continues 202
Summary: The Focal Treaties 203
The Bottom Line: The Lessons of Rio 206
Politics and National Interest 208
Questions for Discussion and Reflection 210

EPILOGUE 215
Summation and Portents

Environmentalism Turns Radical 217
Earth First! 219
The Wise Use Movement 221
The Environment as Military Hostage 224
Concluding Postscript on the Unscientific Method 227

Bibliography 231

Foreword

We would much rather read books than write them. The only good reason to write a textbook is you need something to teach with and there's nothing available or else the material is there in such scattered and inconvenient form that you can't use it for a large class. Such was the situation with the classic cases of environmental ethics—the "defining moments" when human technology trips over itself and sprawls into an ungainly heap of poisoned soil, polluted water, human injury, and death, with no one to explain it or to pay for it. In such moments, we can focus the student's wandering attention on the real problems of environmental complexity—the biological, economic, and legal issues underscored with the damage irrevocably done to real people and the land they depend upon. For our own purposes alone, then, we needed to assemble the snippets of newsprint that hold the information for these cases; from there, it was a short step to put the cases together in a book for our colleagues.

A case is just a story. We deal with theories in our classrooms, but we anchor our theories in stories, for if a theory cannot find illustration in the things that actually happen to us, the theory is bound for the dustheap. Stories are easy to remember, fun to talk about, and form the foundation of insight. With these classic stories, familiar to all, that insight is generalizable and good for the foreseeable future. Assembling them for practical use each semester has made our work as instructors considerably easier for us. We trust it will do the same for you.

We would like to thank our editor, Ken King, for his patience and helpful suggestions in the course of the preparation of this manuscript. We would also like to thank the reviewers for Wadsworth Publishing Company: John Ahrens, Hanover College; Susan J. Armstrong, Humboldt State University; Ned Hettinger, College of Charleston; Frederik Kaufman, Ithaca College; Donald Lee, University of New Mexico; and Louis P. Pojman, University of Mississippi; who gave us encouragement and constructive criticism on the chapters as they emerged. Above all, we gratefully acknowledge the help and support of our families (especially Victor Newton and Bruce Dillingham); without their forbearance and support, the completion of this project would not have been possible.

Lisa Newton
Catherine Dillingham

Watersheds

THE NATURE OF
THE PROBLEM

The natural world seems to be deteriorating around us, and it seems to be our fault. We are uncertain about the extent of the deterioration, the means of reversing it, and the prospects for human life in the future if those means are undertaken. We are not sure that we have the political will to pay what this would cost, and we strongly suspect that the costs may be unthinkably high.

This must be the best of times and the worst of times for environmental consciousness and conscience. On the positive side, our nation has never been more aware of the importance of an enlightened environmental policy. On all sides, alarming accounts of "environmental crisis" and "disaster" greet the eye and ear and demand some sort of response from us. Environmental organizations proliferate almost as fast as do the alarms in the headlines. We have just elected a Vice President for the United States who has written an excellent book (that is in itself worthy of note) on the relation between civilization and the natural environment, strongly urging protection of our remaining natural resources and wiser policies on energy use and consumption.

On the negative side, the confusion caused by all this change—all this new attention to something that has never really occupied our attention before—has muddied the debate. The very passion that newly converted environmentalists—or just alarmed citizens—bring to the discussion of environmental policy can work against effective action, by antagonizing quieter sorts of citizens and by encouraging cynicism when the worst predictions do not immediately come true. Attempts to produce good scientific proofs of the state of the environment, that will make sense to the public, run into the perpetual dilemma of popular science: When the projections are accurate and responsible, they tend to be misunderstood and distorted by press and politics; when they are simplified for a mass audience, they tend not to be strictly true and often cause alarm. That alarm itself is new: It is a type of formless apprehension that could define the century to come. We are frightened, and we do not know how frightened we should be; this is not the best condition in which to formulate policy.

So the first assignment for any work on the environment is to clarify questions, sort out fact from judgment and opinion, analyze terrors into workable tasks, and focus emotion through the lens of logic into practical policy. Since the time of Socrates, that happens to be the traditional assignment of the discipline of philosophy. The question that lies before the people, not just of the United States but of the world, concerns the search for moral imperatives: What is to be done? What are our duties in this new and confusing age—to ourselves, to our children, to other nations, to all living things, to the planet? What policies should we adopt to promote the greatest happiness of the greatest number of people in the long run? Must that happiness be balanced against the welfare of the biosphere? May we give the happiness of our own countrymen some special weight in the calculation? What type of humans will we have to be to carry these new imperatives into practice? While we work to change the relationship between our own very recently evolved civilization and a natural world that has been evolving over eons of time, how will we need to change our accounts of human virtue, aspiration, and self-realization?

These are the classic questions of ethics. The crises of the environment, the headline catastrophes, have posed new ethical questions, and those questions have spawned a new literature, indeed a whole new academic discipline. Although the first effect of any environmental catastrophe, accomplished or impending, is to throw all policy and prudence into question, the second effect is to throw all philosophy into question. Let us discuss these effects one at a time.

First, disaster demands reevaluation of all policies effective at the time. Decisions that seemed prudent and cost-effective at the time they were made—the decision to build a school over an old dump, to prune excess manpower from a little-used oil-spill response team, to defer maintenance on some backup safety systems at the chemical factory—these can suddenly seem terribly unwise or even criminally negligent. Our response is, appropriately, to develop more stringent and far-reaching policies, to introduce new probability calculations into business prudence, and, in effect, to transfer some of the costs of cleaning up a disaster to the safety preparations before it happens, hoping to avoid the majority of these costs entirely.

The debate (if so polite a word is appropriate to describe the aftermath of an environmental catastrophe) is centrally ethical, a debate on the appropriate balance between individual rights and the common good, between short-term and long-term benefit, and among the interests of all parties to the activity. We have a discipline, Applied Ethics, that encompasses all such ethical inquiries in practical issues; another new field of inquiry, Environmental Ethics, includes these ethical issues as they extend to take into account the interests of the biosphere itself.

Second, that last modification—the move to consider the interests of the environment for its own sake—raises conceptual problems that go beyond policy and prudence. The next effect of environmental catastrophe is philosophical inquiry, especially when the event is generalized to the ongoing catastrophe of the last days of the twentieth century: an end to all frontiers, the threat to the last wilderness, the incredible rate of consumption of nonrenewable resources, the depletion of the ozone layer, and the extinction of species. We always knew that we would make mistakes, that accidents would happen, and that humans might cause isolated disasters through carelessness or venality, but only recently has it occurred to us that our entire approach to the natural world could be a disaster in itself and a crime—not just imprudent but conceptually and morally wrong, like slavery. Perhaps humans should not treat Nature as something to be exploited without limit. Maybe Nature should be part of our community, like us, deserving respect and nurture rather than mindless use. We are beginning to realize that our resources are limited; it is even possible that they are not just *resources,* in the sense of material available for the taking. Perhaps we will need to learn to live as part of all life, subordinate to the natural workings of the natural world that sustains us, if we are to continue to live at all.

This philosophical doubt on the environmental front has occasioned some genuinely original inquiry. One of the most interesting movements in philosophy since the dawn of this newer, more acute, environmental consciousness, has been "ecofeminism," a fusion of environmentalism with feminism that distinguishes approaches based on *life taking* (the exploitation of resources) from those based on *life giving* (partnership with Nature) and argues for the superiority of the latter. Another interesting movement identifies all living matter as part of the biosphere (occasionally personalized as "Gaia"), a nurturing, life-giving superorganism, within which we live, and which alone allows us to flourish as fully realized people.

Whatever destroys this organism, destroys humanity; as long as we continue to imagine Nature as something to be commandeered to our purposes and to conceive of living organisms other than ourselves as mere objects, the destruction will continue; therefore, the human imperative for survival demands a total revision of our uses of nature and of our conception of the natural world. This organic approach is one of several that presently form the "deep ecology" movement.

The field of philosophy has expanded, very recently, to include careful treatments of the new philosophical approaches to the natural environment.[1] For this reason alone, these developments in philosophy, fascinating as they are, will receive very little attention in this book. Beyond the superfluity of one more theoretical analysis, when the thick mousse of oil is spreading toward the pristine beaches of Prince William Sound, it matters very little whether we approach the problems created by the spill from the perspective of ecofeminism or deep ecology, or (for that matter) from Kantian or utilitarian perspectives. Sound policy is needed—policy that brings the costs of predictable malfunctions forward into the making of the economic arrangements in the first place—and rigorous enforcement of that policy. It should be noted that, in the course of developing that policy, however, we will have to go deeper than the immediate surface causes of the incident that has focused our attention, to examine the political and economic practices that made it inevitable. These inquiries can be penetrating, even radical: For example, to develop a policy that will be effective in preventing oil spills, we must reexamine our entire pattern of energy use, extraction, and transport, giving special attention to our fondness for the private automobile. To develop a policy that will prevent the destruction of the ancient groves of trees in the Pacific Northwest, we might have to bring into question the whole institution of private land ownership.

Nothing should prevent either the student or instructor from going beyond the concerns of public ethics raised by these cases to fundamental considerations of the deeper philosophical issues mentioned above—the moral and metaphysical status of Nature and its relation to the humans that temporarily inhabit the Earth. Attempts to deal directly with the distortions of our national and international life caused by short-sighted energy policies will not be helped by bouncing the problem back to the conceptual level; indeed, such attempts might be significantly hindered by such redirection. Ultimately, though, we will have to engage in just such reconceptualization. As Vice President Al Gore said in his best-selling book, *Earth in the Balance,*

> The strategic nature of the threat now posed *by* human civilization to the global environment and the strategic nature of the threat *to* human civilization now posed by changes in the global environment present us with ... challenges and false hopes. Some argue that a new ultimate technology, whether nuclear power or genetic engineering,

will solve the problem. Others hold that only a drastic reduction of our reliance on technology can improve the conditions of life—a simplistic notion at best. But the real solution will be found in reinventing and finally healing the relationship between civilization and the earth.[2]

THE RATIONALE OF THIS BOOK

Al Gore's formulation raises the most serious aspect of the environmental crisis. We can be very good at developing new technologies, or at least new wrinkles on existing technologies, but therein lies the problem: We have never thought of the Earth as anything but the raw materials for our technologies, and we are a total failure at reinventing and healing relationships—in our families, our communities, our nation, and between the peoples of the world. Adding the planet Earth to our list of failed relationships only takes us farther out of our depth. The question is not yet how to *solve* the problem of the environment, but how to get a handle on it, how to think about it, how to begin to comprehend its complexity.

This book begins at that point. Faced with global dilemmas of indescribable complexity that do not demand new gadgets to solve immediate problems but new ways of relating to the globe itself, we look for microcosms in which the dilemmas can be faithfully reproduced within a limited time and place and thus easier to grasp. Each one of the cases in this book is a "defining moment," in Al Gore's formulation, that "focuses media coverage and political attention, not only on the environment itself, but also on the larger problems for which it is a metaphor ..."[3]

Whenever we debate environmental problems on the global level, we find we cannot agree on anything—neither on the facts nor the prospects for the future nor the ethical and political principles that should govern any solution. But with concrete cases (Love Canal, for example, or the Exxon Valdez, or the gas explosion at Bhopal), we can reach certain very basic agreements—at least, that whatever happened is unfortunate and should not be allowed to happen again in the future—and we can use that agreement as the foundation for further explorations of the issues. If nothing else, a knowledge of the headline cases—the cocktail-party conversation cases, those that are broadly known—can supply a common currency for an ongoing discussion, at whatever level.

This book aims to be useful for a variety of purposes, academic and otherwise. It is primarily designed as a supplement to all college and graduate-level courses in Environmental Ethics, Business Ethics, Ecology, Environmental Law, Social and Legal Environment of Business, Energy and the Environment, or Environmental Economics. Five or six academic departments are represented right there: Perhaps these cases will prove sufficiently interesting to extend that range. These stories are not, after all, the private property of any academic elite or approach. They are, for better or worse, the property of us all, as unwitting and unwilling indirect agents of their occurrence and along with our children, as heirs of their consequences. We had best get to know them well.

NOTES ON THE TEXT

We have tried to keep all chapters to a length that is convenient for reading and discussing in the course of a single class assignment, prefaced by some questions to focus the student's attention as the chapter is read and concluding with questions for reflection and with a synthesis of the material, to encourage more general insights on ethics and the environment. A short list of books and articles for further reading ends each chapter. A more complete bibliography can be found after the Epilogue.

Notes

1. See Bibliography. One excellent introduction to this literature is a fine collection of essays edited by Peter List entitled *Radical Environmentalism* (Belmont, Calif.: Wadsworth, 1993).

2. Al Gore, *Earth in the Balance* (Boston: Houghton Mifflin, 1992).

3. Cited in E. J. Dionne, Jr., "Big Oil Spill Leaves Its Mark on Politics of Environment," *The New York Times* (3 April 1989): p. A12.

CHAPTER I

Toxin's Halloween
The Story of Love Canal

PREFACE: QUESTIONS TO KEEP IN MIND

Risk

What is risk? What kinds of risk are acceptable, and why? What kinds are not? What role is played in my assessment of the acceptability of risk by (1) knowledge (for example, the known risk involved in rock climbing: I might fall to my death on the rocks below) and (2) voluntariness (yet I voluntarily undertake to engage in that risky activity)? Contrast, on both dimensions, the position of a homeowner living near Love Canal.

What risks, if any, should the community (state, government, or society) protect us from—not allow us to assume voluntarily? Why?

May the society as a whole (as opposed to an individual or individuals) voluntarily assume a risk? For instance, may it adopt a whole new technology, such as gene splicing or, as in this case, the fabrication of petrochemicals?

How do we measure *increased* risk from environmental hazard against a high-risk background (like the one chance in three we all have of getting cancer)?

Accountability and Blame

How do we assess blame in general? How do we assess blame for unforeseen events in particular? What constellation of factors suggests that the company ought to take the blame (and pay the price) for the incidents at Love Canal? What constellation of factors suggests that the public, in the form of the city (or New York State), ought to take the blame and pay the price for the cleanup?

The Media

What was the role of the mass media in the events at Love Canal? Does *the press* (including all forms of communications) ever have a duty to the public, with respect to the information it generates? Did it have such a duty in this case? Was it fulfilled?

Government

What role did government agencies (local, state, and federal) play in the incidents at Love Canal? Is there any way of discerning and preventing the pursuit of self-interest by government agencies? How might this self-interest have affected the outcome of these incidents?

Love Canal, the Event: A Chronology[1]

May, 1892: William T. Love plans to build a model industrial city. The technology of the time allows only for transmission of power by direct current, not economical over long distances, so the Niagara Falls region, rich in hydroelectric power, is ideal. Love starts to dig one of several planned canals, then is stymied by recession and the development of alternating current in 1894. Love eventually goes bankrupt.

April, 1942: Hooker Chemical acquires the property, gets the necessary permits, and in 1947 starts dumping wastes (ultimately 21,800 tons) into the old canal. So do several federal agencies, especially the Army: Clay lining provides an ideal spot for getting rid of toxic wastes where human beings will never be exposed to them.

1951: A housing development begins near the canal.

April, 1953: Hooker closes the dump and seals it with a clay cap. With the increase in population of young families in Niagara Falls in the 1950s, the Board of Education needs more land for schools, and asks Hooker Chemical to turn over the Love Canal area, which it does, under threat of seizure, for the sum of $1.

November, 1957: Public hearings are held on the use of ceded land.

Hooker issues warnings not to cut into clay cap because of danger from toxic wastes.

June, 1958: By this time, roads and sewers are cut through the Canal area, and homes are built. Children are burned after chemical exposure (probably to lindane). Hooker Chemical reissues warnings about waste.

1971–1977: The presence of chemicals in basements on school grounds is noted and mentioned publicly on occasion.

April, 1978: New York State restricts access to the area; buried chemicals are to be removed.

June, 1978: After two years of occasional articles in the media concerning the fears and odors of Love Canal, Michael Brown of the *Niagara Gazette* begins chronicling sick individuals who attribute their ills to Love Canal exposures; national media attention follows.

August, 1978: The New York State Commissioner of Health declares a health emergency at Love Canal and orders evacuation of some 20 families.

Governor Hugh Carey announces that the state will fund relocation of 236 families. The Love Canal Homeowners Association is formed.

President Jimmy Carter declares Love Canal a disaster area.

February, 1979: Dr. Beverly Paigen of the Roswell Park Memorial Institute in Buffalo urges further evacuations based on an in-depth study of several families living near the pollutants. A high incidence of hysterectomies, asthma, and mental instability was found in these families.

November, 1979: A federal report indicates that the odds of Love Canal residents contracting cancer "are as high as 1 in 10."

December, 1979: The Justice Department files a $124.5 million lawsuit against Hooker Chemical.

May 15, 1980: Dr. Dante Picciano, on commission from the Environmental Protection Agency, finds an elevated level of chromosome damage among families in the Love Canal area. This report is leaked to the media on May 17.

May 19, 1980: Dr. Steven Barron, on commission from the EPA, finds some peripheral nerve damage to Love Canal residents. Love Canal residents mob the streets and seize two EPA inspectors hostage. Homeowners Association President Lois Gibbs telephones the White House to describe the situation.

May 21, 1980: President Carter declares a state of emergency at Love Canal; 2,500 more residents are to be permanently relocated at an ultimate cost of about $30 million.

June, 1982: The first of 227 houses is demolished.

July, 1982: New York State Attorney General Robert Abrams says two studies show levels of dioxin in homes next to the canal were "among the highest ever found in the human environment."

EPA declares that homes at least a block and a half away from the canal are safe enough to live in; members of the panel originating the report differ on the conclusions.

May, 1983: Findings of chromosome damage are contradicted.

September, 1983: EPA finds new chemical leaks.

October, 1983: A lawsuit is brought by Love Canal residents against Occidental Petroleum, the City, the County, and the Board of Education; the suit is settled for $20 million.

December, 1984: A new clay cap is installed over the canal.

February, 1985: Former residents of Love Canal receive settlement shares averaging $14,000.

January, 1986: The cleaning of the sewer system begins.

October, 1987: EPA decides to burn all dioxin-contaminated soil taken from the area.

February, 1988: Judge John Curtin of the Federal District Court finds Occidental Petroleum liable for the cost of the cleanup, estimated at $250 million.

INTRODUCTION

For most Americans, the words "Love Canal" represent the emerging awareness that a price tag is attached to the conveniences provided by the chemical technology of our time. Love Canal was the warning trickle that became a flood of chemical stews in open pits, rusting steel drums leaking toxins, dirt roads sprayed with PCB-laden oil, radioactive and chemical contamination at nuclear weapons facilities, PCB-contaminated fish in the Hudson River, Vietnam veterans contaminated with Agent Orange, and—finally—an explosion of popular protest, manifest in legislation (Superfund) and the self-protective fear of local pollution that we came to call NIMBY (Not In My Back Yard).

After the first evacuation in 1978, Love Canal disappeared (temporarily) from the news—but not before entering our vocabulary as a universal designator of a new kind of evil. A recent *TIME* magazine article quotes the director of a Mexican research facility, speaking about mostly U.S.-owned industries on the Mexican border: "These are all Love Canals in the making."[2] A news report on June 24, 1991, referring to a toxic event, stated that it "might become another Love Canal." In a 1990 *Newsweek* article, Anne Underwood captured the significance of the events at the canal: "Love Canal became a national story, a byword, because it radicalized apparently ordinary people. Love Canal severed the bond between citizens and their city, their state, and their country. The battle...was fought in public, through protest marches and press releases, because the public, not the state, was at risk."[3]

From another perspective that emerges in sharper focus in retrospect, Love Canal has another significance. As Elizabeth Whelan pointed out,

> Love Canal...serves well as the focal point for an exposé of the questionable, indeed, immoral and dishonest tactics of those individuals who term themselves "environmentalists" but who are in fact mostly a group of anticorporation, antitechnology advocates. Love Canal is a classic story of half truths, distorted historical facts, unprecedented media exaggeration, and misguided government intervention, all of which caused substantially more human upset and misery than did even the most toxic of Hooker's chemicals.[4]

These two perspectives are clearly in conflict, but are not necessarily contradictory; both can be true and valuable. Public ethics is often best understood as the skill of making judgments without assigning blame. The following inquiry is an attempt to reach judgments that will help us understand both perspectives.

BACKGROUND

Petroleum was discovered in 1859. Soon after this discovery, it was found that petroleum could be separated by a distillation process (cracking) into various components, such as gasoline, kerosene, and other hydrocarbons. Kerosene soon replaced whale oil as fuel for lanterns. The other hydrocarbons included the olefins,[5] such as ethylene (CH_2CH_2), that became the feedstock for petrochemicals—from plastics to pesticides, synthetic drugs to synthetic fibers. In 1927, a combination of ethylene and benzene was found to produce another basic petrochemical, styrene. By 1937, the chemistry was worked out for connecting these individual basic molecules to each other in very long chains. Thus polymerization was born, bringing with it polyethylene, polystyrene, polyvinylchloride, and also thousands of new solvents, films, fibers, plastic, adhesives, and synthetic rubber products.

Petrochemicals began to dominate the chemical industry in 1920, but World War II first brought them into prominence. When natural rubber and silk were no longer available, the Allies turned to the chemical industry for synthetic rubber and nylon to provide tires and parachutes. They rediscovered the chlorinated hydrocarbon, Dichlorodiphenyltrichloroethane (DDT), which had been gathering dust on an English chemist's shelf, and used it to kill the anopheles mosquitoes that carried the malaria parasite. In the thirty years following World War II, the petrochemical industry expanded by a factor of 60.

Actually, 95 percent of synthetic organic chemicals are petrochemicals. The problem is that many of them are suspected of being toxic. Many are considered to be carcinogens, that is, substances associated with the onset of cancer, by the usual methods we employ to determine toxicity of various kinds through research on animals. Other petrochemicals seem to damage the nervous system, the liver, and other human organs and systems. Pesticides are clearly toxic and designed to be. Chemicals that are designed to kill might well kill other species than the targeted ones. The history of the harmful effects of DDT on wild birds, especially raptors, is well-known and parallels the histories of many other pesticides.[6] Hundreds of thousands of pesticide poisonings are estimated to occur each year; most of them affect agricultural workers in the Third World.[7] Yet pesticides make up only a small portion of the synthetic chemicals produced by the industry: Some 70,000 chemicals are used every day, and up to 1,000 new ones are added to the environment each year.

Once these chemicals, or those used to produce them, are discarded, a toxic waste site has been created. The word "toxic" is used because data, usually not data collected from research on human beings, suggest that some components of these chemicals do harm to those exposed to them. Unfortunately, hard scientific data on the vast majority of them is lacking. According to Sandra Postel, "the National Research Council estimates that no information on toxic effects is available for 79 percent of the more than 48,500 chemicals listed in EPA's inventory of toxic substances."[8] An estimated 229 chemicals have been disposed of in 546 toxic waste dumps, but 25 of these chemicals are responsible for two-thirds of the identified toxic waste "occurrences" (incidents in which toxic chemicals are brought to public notice because of some cause for alarm). Of these, eleven are chlorinated hydrocarbons, accepted as toxic; four are hydrocarbons (many of which are toxic); and seven are heavy metals (lead, cadmium, mercury), which are naturally occurring (as opposed to synthetic) but nevertheless generally toxic.[9] We do not yet know what sort of toxicity is created when these chemicals are mixed together in a dump.

In the midst of this toxic stew, we should note that "...epidemiological studies have shown very little evidence of a hazard to human health resulting from exposures to chemical disposal sites." The fear that drives people from their homes is primarily fear of the unknown: We simply have no data on the delayed effects of exposure to these chemicals.[10] Thus, no verdicts have been reached on many aspects of the toxic waste dilemma, as we shall see.

THE EVENT: THE SITE

There is no typical hazardous waste site. There is not even one accepted definition of a hazardous waste site. There are 20,000 sites being addressed by the EPA as part of the "Superfund" legislation, but these sites vary tremendously in terms of their geological, hydrological, ecological, physical, and chemical characteristics. The problem of hazardous waste disposal is too new (or, rather, too recently recognized) to have generated the research that will allow us to categorize the problem. The "failure of U.S. society to assess and manage the issue of hazardous waste"[11] is shown first and foremost in the failure to engage in basic research on site characteristics.

The 16-acre Love Canal site is located in Niagara Falls, New York. In 1892, William T. Love began the development of an industrial site along the canal that connected the Niagara River to Lake Ontario. Two years later, the project was dropped for lack of interest. The Hooker Chemical Company received permission to use the isolated, abandoned canal in 1942 and took it over in 1947. The company had complied with the few requirements that were necessary for waste disposal at that time.

The bottom of the canal consisted of a soil containing clay. Among natural soils, solid clay is the preferred liner for waste sites because it is virtually impermeable to water. (Because some chemicals will diffuse through it—a three-foot clay barrier will leak mobile chemicals in five years—most modern sites now use a mixture of clay and synthetic materials.) Was this natural clay lining cracked and permeable? Hooker Chemical certainly did not think so at the time the dumping began, but this became an issue in the legal arguments when the wrangling began. By 1952, the company had dumped 21,800 tons of chemical wastes into the site. Incidentally, Hooker was not the only source of chemicals in that dumpsite; several federal agencies, principally the Army, arranged with Hooker to dump residues of wartime production in the same spot. Meanwhile, residential building had begun nearby, as the city of Niagara Falls expanded outward. In 1953, the canal could accept no more waste, so the company covered it again with a cap of what they thought was solid clay.

Soon afterward, the expanding population in the area required more schools, so, in 1953, the company sold the site (reluctantly and under threat of condemnation) to the Niagara Falls Board of Education for $1. At that time, the School Board apparently wanted the site only for a playground, and that was fine with Hooker. They made sure to insert into the deed of sale a strong disclaimer regarding any injury to come from the wastes:

> Prior to the delivery of this instrument of conveyance, the grantee herein has been advised by the grantor that the premises above described have been filled, in whole or in part, to the present grade level thereof with waste products resulting from the manufacturing of chemicals by the grantor at its plant in the City of Niagara Falls, New York, and the grantee assumes all risk and liability incident to the use thereof. It is therefore understood and agreed that, *as a part of the consideration for this conveyance and as a condition thereof*, no claim, suit, action or demand of any nature whatsoever shall ever be made by the grantee, its successors or assigns, against the grantor, its successors or assigns, for injury to a person or persons, including death resulting therefrom, or loss of or damage to property caused by, in connection with or by reason of the presence of said industrial wastes. It is further agreed as a condition hereof that each subsequent conveyance of the aforesaid lands shall be made subject to the foregoing provisions and conditions.[12]

There matters stood for four years; then, the School Board decided to build on part of that site and sell the rest of it. A. W. Chambers of Hooker Chemical showed up at the hearings; his company, he said, was insistent that hazardous wastes were underground, and he conveyed their dire warnings about what might happen if the clay cap were pierced. The minutes of the School Board's meeting on November 7, 1957, indicate that Chambers was present at the meeting, specifically to warn about the dangers of disturbing the site of those buried chemicals. He conceded that the company had no further control over the use of the property, but strongly urged that none of the land be sold or used for building houses or other structures.

At the time that the School Board decided to build an elementary school on the site, it was clearly on notice that chemicals were buried there. Hooker Chemical had not told the School Board what the chemicals were, however, or to what extent they were toxic; nor did the company tell them what quantities of chemicals were buried there.[13] It is not clear whether company officials knew any of this information. A later review of the situation revealed quite an assemblage. When the contents of the dump were made public, there was clearly cause for alarm:

> What lay beneath the surface was 43.6 million pounds of 82 different chemical substances: oil, solvents and other manufacturing

residues. The mixture included benzene, a chemical known to cause leukemia and anemia; chloroform, a carcinogen that affects the nervous, respiratory and gastrointestinal systems; lindane, which causes convulsions and overproduction of white blood cells; trichloroethylene, a carcinogen that also attacks the nervous system, genes and the liver…The list of chemicals buried in the Love Canal seems endless, and the accompanying list of their acute and chronic effects on human beings reads like an encyclopedia of medical illness and abnormality.[14]

Trouble could be expected. Before any of this was known, an elementary school was built and house lots were sold. As early as 1958, children were getting burned from playing in the dump, probably from the pesticide lindane (Hooker had buried some 5,000 tons of it there), which surfaced in a cake-like form.[15]

TROUBLE MATERIALIZES

Sporadic appearances of chemicals from the dumps began in neighborhood basements during the 1970s—the chemicals leaching out of their graves after heavy rains like apparitions of spirits of industry on a ghastly chemical Halloween. Michael Brown documented in the *Niagara Gazette* the residents' complaints of chemical stench, dizziness, respiratory problems, and pets losing their fur.[16] In 1978, national publicity prompted both state and federal action. As the complaints continued, there appeared to be an increased incidence of breast cancer among the population.

What did the government agencies find in the schoolyard? Some 200 chemicals were identified on the grounds around the school that had been built over Hooker's protests: Benzene, a known carcinogen, was prominent among them and is credited for initiating government action. New York State began studies of the site to supplement the newspaper anecdotes prevalent at that time. An atmosphere of panic, however, is not ideal for scientific study. Before any actual studies were conducted Robert Whalan, New York State commissioner of health, declared an emergency and moved to evacuate about 20 families. On August 9, 1978, Governor Hugh Carey visited the site and declared that all 236 families living along the affected streets would be permanently relocated, at state expense. At that time, a new clay cap was placed over the old canal area. Then, residents of the houses just outside those evacuated by the state began to notice more and more ailments among themselves; Dr. Beverly Paigen, a biologist with the Roswell Park Memorial Institute in Buffalo, issued her own study of a few families and their ailments. Her evidence was largely anecdotal, but it triggered enough interest to bring the Environmental Protection Agency into the case.

Early in 1980, the EPA commissioned Dr. Dante Picciano to conduct a study on chromosome damage in the area; he claimed to find elevated damage. Hard on the heels of this study came another by Dr. Steven Barron on nerve damage among inhabitants of the Love Canal area; he also claimed to find elevated levels of damage. In the wake of these two reports, at a time of great tension, came a full-scale riot, in the course of which two EPA officials were taken hostage by the local Homeowners Association. Within days, President Jimmy Carter declared a state of emergency at Love Canal and announced the relocation of another 2,500 residents—temporary relocation, at a cost of $3–$5 million; then permanent relocation, at a cost of $30 million.

There are varying interpretations of these events. On the one hand, we can see an appropriate response, possibly a warm-up for more serious matters, in the way the public, the press, and the government worked together to address a situation that was certainly perceived to be dangerous. Between 1978 and 1980, federal, state, and local authorities worked with rare cooperation to get the people out of danger—goaded by the press and encouraged, to say the least, by local voluntary organizations. Government agencies had moved quickly and thoroughly, as before: The state closed the school and evacuated the families next to the canal; the presidential declaration provided funds for additional evacuations; the state recapped the canal and installed a drainage system that pumped any leaking material to a new treatment plant. Soon, the most contaminated houses were demolished, and the abandoned ones bought by New York State. By 1990, everything west of the street that bordered the canal, for one-quarter mile, had been buried and fenced off, and the state owned 789 single-family homes. The total cleanup costs were estimated at $250 million at that point.

On the other hand, there might have been no real danger. None of the studies has withstood scientific scrutiny—not Beverly Paigen's anecdotal study of epilepsy, mental illness, and reproductive difficulties (including miscarriages) in a few families; nor Dante Picciano's studies, which lacked controls; nor Steven Barron's study, which was admittedly a pilot study leaked to the press when the others became public. Perhaps a word about scientific testing is in order at this point.

THE CHEMICALS, THE ILLNESSES, AND THE TESTS

Determination of toxicity is difficult and expensive and, unless we start experimenting on humans, the results will always be controversial. The most common technique used to determine the toxicity of a chemical is animal testing, although there are also techniques that use bacteria and other organisms or tissues. The smaller the population tested and the less time taken to achieve significant results, the less expensive the test will be, so these tests are typically conducted on animals (frequently, white mice bred for genetic sameness), which are exposed to a much larger quantity of the chemical, over a much shorter period of time, than any human population would ever experience. The lethal dose to all, the lethal dose to half (LD_{50}), and the dose that causes no effect are recorded, and those figures are extrapolated to humans.

On the basis of such testing, we are prepared to say that many of the substances found at the Love Canal site—including benzene, dioxin, toluene, lindane, PCBs, chloroform, trichloroethylene, trichlorobenzene, and heavy metals—are certainly capable of causing harm; 13 of them are known carcinogens. Most of the chemicals found at the canal would be liquid at room temperature and soluble in water, increasing the chances of their migration away from the site. Also, chlorinated hydrocarbons are more dense than water, so they would sink and migrate toward groundwater.

It is difficult to prove cause and effect in these cases—to prove that exposure to a given chemical at a given time causes a specific symptom. To determine causality, it would be necessary to know the quantity of the chemical to which each sufferer was exposed and the duration of exposure for each individual within the exposed population. In addition, the findings should be repeated in a statistically significant number of exposed individuals, other causative factors must be ruled out, and the cause should make physiological sense. There were 200 chemicals at Love Canal and an exposed population that occupied about 800 homes. To separate each chemical and its related symptom from the others would be a monumental task and, given the number of chemicals involved, synergistic and antagonistic reactions cannot be ruled out.

No one has ever conducted a comprehensive study of the health effects purported to have resulted from chemical exposure at Love Canal. Of the less-than-comprehensive studies that *have* been done, however, those that attempted to connect the chemicals to the previously mentioned symptoms have not been accepted by the scientific community.

Many early accounts, those that first drew media attention to Love Canal, were informal surveys done by the residents themselves. Few governmental studies were done. Of the state and federal studies mentioned earlier, Paigen's results were anecdotal and impossible to interpret; Picciano's findings on chromosomal damage were the result of a study that lacked controls. A group of 17 scientists from the Centers for Disease Control, Brookhaven National Laboratory and Oak Ridge National Laboratory attempted a follow-up study on chromosome damage in 1983 and found that, if anything, the chromosomes of Love Canal residents were healthier than the norm.[17] As for the miscarriages, those results were specifically addressed by Dr. Nicholas Vianna of the New York State Department of Health:

> Efforts to establish a correlation between adverse pregnancy outcomes and evidence of chemical exposure have proven negative. Comprehensive studies of three households with unusually adverse reproductive histories did not produce evidence of unusual risk of chemical exposure...We have not yet been able to correlate the geographic distribution of adverse pregnancy outcomes with chemical evidence of exposure. At present, there is no direct evidence of a cause-effect relationship with chemicals from the canal.[18]

Meanwhile, anecdotal evidence continued to accumulate; included were stories of seizures, learning disabilities, eye and skin irritations, incontinence, abdominal pains, lung cancer, non-Hodgkins lymphoma, and leukemia. In children, birth defects, low birth weight, and hyperactivity were noted. One child from the area was born deaf with a cleft palate, deformed ears, a hole in the heart, and impaired learning abilities.

Such anecdotal evidence carries little weight in scientific circles. Even if it could be shown that the incidence of such ailments is statistically higher in the Love Canal area than elsewhere—and this has not been shown—no connection to exposure to the chemicals could be demonstrated. The residents, as might be expected, dismiss all denials of this type as politically motivated (like the Tobacco Institute's disclaimers on the link between smoking and cancer) and continue to insist that the New York State Department of Health (DOH) underestimated the health effects of the event. The DOH scientists, for their part, believe that the health effects were *overestimated* by unqualified independent investigators and that the second evacuation in 1980 was unnecessary.

There seems to be general agreement that the psychological toll on the residents has been immense. Any slight physical symptom becomes a cause for concern; as one former resident said, "It's like AIDS."

LEGISLATION

No one disputes that the publicity given to the symptoms reported by Love Canal residents and the eventual abandonment of the area was the driving force behind Congress' enactment of the Comprehensive Environmental Response, Compensation and Liability Act (CERCLA or "Superfund"), which was designed to assess liability for hazardous waste sites and clean them up. With this legislation, the EPA is empowered to sue the owner, or the dumper, for the cleanup costs; if the site is significant, the responsibility for payment is usually settled in court.

The other piece of legislation that controls hazardous waste is the Resource Conservation and Recovery Act (RCRA, 1976, 1984), which requires dumpers to obtain permits and to describe how the material will be treated before being dumped. It also requires "cradle-to-grave" reporting of waste, from origin to final disposal. This last requirement is generally acknowledged to be unenforceable, given the estimated 750,000 hazardous waste producers and 15,000 hazardous waste carriers.

In short, by the time the fallout from Love Canal had fallen out, the federal government, in general, and the EPA, in particular, were much more centrally situated in the lives of our neighborhoods than they had been before. Is that *why* the publicity happened?

Let us make the question a bit clearer. The actions taken by the EPA in this case are subject to two interpretations:

On the one hand, the EPA is charged with protecting the public from environmental dangers. When evidence came to their attention that an environmental hazard existed at Love Canal, the agency acted appropriately by commissioning studies and by cooperating with state and local agencies to act on the results of those studies. Indeed, the EPA acted before all the data were in, and scientific nitpickers might continue to find flaws in the research designs but, given that lives were apparently in danger, the inconclusive results—if only suggestive—were adequate basis for taking action.

On the other hand, any responsible public agency should have thought long and hard about the "panic factor" in such a situation. Any official action as extensive as this—including massive relocations and repossessions—is certain to cause fear and injury, if only to property values. Why did the EPA gamble on uncertain results? Hank Cox, writing for the *Regulatory Action Network,* suggests that

> [t]he answer may lie in EPA's awareness of the growing tide of public opinion opposed to excessive regulation and the agency's desire to deflect political pressure for reform. At the same time it was creating the Love Canal panic, the EPA came out with another report showing that there were an estimated 50,666 hazardous waste sites similar to that in Love Canal around the country, thereby laying the groundwork for [the creation of] a "superfund" to clean up this alleged danger to the American people.[19]

"Were EPA's actions at Love Canal self-serving, simply to stimulate more federal laws, activities, and, most important, budgetary revenues for itself?" wonders Elizabeth Whelan.[20] Superfund was a major triumph for an agency worried about its legitimacy. We tend to think of individuals as self-interested and corporations as profit-oriented, but government agencies can be as self-interested as private parties: In government, as in business, success is measured not simply by large salaries or prominence in the press, but by the extent of office space, number of secretaries, computers, rugs on the floor, number of staff—in short, by total budget. An agency will stay in business only as long as it finds work to do, dragons to slay, and maidens to save. Therefore, finding that the evil that the agency is set up to fight is really minimal right now will lead straight to budget cuts and layoffs. The detection of violations is in the hands of those who will prosper if violations exist and be off looking for a new job if there are none. A worrisome bias has been built into the system: The regulators are acting as judges in their own cause.

LIABILITY

Of course, there were (and are) lawsuits against the dumper. Let's for a moment review to see what a lawsuit would have to establish. Whether the suit is brought by a public or private party, the kind of negligence that is being alleged requires the establishment of four points:

1. that there was injury (someone got hurt—the plaintiff, generally)
2. that the defendant had a duty to the plaintiff that preexisted the injury, either under existing law governing that sort of conduct or just the common-law duty to exercise "due care" in all actions that might affect others
3. that the defendant breached that duty by some act or omission that figured in the injury
4. that, indeed, that act or omission was the proximate (nearest, most immediate) cause of the injury.

Accordingly, any defense against charges of negligence will argue that there was no injury, or that no duty existed between defendant and plaintiff, or that, if there had been a duty, then there was no breach (that is, the defendant obeyed the law, was within his or her rights, and exercised due care), or, finally, that so many other causative factors were present that the defendant's contribution could not possibly be sorted out from all the others.

Occidental Chemical, which had bought out Hooker Chemical in 1968, argued all of those things, and very cogently. They obviously could not argue that whatever had happened was Hooker's fault and Occidental was scot-free; in acquiring Hooker's assets, they also had acquired Hooker's liabilities. So Occidental was forced to argue that Hooker was not to blame for whatever damage had been done. They continued to claim that there were no documented health effects attributable to the leakage of chemicals from Love Canal, other than the dogs with chemical burns discovered in 1977. Psychological distress counts as an injury, of course—but again, only if the company was its proximate cause, and they could argue convincingly that the publicity, not the chemicals, had caused the distress. In any event, Occidental maintained that Hooker had been under no obligation of any kind to anyone regarding that site after the compulsory sale of the site to the City of Niagara Falls, especially given the disclaimers written into the deed of sale.

It is unclear what obligation companies have to people in general regarding the safe disposal of toxic wastes. That obligation is generally determined by the law at the time the wastes are dumped (the 1940s, in this case), added to the general duty of due care, which Occidental claimed was satisfied by the choice of an impermeable clay receptacle and the placement of an impermeable clay cap on the dump when it was full. They contended that the landfill had been perfectly secure when Hooker sold it, demonstrating good corporate citizenship by turning it over to the city without a fight and by warning city officials about the toxic chemicals buried there.

Finally, the event that disseminated the chemicals was the piercing of the clay cap when the school and neighboring houses were built in the canal area. Once the cap had been pierced, there was no longer any way to keep water from seeping into the dump; given that the floor of the canal was impermeable clay, the water could not get out except by overflowing the top, carrying all manner of dissolved chemicals along with it, just as Hooker had warned at the time of the sale. Surely, the company argued (argues), whatever did happen (and it is not clear that very much did happen, beyond a feeding frenzy for the press), the company is not to blame.

The courts have not favored Occidental's assessment of the case. Companies may decide to settle civil lawsuits for a variety of reasons, of course, but when Occidental settled a $20-million suit brought by the residents in 1983 (disbursing payments from $2,000 to $400,000), they must have foreseen a court decision going against them.[21] In February, 1988, Federal District Court Judge John T. Curtin found Occidental liable under CERCLA for all cleanup and resettlement costs, about $250 million.[22] (That amount may be appealed, but the judgment still stands.[23]) The State of New York, encouraged by that result, sued Occidental in the fall of 1990, asking another $250 million in punitive damages for "recklessly disregarding public health." The suit was brought despite the clause in the deed of sale from Hooker to the Board of Education that protected Hooker from liability; such clauses are not binding on third parties like New York State.

The state has brought new claims to this trial. In particular, the state claims that the landfill was never secure—that the canal bottom is really cracked and permeable, that sandy loam replaces clay halfway up the sides of the canal, and that the covering (cap) was nothing like impermeable clay. Hooker personnel have testified that they knew the cover was not secure and that they found the situation "scary," given the chemicals that had been stored there.[24] The state now claims that the chemicals would have leaked even if the new construction had not opened the top and, more to the point, Hooker knew all about this; they saw trouble coming and were very glad to get rid of the property and all liability for it as soon as the opportunity arose.[25] The state claims to be in possession of internal memos from Hooker Chemical that support their accusations.

The state is *not* trying to establish that a specific disease was caused in specific individuals by the Love Canal event; it would be difficult to prove this, especially since so many symptoms turn up years after exposure to the chemicals. (In other words, the state will not attempt to prove "proximate cause" for any given injury.) There is extensive laboratory evidence of injury caused to organic systems, especially the nervous system, by the chemicals found in Love Canal, but it is still very hard to establish direct causal links to specific impairment. Nevertheless, the state argues that the mere creation of a risk is a punishable action. The purpose of this suit is twofold: to deter future reckless corporate behavior and to use the resulting fine for the creation of an Environmental Remediation Fund.[26]

RESETTLEMENT

After the canal was resealed in 1978, New York State conducted a five-year study to determine the potential for resettlement of adjacent areas. About 2,300 soil, air, and water samples were analyzed for contamination and compared to control samples from comparable areas in Niagara Falls. This testing, incidentally, cost the state $100 million, thus bringing to $375 million the total amount spent on the event by the state.

As a result of this five-year study, Dr. David Axelrod, the New York State Health Commissioner, announced in September, 1988, that 220 houses were safe enough to be reoccupied, whereas 250 were not yet habitable. The Love Canal Area Revitalization Agency (LCARA), a state agency that owned some 400 houses by that time, began to develop a land-use plan and to renovate the houses, which were to be sold for between $35,000 and $100,000. The cleanup and containment would continue while the sale was going on.

This announcement immediately drew sharp reactions, ranging from dismay to strong interest from bargain hunters. Six months later, however, soil samples from neighboring control areas were found to be contaminated with toluene and dichlorobenzene, which seemed to negate the value of the comparison. The sale had to be delayed. "The real sad message here," commented Peter Slocum of the New York State Health

Department, "is that there might be no place in Niagara Falls that is not within spitting distance of chemical waste."[27]

The following year, this decision was reversed again. In May of 1990, William K. Reilly, Administrator of the EPA, reassessed the studies and found the originally affected area to be safe; there had been, after all, only one contaminated sample, and that one did not originate in Love Canal. Reaction was mixed: The mayor of Niagara Falls and chairman of LCARA predictably insisted that the houses were perfectly safe; the Natural Resources Defense Council, an advocacy group, predictably protested that the "EPA has given a narrow, legalistic reading" of the data and that "Love Canal is a ticking time bomb." Since there are more than 200 toxic waste sites within 50 miles of Love Canal and 23 of these were leaking, another activist complained that comparing the soil around Love Canal to soil elsewhere in the area is like "comparing rotten oranges to rotten oranges."[28]

Over the protests of six environmental groups, the LCARA went forward with its plan to sell 70 houses in the summer of 1990, the first ten to be offered in August. More than 200 people were willing to accept the risk (and stigma) of a house at Love Canal and applied for homes selling between $30,000 and $80,000, about 20 percent below the local current market price. For many prospective buyers, who were generally working-class people, this sale might be their best or only chance to own their own homes; they also felt that the hazard might have been overrated in the first place—and a government statement that it is safe to move in should certainly be an adequate guarantee. The advocacy groups' plea for an injunction was denied by the state court; 24 houses have been sold since August, 1990.

CONCLUDING REFLECTIONS

The final phase of the Love Canal cleanup will occur over a five-year period while the rehabilitated houses continue to be reoccupied. An incinerator will be built to burn the 35,000 cubic yards of dioxin-contaminated soil and sediment that resulted from earlier dredging of creeks and sewers. The residual ash will be buried in a newly designed landfill. The cost is predicted to be between $26 and $31 million, to be added to the amount already spent and the cost of relocating about 1,000 families.[29]

The influence of the Love Canal story has been considerable. This story is responsible for the emergence of popular awareness about the threat of toxic chemicals, for the consequent "Superfund" legislation, and for strengthening the Resource Conservation and Recovery Act. With that awareness also came increased fear (some of it justified but much not) that led to the syndrome known as NIMBY (Not In My Back Yard).

It has become enormously difficult to find an acceptable place to dump toxic wastes. As a result, we are resorting to increasingly expensive means of disposing of the stuff: A ton of hazardous waste could have been disposed of for $10 before Love Canal but cost $500 by 1988.[30] Unfortunately, as the expense rose, so did the incidence of illegal dumping, which has reached scandalous proportions in some parts of the country.

Ironically, although hazardous wastes are among the environmental issues that have "aroused high emotions, generated reams of reports and prodded Congress to spend billions of dollars...scientists rate them at near the bottom of a broad array of environmental threats."[31] The acute health threat posed by hazardous wastes is uncertain, limited, possibly inflated, and relatively short-lived, compared, for instance, to ozone depletion. We still have no more useful data than we did years ago on how, or whether, small amounts of toxic chemicals in the environment cause damage to human health. The National Research Council issued a report on October 21, 1991, arguing that the national effort to clean up toxic waste was "hampered by its inability to tell the difference between dumps posing a real threat to human health and those that do not."[32]

> Almost nothing is known about the effects on human health of most chemicals found in hazardous waste sites, the study said. Most people exposed to hazardous waste at those sites come in contact with minute amounts of chemicals, but very little is known about how they are affected, [the report] continued. Another gap in the Government's data is that scientists have virtually no idea of the risks posed by two or more chemicals that react in a waste site to form another toxic compound.[33]

Yet it is clear that exposure to some (perhaps most) chemicals, in high enough amounts, will cause health problems. The danger must be taken seriously, at some level. If there is a danger, the greatest long-term threat posed by these wastes might be their migration to groundwater, because the seepage will move as a unit, very slowly, and the chemicals are very long-lived and hard to detect, thus making cleanup very difficult.[34]

The hope that strict regulation would reduce the amount of hazardous wastes has not been realized.[35] Figures on waste disposal are hard to amass but, with 70,000 chemicals in daily use and 500–1,000 new ones added each year, it is reasonable to assume that the 1983 figure of 266 million tons per year is much higher now.[36]

What, then, is the legacy of Love Canal? That will not be completely known for years. On the positive side, the increase in the difficulty and costs of waste disposal have brought the issue of hazardous-waste generation full circle to source reduction. Industries are finding that, by recycling and changing some procedures, they can reduce their waste considerably and save significant dollars. One EPA study showed that, of 28 firms investing in waste-reduction techniques, 54 percent recovered their investment in less than one year and another 21 percent recovered it in less than two years.[37]

As with many other environmental issues, encouraging the positive effects depend upon the negative: The fear of "another Love Canal" propels communities to prohibit disposal of toxic wastes except at ridiculous cost; this cost in turn, provides an economic incentive for industry to experiment with new and costlier methods of manufacture that eliminate the production of that waste; and the overall result is a cleaner industry.

On the other hand, some of the results of this fear are clearly undesirable. Unrealistic and counterproductive requirements exist for the handling of any land found stained with toxins, such as the requirement that all hazardous wastes found on any building site must be cleared away, transported to a disposal site, and burned, before the title can be cleared and building can begin. That particular rule results only in increased hazard, because the exposed, exhumed, and transported waste is picked up by wind or rain in transit and disseminated more widely than if it had been left alone. Also, the NIMBY syndrome makes all municipal efforts at safe disposal of toxic wastes unnecessarily difficult. There is now a stigma surrounding chemicals and a reinforced tendency for the public to accept any fearfulness as the gospel truth and any reassurance as political coverup. All of these, especially the last, are results that we may find difficult to overcome while we adapt to the necessities of handling toxic wastes.

QUESTIONS FOR DISCUSSION AND REFLECTION

✦ What values are in dispute in the case of Love Canal? What are their limitations? How can we factor in, and compare ... ?

> the property values of the owners
>
> the health of the residents
>
> the public image of the town
>
> the preservation of contractual agreements
>
> the health of the ecosystem
>
> the integrity of the local aquifers

✦ Was there, in all this, a duty not to pollute or otherwise hurt the soil, for the sake of the soil itself, in advance of legislation on the subject? If so, why? To what or to whom was that duty owed?

✦ Who should pay for the cleanups and other economic consequences now and in the future? Who was really responsible for the leaking chemicals? Who was responsible for the panic? Who was responsible for the economic loss?

+ And most basically, what *did* happen? Was it worth all the fuss? What counts as "acceptable" risk and damage?

Notes

1. Parts of this chronology are taken from one compiled by Dennis Hevesi for *The New York Times,* September 28, 1988.

2. Philip Elmer-Dewitt, "Love Canals in the Making," *TIME* (20 May 1991): p. 51.

3. Anne Underwood, "The Return to Love Canal," *Newsweek* (30 July 1990).

4. Elizabeth Whelan, *Toxic Terror: The Truth About the Cancer Scare* (Ottawa, Ill.: Jameson Books, 1985).

5. Olefins are compounds consisting of carbon chains in which some of the carbon atoms are connected by double bonds, that is, they have room for more hydrogen atoms and are therefore called *unsaturated.*

6. If you have forgotten the history, reread Rachel Carson's *Silent Spring* (Boston: Houghton-Mifflin, Anniversary Edition 1962).

7. Sandra Postel, "Defusing the Toxics Threat: Controlling Pesticides and Industrial Waste," *Worldwatch Paper* 79 (Washington, D.C.: Worldwatch Institute, September 1987).

8. *Ibid.,* p. 15.

9. Philip H. Abelson, "Chemicals from Waste Dump," *Science,* vol. 229, no. 4711 (26 July 1985).

10. *Ibid.*

11. "Health Aspects of Hazardous Waste Disposal" (summary of report of the same name from Universities Associated for Research and Education in Pathology), *Environment* 28: 3 (April 1986) p. 38.

12. Deed of Love Canal Property Transfer, Niagara Falls, New York (28 April 1953). Emphasis added.

13. Telephone conversation with Eugene Martin-Less, Esq., Environmental Bureau of the Attorney General of New York State, Albany, New York, Senior Attorney, *New York State vs. Occidental Chemical Company* (suit pending), asking $250 million punitive damages relative to Love Canal dumpsite.

14. Ralph Nader, Ronald Brownstein, and John Richard, eds., *Who's Poisoning America? Corporate Polluters and Their Victims in the Chemical Age* (San Francisco: Sierra Club Books, 1981).

15. Gary Whitney, "Hooker Chemical and Plastics," *Case Studies in Business Ethics,* ed. Thomas Donaldson (Englewood Cliffs, N.J.: Prentice-Hall, 1984).

16. Michael H. Brown, "A Toxic Ghost Town: Harbinger of America's Toxic Waste Crisis," *The Atlantic,* vol. 263, no. 1 (July 1989) pp. 23–24.

17. "CDC Finds No Excess Illness at Love Canal," *Science,* vol. 220 (17 June 1983).

18. Nicholas Vianna, Report to the New York State Department of Health; Reported in *Science* (19 June 1981), p. 19.

19. Hank Cox, *Regulatory Action Network: Washington Watch,* September 1980.

20. Whelan, *Toxic Terror,* p. 99.

21. Brown,"Toxic Ghost Town," *supra.*

22. *Ibid.*

23. Interview with Attorney Eugene Martin-Less, cited earlier.

24. *Ibid.*

25. "Love Canal Suit Threatens to Make Old Errors Costly," *Wall Street Journal* (24 October 1990).

26. Martin-Less, Esq. Environmental Bureau of the Attorney General of New York State.

27. Peter Slocum, New York State Health Department. Quoted in *The New York Times* (15 April 1990).

28. *The New York Times* (15 May 1990).

29. *Science News* (14 November 1987): p. 319.

30. Joel S. Hirschhorn, "Cutting Production of Hazardous Waste," *Technology Review,* vol. 91, no. 3 (April 1988).

31. William K. Stevens, "What Really Threatens the Environment?" *The New York Times* (29 January 1991): p. C4

32. Keith Schneider, "U.S. Said to Lack Data on Threat Posed by Hazardous Waste Sites," *The New York Times* (22 October 1991).

33. *Ibid.*

34. "Health Aspects of Hazardous Waste Disposal," *Environment* (April 1986): pp. 38–45.

35. *Ibid.*

36. Postel, "Defusing the Toxics Threat," *supra.*

37. Hirschhorn, "Hazardous Waste," *supra.*

Suggestions for Further Reading

Beauchamp, Tom. "Love Canal." *Case Studies in Business, Society, and Ethics.* Englewood Cliffs, N.J.: Prentice-Hall, 1983.

Brown, Michael. *Laying Waste: The Poisoning of America by Toxic Chemicals.* New York: Parthenon, 1980.

Brown, Michael H. "A Toxic Ghost Town: Harbinger of America's Toxic Waste Crisis." *The Atlantic,* vol. 264, no. 1 (July 1989): pp. 23–24.

Carson, Rachel. *Silent Spring.* Boston: Houghton-Mifflin, Anniversary Edition, 1962.

Cox, Hank. "Love Canal Special Supplement." *The Regulatory Action Network: Washington Watch* (September 1980).

Epstein, Samuel. *Hazardous Waste in America.* San Francisco: Sierra Club Books, 1982.

Gibbs, Lois Marie. *Love Canal: My Story.* Albany: State University of New York Press, 1982.

Griffin, M. "The Legacy of Love Canal." *Sierra,* vol. 73 (Jan.–Feb. 1988), pp. 26–27.

Kadlecek, M. "Love Canal—10 Years Later." *The Conservationist,* vol. 43 (Nov.–Dec. 1988): pp. 40–43.

Klinkenborg, Verlyn. "Back to Love Canal." *Harpers* (March 1991).

Levine, Adeline Gordon. *Love Canal: Science, Politics, and People.* Lexington, Mass.: Lexington Books, 1982.

Nader, Ralph, Ronald Brownstein, and John Richard, eds. *Who's Poisoning America? Corporate Polluters and Their Victims in the Chemical Age.* San Francisco: Sierra Club Books, 1981.

Postel, Sandra. "Defusing the Toxics Threat: Controlling Pesticides and Industrial Waste." *Worldwatch Paper 79,* Washington, D.C.: Worldwatch Institute, September 1987.

Regenstein, Lewis. *America the Poisoned.* Washington, D.C.: Acropolis Books, 1982.

Revkin, A. C. "Trapping Toxics in the Trenches." *Discover,* vol. 9 (Nov. 1988): p. 10.

Whalan, Robert. *Love Canal: A Public Health Time Bomb.* Report of the New York Department of Health, 1978.

Whelan, Elizabeth. *Toxic Terror: The Truth About the Cancer Scare.* Ottawa, Ill.: Jameson Books, 1985.

Whitney, Gary. "Hooker Chemical and Plastics." *Case Studies in Business Ethics.* ed. Thomas Donaldson. Englewood Cliffs, N.J.: Prentice-Hall, 1984.

CHAPTER 2

A Cloud of Poison

The Disaster at Bhopal

PREFACE: QUESTIONS TO KEEP IN MIND

Bhopal is the story of an American company abroad, subjected to a series of mishaps that might have been otherwise. As you read, ask yourself:

If the company had been in the United States, would the safety standards and work practices have been different? What makes you think so (or not)?

Would the government have reacted differently in the U.S.? Would government reaction have been different if the company had been culturally—as it was legally—an Indian company, rather than an American company?

The company was American, in origin and culture. How did this influence the press and the attorneys for the plaintiffs? How would the press and the legal profession have treated a similar incident in an Indian company?

What ethical imperatives are binding on an American company abroad? How do we strike a balance—neither exploiting nor being exploited by the host country?

How significant is the fact that this plant makes insecticides? What were they used for? Did alternatives to this kind of industry exist?

How do we assess blame in such catastrophes? Who should be held accountable for the damage? How should monetary damages be assessed?

BHOPAL AND THE ENVIRONMENT

Bhopal is the story of the leak of methyl isocyanate (MIC) from the United Carbide India Ltd. (UCIL) plant in Bhopal, India, and the subsequent deaths, injuries, cover-ups, firings, lawsuits, political maneuvering, and inflammatory books and articles. This might seem to be just another story of an industrial accident, this one replete with the colorful politics of international rivalries, possibly of interest to students of tort law and to those who coach CEOs on the proper responses to adverse publicity but of no immediate import to the ethics of the natural environment. But that interpretation would miss the most important aspect of the whole affair: The real questions arising from Bhopal have to do with the existence of the factory in the first place and our alleged reliance on "development strategies that are inherently violent, manipulative, and wasteful."[1] As the commentator suggested, these questions might be part of a larger question on technological civilization in general: "How can man [sic] use his most modern and ingenious developments in ways that will not turn upon his fellows and destroy them?"[2] But that question is beyond the scope of this volume.

It is hardly surprising that chemicals formulated to kill other species would also kill our own. Is there no other way to feed ourselves than by slaughtering all species who eat the same food we do? If we must keep insects and rodents at bay to ensure an adequate harvest, are there no alternatives to the use of deadly chemicals? On the plausible hypothesis that those chemicals are poisoning the soil in the long run, are we not doing more harm than good? Should we rethink our mass industrial approach to agriculture—the chemical-dependent "factory farm"—to see whether we can find more environmentally friendly ways to get our food? All these questions emerge in the wake of Bhopal, calling our attention to the need to reconsider our stewardship of the land.[3]

THE STORY OF A DISASTER

On December 2, 1984, about 11:00 PM, a discontented employee (whose name is known but has not been made public) removed the pressure gauge from MIC Storage Tank #610 on the grounds of a pesticide plant run by Union Carbide India Limited (UCIL). The employee knew, or had very good reason to believe, that the tank contained about 41 metric tons of MIC and that it was very important not to let water get into it. He almost certainly did not know *why* contact with water must be prevented; his home and his family were probably nearby, and injury to the people of the area was surely no part of his intent. He did know, though, that water contamination would ruin the batch of pesticide being prepared from that MIC. That is apparently what he intended when he attached a hose, already connected to a water faucet in the corner of the yard, to the hole where the pressure gauge had been and turned on the water.[4] Within hours, the ensuing chemical reaction had exploded the safety valve in the tank and allowed a lethal cloud of poisonous gas to spread over (ultimately) about 25 square miles of the area downwind of the plant,[5] killing about 4,000 people[6] and causing an undetermined number of injuries.[7]

In the aftermath of this simple-minded act of destruction, the name of Bhopal became an international symbol for the senseless, unexpected devastation that can follow upon industrial accidents in advanced industrial settings—not to mention the economics, law, and politics of compensation for injury. The drama attracted a large and continuing amount of public interest and acrimony: Within a few years of the incident, with lawsuits still pending, at least three books had been written about the incident, none of them friendly to Union Carbide and corporate enterprise in general. Two of these books, Dan Kurzman's *A Killing Wind,* and David Weir's *The Bhopal Syndrome,* have been consulted extensively, along with materials from Union Carbide, as primary sources for the account that follows.

In considering the ethical dimensions of the Bhopal incident, we will divide the discussion into three parts: We will begin by examining the conditions and events at the time of the incident—a disaster, as one author describes it, waiting to happen.[8] We will go on to consider the sequel to the accident—a sad chronicle of finance and politics where the victims are lost in the process—to see what we might learn from this experience that could be applied to similar situations in the future. We will conclude with some further reflections on pesticides and agriculture in a technological age.

THE INCIDENT: UNION CARBIDE IN INDIA

Why was the Union Carbide factory in India to begin with? Why is methyl isocyanate worth manufacturing despite its known tendency to explode and kill people under certain circumstances? Given that such a lethal chemical was being manufactured, was it right for Union Carbide to maintain the relatively low level of security that permitted the sabotage to take place? Could the incident have been prevented?

Despite the company's American name, it was largely Indian-owned and completely Indian-operated. The company had been founded as a branch of an American corporation almost 50 years ago to provide pesticides for India's agricultural "green revolution"; the plant at Bhopal dated from 1969.[9] There was nothing exotic or extraordinarily dangerous in the operation of Union Carbide's plants; the most common pesticide they produced was carbaryl, an ester of carbamic acid, a reliable and relatively safe product that is marketed in the United States under the brand name SEVIN.[10]

THE CHEMISTRY OF DISASTER

The chemicals employed in the process of making the pesticide are undoubtedly dangerous. Phosgene, the deadly gas briefly used in World War I on the battlefield (and also in the gas chambers of the Third Reich), is a precursor of SEVIN. The Union Carbide process for the manufacture of SEVIN uses phosgene ($COCl_2$) and a methyl (CH_3) amine (NH_2) to produce the intermediate compound methylcarbamoyl chloride ($CH_3NHCOCl$). This last compound breaks down with heat into MIC (CH_3NCO) and hydrochloric acid (HCl).

MIC is a variation of the cyanide group (NCN^{-2}); the highly poisonous hydrogen cyanide (HCN) is probably the most famous chemical in that group. MIC is extremely unstable and dangerous and, as such, is not ordinarily studied in a laboratory situation. Its boiling point is 39° C. (102.40 F.). It is lighter than water in liquid form but heavier than air in gaseous form, so it hugs the ground when released. Its breakdown products include carbon dioxide and stable amines (organic compounds of carbon, hydrogen, and nitrogen), but the breakdown process is exothermic—that is, it releases a vast quantity of heat. MIC reacts violently with water (producing breakdown products and high temperatures); in this case, that includes the water that entered the MIC storage tanks and the water in human tissue. Therefore, MIC is a virulent human poison, and there is no known antidote.[11]

Regulations of the Occupational Safety and Health Administration (OSHA) allow human exposure to MIC at 0.02 parts per million (ppm) over an 8-hour period; irritation is felt at 2 ppm and becomes unbearable at 21 ppm.[12] A mere 5 ppm will kill 50 percent of an experimental rat population.[13] No one measured the concentration of the escaped gas at Bhopal but, since 50,000 pounds of it was released,[14] the heart of the cloud must have greatly exceeded those limits.

MIC is used as an intermediate in the production of SEVIN, which is considerably less poisonous than its chemical precursors.[15] Incidentally, this is not the only way to manufacture SEVIN; it can also be produced by adding methylamine to a reaction of phosgene and napthol. Or else, MIC can be produced without using phosgene: In Germany, the Bayer company makes MIC by combining dimethyl urea and diphenyl carbonate. It is not clear just what considerations led UCIL to the choice of this particular method of making SEVIN. Either of the other methods might have been preferable.[16]

A FACTORY IN A FOREIGN LAND

It made a lot of sense to put pesticide plants in India instead of manufacturing the SEVIN in the U.S. for export: It eliminated transportation costs (and dangers), and labor costs were considerably lower in India, making the whole operation safer and more profitable for Union Carbide. Having the plant in India also provided tax revenues and very good jobs in a chronically depressed economy; in consideration for this, the Indian government sought, welcomed, and catered to American companies willing to locate plants in their large and needy country. The land on which the Bhopal plant was built had been given to Union Carbide by the Indian government for an annual rent of $40 per acre. (Bhopal is the capital city of Madhya Pradesh, the largest and one of the poorest states in the nation.)

At the time of the Bhopal incident, there were 14 Union Carbide plants in India. Here, as elsewhere, the host nation insisted on assuming a large share of the ownership of foreign plants; in this case, though, India did not insist on a majority holding, because the plant was a "high technology" enterprise.[17] The Indian government held about 25 percent of the stock, and the rest was owned by Indian citizens.[18] The management of the plant was wholly Indian; the last American employee had left the Bhopal plant in 1982. Still, the operation was widely viewed (at least in that election year in India) as an American colonialist intrusion into the Indian economy, an outpost of foreign capitalist greed in a sovereign state.

Well, was the Union Carbide plant Indian or American? The Americans were responsible for the design, and the Indians responsible for its implementation. This division of responsibility fostered attitudes of mutual suspicion, in combination with complacency and unconcern for the details of the safety arrangement. Those attitudes could have predicted the explosion and the tragic chain of events that followed it: the recriminations, litigation, and political hyperbole, continuing to this day.

Union Carbide is not the only American multinational corporation to have experienced a removal of the welcome mat. What, really, are the obligations of an American corporation in such situations? In this telling of the story, our major concern is environmental safety, and the possibility of environmentally disastrous industrial accidents, which is the domain of the Health, Safety and Environment Department of the corporation; other tellings of the story might examine only the profitability of such arrangements and reach different conclusions. When the forces of nationalism insist that the plant must be run by national managers and that Americans can no longer exert the kind of control that might be necessary to ensure safety, are the Americans obligated to withdraw from the whole operation? Was there a double standard at Bhopal? In other words, did the American parent company tolerate lower safety standards in India because the company was no longer strictly liable for plant safety?

IN SEARCH OF SAFETY

Union Carbide was well aware of the instability of MIC and of the potential for any of a wide variety of contaminants, including water, to set off an explosive and lethal chain reaction. To prevent that reaction, the corporation had instituted a meticulous series of systems and rules all "aimed at preventing MIC from escaping, getting overheated, or being contaminated."[19] In general, these procedures work: Similar plants in the United States have excellent safety records, and there had previously been only one fatal accident at the Bhopal plant (a worker died of phosgene inhalation after cleaning out a pipe without wearing a face mask). Investigations conducted after the Bhopal incident revealed a whole slew of collapsed systems. David Weir gives us a partial list:

> Gauges measuring temperature and pressure in the various parts of the unit, including the crucial MIC storage tanks, were so notoriously unreliable that workers ignored early signs of trouble.
>
> The refrigeration unit for keeping MIC at low temperatures (and therefore less likely to undergo overheating and expansion should a contaminant enter the tank) had been shut off for some time.
>
> The gas scrubber, designed to neutralize any escaping MIC, had been shut off for maintenance. Even had it been operative, post-disaster inquiries revealed, the maximum pressure it could handle was only one-quarter that which was actually reached in the accident.
>
> The flare tower, designed to burn off MIC escaping from the scrubber, was also turned off, waiting for replacement of a corroded piece of pipe. The tower, however, was inadequately designed for its task, as it was capable of handling only a quarter of the volume of gas released.
>
> The water curtain [high-pressure spray], designed to neutralize any remaining gas, was too short to reach the top of the flare tower, from where the MIC was billowing.[20]

What went wrong? One major problem throughout the decision-making preceding the incident was the slim budget available for maintenance. The Bhopal plant had never made very large profits; its projected market had never materialized. The plant had been designed to produce 5,000 tons of pesticides a year, but in 1982 it produced only 2,308 tons; 1,647 in 1983; and in 1984 production dropped below 1,000 tons.[21] Cost-saving measures were mandated; shutting down the refrigeration unit was one of them. As with most cases of cash-flow problems, routine maintenance was deferred. Suggested remodeling (to increase the height at which the "water curtain" could work, for instance) or relocation to the "obnoxious industry" zone outside of town could not be considered.

This is a hazardous industry, and the warnings were readily apparent. A Union Carbide investigative team had visited the site two years before the incident, discovered many flaws in the safety arrangements and recommended changes, which had not been implemented. The enterprising journalist who uncovered the Union Carbide report, Raj Kumar Keswani, had written a series of exposes in the local newspaper on the safety problems at the plant. Weir asks, "Why didn't the insurance companies covering Union Carbide in the event of a chemical disaster require that the Bhopal plant fortify its safety systems? Why didn't the Indian authorities heed the repeated warnings sounded by [Keswani] of the impending danger posed by the Bhopal plant?"[22] Where, in short, were the people *outside* the company who were supposed to be watching the store?

The problems underscored by the Bhopal incident, from the corporation's point of view, involve loss of proximity and control. For instance, before the accident, there was no reason to believe that the Indian managers were unable to maintain the same safety standards that would be possible in a similar plant in the U.S. (All Union Carbide plants were built to the same specifications.) Nevertheless, when the incident happened, the managers on that shift were taking a tea break together, contrary to company rules and explicit instructions.[23] Was that foreseeable? In retrospect, should Union Carbide have terminated the operation in Bhopal as soon as the corporation lost effective control—whatever the loss of jobs in the area and the financial loss to its shareholders?

THE VICTIMS: WORKERS AND SQUATTERS

Why were so many people in the path of the poisonous gas? The Bhopal plant had been built in a small city with perhaps a million souls in it before the establishment of the pesticide operation, but the plant soon found itself surrounded by people. Employees found housing near the plant and brought their extended families with them. Meanwhile, a veritable army of India's homeless constructed shantytowns near the plant and occasionally against the plant walls themselves, which were conveniently solid and vertical. These clusters of shacks amounted to villages with individual identities and names of their own: J. P. Nagar, Kazi

Camp, Chola Kenchi, Railroad Colony. They had grown into crowded slums since the plant arrived and largely because of the plant.[24]

These were the people so horribly gassed when the tank of MIC exploded, and that explains some of the lawyers' efforts to get the litigation transferred to the United States, as we shall see. What were those people doing there, where they did not belong? Presumably, it makes no moral difference that these people were poor and uneducated. Does it make any difference that the people had no particular *right* to be there?[25] Is it appropriate to introduce the notion that people squatting on land that does not belong to them (government land, in this case) are there somehow "at their own risk"?

The suffering of the victims was painfully evident. The MIC exposure was so toxic because it "reacted furiously with moisture in exposed tissues."[26] Moisture in the lungs was first and most affected, although burns also occurred in the eyes; the gas also affected tissues of the cardiovascular, gastrointestinal, neuromuscular, reproductive, and immune systems.[27] Respiratory symptoms (choking and shortness of breath) were most common among the survivors, and might become long-term in some of the victims. Also common were watering of the eyes, lid edema, and corneal ulcerations, but no irreversible eye damage was found. Here, as elsewhere in Bhopal, good data can be hard to come by; clinical studies that have been done on the medical sequel of the incident apparently lacked controls, thus impugning their validity, and show evidence of inherent biases in their design and conclusions.[28]

The Bhopal disaster was compounded, in mortality and morbidity, by the inability of the medical community to offer any real help. MIC poisoning was unheard-of; indeed, the gas was widely believed to be harmless, as Union Carbide's medical director continued to claim for some time after the gas had escaped.[29] Drops for the eyes and oxygen for ravaged lungs were the only palliatives that anyone could offer. Some physicians administered sodium thiosulfate, a known antidote for hydrogen cyanimide, or cyanide poisoning. Later, it was alleged that there had been official reluctance to implicate this most famous poison (for fear of causing panic?), but some attending physicians suspected cyanide poisoning and thought that the antidote should be given.[30] Again, no clinical evidence is available on one side or the other of this question.

Could injuries have been prevented if more attention had been given to warning the public? There had been no drills or dissemination of information. If the people in the path of the gas had known enough to put wet cloths over their noses and mouths, hundreds of lives might have been saved—but no one had thought it might be a useful thing for them to know. Should drills have been held? There would probably never be any need at all to show people what to do in the event of a massive gas leak, and attempts to educate the people might just cause panic. How do you balance the known and certain disadvantages of fearful warnings with the unknown and unproven disadvantages of risking a disaster without the warnings?

Once the chain reaction began, there was no stopping it; the introduction of water to the MIC tank started the runaway reaction. That produced the heat of an intensely exothermic reaction. Apparently chloroform ($CHCl_3$), used as a solvent throughout the process, had already contaminated the MIC; and it had not been removed earlier by distillation because of a higher than normal temperature in the still.[31] That chloroform evidently provided the chlorine ions (Cl) that attacked the steel lining of the tank, which in turn released the iron ions (Fe^{++}) that acted as a catalyst to promote the trimerization (three molecules of MIC reacting with each other in a polymerization reaction), which is also exothermic. The MIC, which is usually held at 20° C. (ideally at 4.5° C.), finally reached 120° C.[32]

By now, of course, the MIC had boiled (vaporized); the pressure exploded the tank, releasing a cloud that covered 25 square miles. None of the safety devices had worked; the emptying of the huge tank—and the resulting devastation—was therefore inevitable.[33]

The workers in the plant were as baffled as the squatters outside the plant. Dan Kurzman documents[34] the frantic efforts of plant managers who were at home at the time of the gas leak to get to the plant through the mobbed streets and the frantic efforts of the employees on the spot to find out what was going wrong with the MIC tank, to drain the tank when they realized that a reaction had gone out of control, to get the caustic scrubber, flare tower, and water curtain working—and, incidentally, to inform their superiors, organize remedial efforts, and prevent panic, including their own.

Not much of this effort was to any avail: The plant and the workers were simply not up to the task of stopping the killer cloud from completing its journey.

THE SEQUEL: THE CORPORATION'S RESPONSE

Union Carbide's response was instantaneous: Warren B. Anderson, Chairman of the Board and Chief Executive Officer of the company, announced that the corporation accepted full moral responsibility for the disaster and that the victims would be compensated. He then personally left immediately for Bhopal. He had been authorized by the Board of Directors to offer anywhere from $1 million to $5 million in aid on the spot, and he had pledged to find out how the company could best help the victims. Did this prompt reaction signify real horror at the human suffering, genuine compassion, and a sincere desire to help? Or was it just a public relations maneuver—a dramatic gesture to protect the shareholders—to evoke sympathy for the corporation and perhaps a little leniency in the lawsuits sure to follow? Who knows? Who cares?

Let us take these last two questions one at a time.

Who knows what motivated Union Carbide's reaction to the disaster? Probably no one, including Warren Anderson; most human motivation is a mixed bag. There is no reason to doubt that simple compassion and a desire to help were significant among Anderson's reasons for making the trip to Bhopal. There is also no reason to doubt that Anderson knew that *his* trip to India would make a clearer statement of the company's compassion than sending a middle manager, no matter how expert that manager might be in the chemistry and medicine of gases, and that he wanted to use this gesture to place the company in control of the handling of the aftermath of the disaster. He also very likely considered that it was important to protect the shareholders' equity and that the company would be in better shape in the long run if he was seen to concentrate on getting aid to the victims rather than circling the legal wagons. After all, CEOs are paid to consider such things at frequent intervals.

Who cares about Anderson's motivation, anyway? We do. We want very much to be able to attach a moral label to the public acts of those who influence our lives, like the CEOs of major corporations. The moral character of a single act is determined less by the effects of the act than it is by the motives on which the agent acted. So we want to find out what the consequences of an act are likely to be and also from what law it flowed—not why anyone should or should not do it but why the agent in fact *did* do it. We are, in the language of ethics, at least as much deontologists as we are teleologists, Kantians as much as Utilitarians. Thus, depending on what we believe about Warren Anderson's motivation in making the trip to Bhopal, we will regard that trip as a courageous and compassionate pilgrimage, appropriately designed to bring the money to the spot where it needed to be spent, and praiseworthy beyond the call of duty for an elderly corporate statesman—or else as cheap public relations showmanship, crocodile tears for the masses to conceal a blatant attempt to pressure India to accept a smaller payment immediately in lieu of the larger payment that Union Carbide would have to make when all the facts had been ascertained.

RESPONSE AND FRUSTRATION: DEALING WITH INDIAN AUTHORITIES

Our conclusions on the last two questions will dictate our reaction to Anderson's arrest by the Indian authorities when he stepped off the plane at Bhopal. Anderson was detained in a company guest house for a few days. He was never allowed to interview the victims or his managers from the plant nor to offer help. Promised interviews with the governor and the prime minister never materialized; not even the environmental minister would talk to him. That arrest, too, could be seen either as a vicious bit of Indian political grandstanding, playing to the nationalistic crowd in an election season, tragically counterproductive for the actual victims—or else as just what Anderson deserved, good medicine for a conceited corporate mogul who was trying to manipulate public opinion to save his profits and his job.

Anderson was further forbidden to talk to the press, which was one of his major objectives in making the trip. That prohibition itself was either a cynical move to ensure that the victims would never know that Union Carbide was entirely ready from the outset to compensate them for injuries sustained (because the politicians wanted to make any eventual settlement look like a triumph for them)—or else simply a refusal to let Anderson convert the press, as he had wanted, into an arm of the Union Carbide public relations department. Your interpretation, again, will depend on your reading of Anderson's reasons for making the trip. (As both the Indians and Union Carbide had anticipated, contemporary sources read Anderson's failure to contact the press as deliberate evasion.)[35]

Thereafter, Union Carbide was forced to conduct its response to the incident from afar, hindered by lack of access to the plant (the Indian equivalent of the FBI had closed it for their criminal investigation) and, for many months, by a prohibition against interviewing the employees who had been on duty the night that the incident took place. Union Carbide devoted an immense amount of time and energy to its response. The company's management split in two: While Anderson and many others assembled a team of scientists and administered the investigation into the causes and cures of the uncontrolled emission of gas (see below), a caretaker administration ran the rest of the company in the meantime. The major effort, for some time, was to get relief for the victims.

The story of Union Carbide's efforts to give money to those who really needed it at Bhopal is a chronology of frustration. As mentioned above, Warren Anderson's initial offer, days after the explosion, of several million dollars was rebuffed. By February, 1985, the Union Carbide Employees' Bhopal Relief Fund had collected over $100,000 for the victims but had no one to entrust the money to. That April, India again summarily rejected any comprehensive settlement. Litigation began, initiated by teams of lawyers who wanted to represent the victims in damage suits against Union Carbide, before U.S. District Court Judge John Keenan, with the object of getting the cause tried in the United States. Judge Keenan himself accepted $5 million from Union Carbide, on behalf of the victims, the first money to be routed toward the sufferers. More significantly, the judge ordered that the cases be tried in India, on the grounds that was the scene of the incident and also the location of the victims, witnesses, documents, applicable laws, and most of the lawsuits. The government of India promptly invalidated all the lawyers' claims, taking on itself the right and duty to speak for the victims.

After more litigation, dragging on for three more years, Chief Justice R. S. Pathak of India's Supreme Court directed a final settlement of all Bhopal litigation in the amount of $470 million, to be paid by March 31, 1989; Union Carbide made full payment by the end of February.[36]

During the course of the litigation, Union Carbide had repeatedly attempted to get funds to the victims through other than legal channels, including at least the International Red Cross and Mother Teresa; all potential channels refused the money on the grounds that the political flak that would accompany any appearance of cooperating with Union Carbide would hurt their own cause.

Why did it take so long to get money to the victims? The answer seems to be: politics and calculation. On the political side, Indian officials gained significant political advantage from portraying Union Carbide as murderers who had knowingly foisted a terribly dangerous operation on an unsuspecting community. The political players were soon competing with each other in a hyperbole of condemnation and blame directed at the corporation, scornful rejection of any proposed settlement as a tiny fraction of what was really owed, and feigned attempts at saving the public from the unimaginable dangers of anything the company might ever again do in Bhopal.

Quite possibly the supreme act of cynicism in the entire Bhopal affair was the evacuation ordered by Arjun Singh, Governor of Madhya Pradesh. Singh created out of whole cloth a full-blown panic in Bhopal when Union Carbide Vice President Van Mynen led a technical team, on December 18, 1984, to convert the remaining MIC to SEVIN, which was the safest way to dispose of it. Singh urged residents to evacuate the town if they could but pledged that he would personally guarantee that these "murderers" would do no harm during this routine operation. He himself ordered the appropriate safeguards, which included closing all the schools and colleges, which were then in the middle of examinations. He then announced that wet cloths would be draped over all the fences, a tent of wet cloths would be erected over the MIC tank and continually sprayed with water, and, just to make sure, "Indian Air Force helicopters would hover overhead and periodically spray the plant with water."[37] The conversion operation was perfectly safe but, in the ensuing panic, more lives and much more property were lost.

In such an atmosphere, who would dare sit down at a negotiating table with Union Carbide and presume to talk about a "fair" settlement?

That was not the only time that political frustration resulted in real damage to the residents: Union Carbide funded a vocational training school to relieve the poverty of the area, but the Indian government ordered it closed. Union Carbide, thwarted in their attempts to go through the government to reach the victims, then provided over $2 million to Arizona State University to build and operate a rehabilitation center for the injured. "The center was built, and operating well, but when the state government learned that Carbide money had funded it, bulldozers were sent in to knock the building down."[38] Union Carbide and UCIL together offered to fund a hospital to treat the victims over the long term and to provide more jobs and better medical care for the area; at last accounting, they had not yet been successful in getting permission to start the hospital.

On the one hand, in light of the political situation, these actions are not surprising, since they were expected to produce a larger compensation in the long run—thus the calculation. On the other hand, the victims of the killer cloud, impoverished Indians sickened by the gas, might have been helped by the vocational school and hospital but could not possibly benefit from acts whose import was wholly symbolic.

THE INVESTIGATION, WITHIN AND WITHOUT

On his return from India, company Vice President Van Mynen led the technical side of Union Carbide's response to Bhopal—the effort to determine just what had happened. By mid-March, the scientific team had determined that the chemical reaction had been triggered by a large volume of water; this was confirmed in July, when they were able to obtain core samples from the plant. By August, they had determined that the only way that water could have gotten into the tank was by a deliberate act.[39] Incidentally, that had been the first impression of the managers of UCIL, on the night of the explosion.[40]

Union Carbide had no access to human sources of information until the Government of India sued them for damages later that year. The court action allowed the company to request the records from the factory, which the U.S. District Court ordered India to make available to them in November. In December, 1985, they obtained access to the plant logs and immediately noticed a pattern of changing and falsifying records; that pattern was confirmed almost a year and a half after the incident, when the company was finally permitted access to plant-employee witnesses.

Three obstacles hindered their fact-finding through interviews: First, after a year and a half, the plant was now closed and all employees had been laid off; simply finding the employees that had been on duty on the night of the explosion, and persuading them to talk to the investigators, was a major task. Second, for those only peripherally involved in the incident, memories had faded, their sense of what was really relevant had dissipated, and accounts had to be reconstructed slowly and patiently by sifting through countless details. Those very fragmentary accounts, once reassembled, however, turned out to be the most reliable sources of information, because the most centrally involved parties had a tendency to lie. Ashok Kalelkar, a member of the investigating team, describes the team's experience during the interviews:

> ...As the interviews with the operators and supervisors directly involved progressed, it became apparent that there were massive contradictions in their stories. For example, operators and employees from other units and another plant downwind of the MIC unit, together with some MIC operators, reported sensing small MIC leaks well before the major release occurred, and they notified their shift supervisors. However, those Bhopal plant supervisors denied hearing any reports about earlier leaks. In addition, the supervisors were unable to plausibly account for their activities during the 45-minute period prior to the release. They placed themselves with people and in locations for reasons that were entirely different from those that had been given by those individuals they were supposedly with.[41]

Why the discrepancies? The managers had apparently wanted to cover up the fact that several of them had taken their tea break together, contrary to instructions. The other discordances in the logs and in the interviews, too, can be readily explained as consistent attempts to place the person giving the account as far away from the scene as possible or as completely ignorant as possible, as long as possible, of any trouble brewing.[42]

ACCIDENT OR SABOTAGE?

By the time these interviews took place, a long time had passed since the incident, and the journal readers of the world had meanwhile accepted an inaccurate theory of its cause. Unlike Union Carbide officials, journalists had full access from the beginning to anyone they could find who would talk to them. Some of them brought their own agendas with them. Journalists operate under certain unique constraints. They must file stories quickly for an impatient audience. They want their stories to be exciting, and they want them to be true, and if the two conflict, the exciting versions get at least a shot at acceptance. Above all, they want the stories fast, and they draw their conclusions quickly, for deadlines await at home.

Thus the imperatives of journalism worked against Union Carbide and the truth in the complex aftermath of the Bhopal incident. Isolating all company spokespeople from the Indian press ensured that unlimited speculation would rule the background stories. "It is remotely possible," Alfred de Grazia pointed out, writing less than a year after the incident, "that the research facility [on the factory grounds] was being used or intended for use to test the chemical warfare potential of MIC or to develop other chemicals that would be hazardous in themselves or when compounded. Indian journalists have raised such issues, and have found a large audience receptive to the theories."[43]

Even more bothersome than these fantasies was the early acceptance, before exhaustive investigation, of the theory that worker negligence was responsible for the water entering the tank. For months, the account of the incident faulted a missing "slip blind" for the explosion. (The slip blind, a circular disc inserted in a pipe while it was being washed, was supposed to isolate the piping being washed to keep the water from leaking backward past the valves into the tanks of chemicals.) For that matter, the first report issued by Union Carbide, in March, 1985, was noncommittal about the source of the water that caused the chemical reaction and noted that the relevant slip blind appeared to be missing.

During this period, theories jostled for newsmagazine space. The amount of water necessary to trigger the reaction became a serious question, as was the timing of the entry of the water. The Indian investigating team hypothesized that only a small amount of water would be necessary to cause the reaction via one possible chemical route (and therefore it could easily have been an accident), but the Union Carbide team hypothesized that 120 to 240 gallons of water must have entered the tank to cause the reaction by a different chemical route, and that it therefore had been a deliberate act.[44]

Additional questions arose about the amount of time necessary for the reaction to produce the temperature necessary to corrode the steel tank and release the catalytic iron ions. If, as the Indian team hypothesized and as one Union Carbide manual described, it would have taken more than 23 hours for the heat to rise sufficiently, the saboteur must have allowed the water to enter the tank the day before (and, presumably, risk being found out). Union Carbide figured that if the amount of water that they hypothesized had entered the tank, it would have caused the reaction in two hours.[45]

At this point, journalists had every reason to accept the accident theory and to suspect the sabotage theory; in a typical comment from that period Anantha K. S. Raman, commenting in April, 1985, dismissed Union Carbide's claim that the cause of the disaster was sabotage as "a carefully orchestrated attempt to influence the upcoming legal hearings."[46] By August, however, when Union Carbide had been able to obtain core samples, they realized (and proved) that the sheer amount of water needed to cause that kind of reaction could not possibly have come from pipe-washing leaks. (There were also many other reasons to reject the slip-blind or "water-washing" theory.[47]) Two years later, when Union Carbide's eventual access to plant workers for interviews spotlighted the missing pressure gauge and made the cause of the accident quite clear, some journalists still defended the slip-blind theory, apparently (with Raman, above) under the impression that

Union Carbide's responsibility for the accident would be lessened if it were established that the water had been introduced into the tank deliberately.[48]

Would this have lessened the company's responsibility? There is some punitive part of each of us that would say yes: that if the leak had been caused during water-washing (involving faulty valves and the like), the plant was primarily to blame, and the careless worker, only secondarily; in the case of sabotage, the perpetrator of the act was to blame, and it was no more than a regrettable shame that no one caught him at it. That part of us tunes easily to the criminal law and the *mens rea* ("guilty mind," or intent to do wrong) that, except in rare instances, is necessary for the existence of a crime. Criminal law thus holds the guilty saboteur responsible, and no one else; in cases of ordinary negligence, no one is held to be guilty (although the negligent tortfeasor might have to pay the bill for the damages), and it is psychologically easier to blame the surrounding circumstances—in this case, the factory—for whatever happened.

From the perspective of the civil law and Union Carbide, however, there is no distinction between responsibility in the one case and in the other: Both cases involve sloppy procedures (careless washing and omission of the slip blind in the "accident" scenario and no security around a tank full of dangerous chemicals in the sabotage scenario) and bad personnel practices (inadequate training and supervision of the washer in the accident scenario and inept handling of an employee demotion in the sabotage scenario). Both of these factors are culpable deficiencies in plant management. Besides, Union Carbide had been quick to admit full responsibility for the disaster; as soon as the actual, real damages had been established, they would be paid in full.[49]

SORTING OUT THE DEMANDS FOR COMPENSATION

Of course, not everyone thought Union Carbide should pay only the actual, real damages in the case. Efforts to attribute fair liability and to determine compensation, in the aftermath of the explosion, rapidly drowned in exaggerated estimates of the amount of money that could be expected from the company. In a poor country, the amounts being demanded in compensation were unrealistically high and not at all in line with precedents within the Indian justice system.

Since justice is the issue here, this controversy deserves a closer look: First, the estimates of damages due and payable were high by any standards. Within a year after the incident, Alfred de Grazia, writing on behalf of the India-America Committee for Bhopal Victims, devoted a chapter to "Damages and Compensation" and concluded with unconcealed glee that the company owed the victims and their survivors $1,318,650,000 in U.S. dollars.[50] Had de Grazia known that more were to die, the estimates would doubtless have been higher.

People discovered or invented reasons for believing that they were owed particularly large amounts of money. Depending on the political advantage of the moment, Indian officials alternately dangled and withdrew promises of much more money for the victims.[51] Because records of deaths and injuries were woefully inadequate, it was almost impossible to verify who had actually suffered from the gas and who had suffered (only!) from the preexisting poverty, malnutrition, and disease.[52] Emergency measures that were supposed to save lives, at the hospitals and in the town, were impossible to coordinate in the heat of the incident itself; it was thus impossible to attribute blame for injury and death with any reasonable certainty. After the incident, attempts to register those who deserved compensation were shot through with bureaucratic inefficiency and blatant corruption. With Union Carbide money looming in the background to pay all damages, large numbers of officials and secretaries—and even an occasional doctor or police officer—sought maximum financial reimbursement for performance of their duty.[53]

The lawyers played a large part in these monetary demands. Whenever the ethical dimensions of Bhopal are discussed, the lawyers always merit a chapter of their own. These lawyers—international "ambulance-chasers" of the stripe of Melvin Belli, John Coale, and, eventually, Stanley Chesley—claimed that they only wanted to represent the helpless widows and orphans, to make sure that the poverty-stricken victims got their due. But the lawyers' plans to keep 30 percent of each award for themselves (or at least as much of that as they could persuade a judge to allot them) were openly discussed from the time they first laid foot in India. First, they went from door to door on their own behalf, persuading the poor of Bhopal to sign retainers appointing them as their attorneys; later (after the Indian government took over that role), they attempted to persuade the Indian government to hire them as their representatives in the American courts. The lawyers had mentioned sums beyond anyone's imagination: millions for the victims, billions for the government. They were taken all too literally.

It is perhaps too tempting to be cynical about the lawyers. On a memorable bus ride through San Francisco, Stanley Chesley once described himself, with all apparent sincerity, as a man who just cannot resist a chance to help the underdog. It is surely part of the American tradition that one can do good and do well at the same time, and these lawyers were just doing their job.

More importantly, it is certain that, if American lawyers had not brought the victims' cause to the fore, no one else would have done it. No Indian lawyer (or, indeed, the Indian government) showed real interest in compensation for the victims until the American lawyers arrived on the scene.[54] Melvin Belli explained why he wanted the cases tried in the U.S., in a telling comment to the press soon after his arrival in India "...in court, you [Indians] don't appreciate the dignity of a man as much as we do."[55] By "dignity" he meant *worth*: worth as an autonomous individual, worth as a human life, worth in court in terms of monetary compensation. (Kant's arguments to the contrary notwithstanding, "price" and "dignity" are not incompatible in the courts of law.) For this is India, "steeped in poverty, apathy, corruption, and greed, an India that, while laudably dedicated to democratic freedoms, still judged the value of a life by the kind of work a person did."[56] And where tort law is concerned, that judgment is crucial.

Tort law is undeveloped in India: Compensation for injuries is not a fundamental right where injuries occur so often to so many. "Since there are no civil juries in India, judges determine liability and damages, and they are not overly impressed by calamities that kill thousands and simply punctuate the rough rhythm of survival in India."[57] According to all cited sources, India is not the appropriate place to mount tort action on behalf of the poor: The poor are expected to accept their lot. Victims and judges agree that most injuries are a matter of fate and could not have been avoided and, in any case, the value of what was lost in the Bhopal disaster—scraps of property, time, health, limb, life—is so small in the social reckoning that the suit would hardly be worth a lawyer's efforts. Until the Americans arrived and talked of infinite money, no one else was talking about the infinite value of human life. (And why should the value of an Indian life not be just as infinite as the value of an American life?) The lawyers were undoubtedly very interested in high fees, but they were also interested in Western law's historic recognition of the rights and value of the individual. If Warren Anderson can have mixed motives for his actions in the matter, so can the lawyers.

THE INCIDENT CONTINUES

The situation did not notably improve after the first shock of the incident. Indian fatalism might be the most appropriate philosophical orientation for the poisonous waves of disruption and destruction that followed the killer cloud. These included the maneuvering of the politicians; the assaults of the lawyers; the arrival of the political activists who took over part of the UCIL grounds, temporarily, to set up a People's Hospital; the best-selling journalistic accounts of the incident (some of which have been used extensively for this account), all of them hostile to business in general and Union Carbide in particular; and the hostile takeover attempt by GAF that drained the company's energies, and coffers, just when they were most needed by the victims.

At this writing, few victims have received compensation. The $470 million paid by Union Carbide in 1989, now increased by interest to something between $600[58] and $700[59] million, still sits in the State Bank of India. Some 630,000 claims for compensation by reason of injury or death were brought forward, but only 350,000 can be substantiated on the basis of medical records and other documents. To simplify their task, Bhopal authorities simply declared 37 wards of the city to be damaged by the gas and entitled to compensation, but as Paul Shrivastava, one of the foremost authorities on the incident, points out: "These 37 wards now hold about as many people as made up the whole population of Bhopal of 1984...now it's impossible to find a way to determine who was and who was not living in those wards at the time of the accident...It's become a very political thing."[60]

Fires swept Bhopal in December, 1992, during the riots following the burning of a mosque in northern India. The fires destroyed compensation documents and otherwise slowed the process of disbursing the funds.[61] Attempts by Bhopal activists to reactivate the civil suit in the United States and to increase the amount of the settlement pool have failed, but on Easter in 1993, an Indian court in Bhopal ordered eight officials of UCIL to go on trial for the gas-induced deaths of 3,828 people. For good measure, the judge "also ordered the former chairman of Union Carbide, Warren Anderson; the corporation; and its Hong Kong subsidiary to stand trial." The Indian CBI is to begin extradition proceedings for Anderson.[62]

Most observers assume that U.S. courts will not cooperate in the criminal proceedings, and Paul Shrivastava has expressed doubt that "even the Indian government is taking the criminal trial seriously."[63] Victor Schwartz, a Washington, D.C., attorney estimates that the main purpose of the charges is "leveraging criminal law to force more compensation in the civil case."[64] Whether or not the criminal trial goes forward, the situation of the victims will still be unresolved for some time. Yet, through the lingering cloud of legal and political toxins, two very serious areas of reevaluation are emerging from the agonies of Bhopal.

First, the U.S.-based multinational corporation will have to rethink its relation with the Third World or withdraw its operations aboard. Surveying the problems of the Bhopal plant, Warren Anderson concluded that multinationals "must not simply make improvements; they must demand more control of the plants, especially in the Third World, even if the host government balked" and, if that were impossible, then they should withdraw from the project completely.[65] Anderson was distressed that any Union Carbide plant should operate, as the one at Bhopal had, "with such total disregard for procedures."[66] With nationalism on the rise all over the world, the prospect for control, and for untroubled operation in the developing nations seems remote indeed. One mainstay of the national business scene, the profitable multinational corporation—spanning the world as the British Empire once did—might be destined for obsolescence, in the next few years.

The other lesson—a long-term one—concerns the whole enterprise of manufacturing poisons. These chemicals, designed to be incompatible with life as their very raison d'être, may be for that reason alone more of a burden than the Earth can bear. To that possibility we now turn.

THE POISONS: INSECTS AND PEOPLE

Bhopal is not alone: The pesticide industry is global big business, worth billions of dollars per year, all aimed at killing the insects, molds, weeds, and rodents that compete with the crops for sun and water or compete with us to eat crops. Our own factory farms have become dependent upon pesticides. In the Third World, pesticides are an essential part of the "green revolution" that was expected to feed the hungry of the world. In Africa alone, pesticide use quintupled between 1976 and 1986.[67] Whenever a major corporation moves into the pesticide trade in the Third World, questions of influence immediately arise: "By 1974, a decade before the Bhopal tragedy, for example, Union Carbide was marketing its products in 125 countries, 75 of which had smaller economies than the corporation."[68] The multinationals of all nationalities (the United States is not alone, either) often used or were suspected of using very substantial financial muscle to persuade Cabinet-level officials of the developing nations to allow the establishment of chemical plants in rural areas.[69]

Once those plants are established, poisoning becomes inevitable. Weir quotes a United Nations official who did not wish to be identified:

> Even those companies that say they will maintain the same standards as in the developed world find it difficult to resist the temptation to take a shortcut. Even if they have a good design for their plant, however, there's no good infrastructure in the underdeveloped countries. Even if they put it away from population centers, who will check and control that the people don't come in around it?[70]

Jan Huismans, the United Nations Environmental Program (UNEP) official who maintains the IRPTC (International Registry of Potentially Toxic Chemicals), expands on this point:

> In Africa, for example, they start with a little planning and try to locate these plants outside a populated area. But in no time, these cities grow and the industrial areas are engulfed by population settlement, surrounded by shantytowns. Also, there are no adequate waste disposal facilities for these plants. There is a lack of awareness

generally about how dangerous pesticides are. There's a lack of skilled regulatory personnel and controls. There is, in sum, a whole syndrome of problems.[71]

And that is what we have come to call "the Bhopal Syndrome."

Why do we manufacture these poisons at all? Whether or not the poisons escape from their factories, there are still very serious problems with them.

Consider that insecticides are only the most visible of the pesticides, a billion-dollar industry dwarfed by all other petrochemical operations: plastics, synthetic fibers, and thousands of other chemicals. Insecticides are designed to kill and are therefore toxic by definition. They are distinguishable by the range of their toxicity, their solubility, their persistence, and the breadth of their killing spectrum. If we wanted to kill every insect in or out of our sight (and many other creatures along the way), we would use a broad-spectrum, highly toxic, fat-soluble, and very persistent insecticide, such as DDT.

Historically, that was the approach taken, but its drawbacks soon became apparent. The broad-spectrum insecticides caused the death of non-targeted insects, including the insect pest predators that lived on the target insects and the pollinators essential to the growth of the crop. Fat-solubility meant that the chemical was not soluble in water and therefore impossible to flush out of a system, including organic systems (that is, it cannot be cleared from animal bodies by the kidneys and washed out in the urine). Persistence meant that the poison did not begin to break down into component chemicals for years but instead accumulated and became concentrated in the food chains. This means that each organism higher in the food chain will have a much higher concentration of the deadly stuff than the organisms it just consumed. To survive, consumers must eventually eat more than their own weight of the plants or animals they customarily eat. So a concentration of 0.1 part per million (ppm) of an insecticide in algae becomes 1.0 ppm in zooplankton that eat algae, 10 ppm in minnows that eat zooplankton, 100 ppm in small fish that eat minnows, and 1,000 ppm in large predator fish.

Meanwhile, the undiscriminating toxicity of DDT has threatened numerous unintended species with extinction, especially the birds of prey (the raptors) that ate the owls that had eaten the snakes that had eaten the mice that had eaten the acres of insecticide-treated plants. The next concern is, of course, the effect of this chain reaction on humans, who are high on the food chain. This is precisely why some fish caught in contaminated waterways are banned from human consumption and why some poisons exist in human milk in higher concentrations than allowed in cow's milk.

On top of all this, the effectiveness of these insecticides is really very limited. There are more than one million insect species (*species,* not individuals), and this only includes those that are known to us now. About four billion individual insects can be found per square mile. Given these numbers, it is reasonable to expect that, among an insecticide target species, a certain number will be genetically immune to the poison, just as some humans are immune to poison ivy. Now, if the insecticide is effective, it will kill all individuals that are not immune to it. Left behind will be those unaffected by the poison, who reproduce like crazy, passing their immunity along to a population that will be presented with a feast, such as a corn field, with *no competition* from either their own species or predator species (who have also died from the insecticide).

We have now created an insecticide-resistant strain of an insect species. Next, the farmer will usually try a different, generally more expensive insecticide, and then the process starts all over again. This is often called "the pesticide treadmill."

In 1938, seven insect species exhibited pesticide resistance: By 1984, there were 447 resistant species. Today, about the same percentage of our crops is lost to insects and weeds as before the development of synthetic pesticides.

Yet, how shall we grow our crops without insecticides? Donovan Webster summed up the state of the art for the Mississippi Delta. He predicted what would happen if the crop dusting were stopped:

> Most of the United States rice crop would be destroyed by insects and fungi. Forty per cent of our national cotton harvest would be ruined by bollworm and boll weevil. Roughly a quarter of our national soybean yield would never make it to the silo. The cotton gins would stop, the area's grain elevators would empty, and the farmers would have almost no new produce to sell.[72]

The bottom line? This "would make the price of being an everyday American rise appreciably."[73] The author does not mention this, but such a policy might well make the price of being an everyday inhabitant of the less-developed nations absolutely prohibitive, at least for a while.

Perhaps we shall have to pay that price, however. Alternatives to chemical warfare against insects are under study; some of them are on the horizon. Some very interesting research is being done in the area of IPM (Integrated Pest Management) using carefully measured minimal doses of pesticides along with biological and mechanical controls on insect pests. The cultivation of insect predators is already under way, and perhaps we should explore the capacity of plants to defend themselves, quite without our help: "Besieged by armies of voracious creatures but unable to run away, plants over the eons have evolved cunning defenses that include deadly poisons, oozings of toxic glue and hidden drugs that give leaf-eaters serious indigestion…Many plants…wait until a predator actually starts munching before they unleash their most noxious washes of chemicals."[74] The obvious suggestion is to learn how plants defend themselves and figure out how to teach, or modify, our agricultural staples to do the same; then, we would not have to use chemical pesticides at all. That would be good for the farmers, good for the land, and it would mean good-bye to Bhopals.

QUESTIONS FOR DISCUSSION
AND REFLECTION

✦ What does the Bhopal incident teach us about "responsibility" or "accountability" for things that go wrong? Is it inevitable that attributions of blame will be politically influenced?

✦ What is the difference between the way we ascribe blameworthiness to individuals and to corporations? How does the early controversy about whether the Bhopal incident was an accident or sabotage illustrate this difference?

✦ What would have been the best way to ensure that the victims received speedy and effective medical treatment? What should be done in future incidents of this sort?

✦ What should American companies that wish to operate abroad do to avoid future such incidents? Must we reach the conclusion that capitalism of the U.S. variety is simply unworkable in Third World nations?

Notes

1. Anwar Fazal, foreword to David Weir, *The Bhopal Syndrome: Pesticides, Environment and Health* (San Francisco: Sierra Club Books, 1987).

2. Alfred de Grazia, *A Cloud over Bhopal* (Bombay, India: Kalos Foundation, 1985): Kalos Foundation for the India-America Committee for the Bhopal Victims, 55 Mamta-A, Appasaheb Marathe Marg, Prabhadevi, Bombay 400 025 India.

3. Weir, *The Bhopal Syndrome*.

4. Ashok S. Kalelkar (Arthur D. Little, Inc.), "Investigation of Large-Magnitude Incidents: Bhopal as a Case Study," presented at the Institution of Chemical Engineers' Conference on Preventing Major Chemical Accidents, London, England, May 1988.

5. de Grazia, *Cloud over Bhopal*, p. 12,

6. Denise Lavoie, writing for the Associated Press, "Bhopal still haunts former Carbide chief," *Hartford Courant* (5 April 1992), pp. D1 & D7. Union Carbide estimates a death toll of 3,800. ("Union Carbide Corporation Bhopal Fact Sheet," available from Union Carbide Corporation, Corporate Communications Department, Section C-2, Danbury, CT 06817-0001. Hereinafter, documents obtained from that source will be identified as "UCC.") Dan Kurzman, in *A Killing Wind*, estimates "at least" 8,000 deaths and suggests that bodies were dumped anonymously into the river, to account for the lack of evidence of more casualties. De Grazia estimates 3,000 killed (*A Cloud over Bhopal*, p. 15) but wrote before the toll of indirect death was complete.

7. Lavoie (*supra*) estimates 20,000 injuries; Union Carbide estimates are closer to 3,000 with measurable injury after the fact (*ibid.*; UCC). Kurzman (*supra*) estimates 300,000 injuries; de Grazia gives 30,000 disabled and 180,000 "affected to minor degrees" (*supra*). Such discrepancies are the rule with this issue.

8. Weir, *The Bhopal Syndrome*, p. 36

9. Warren M. Anderson (Former Chairman, Union Carbide Corporation), "Bhopal: What We Learned," distributed by Union Carbide Corporation (Danbury, Connecticut 06817-0001; UCC Document #158); Kurzman, *A Killing Wind*, p. 21.

10. Kalelkar, "Large-Magnitude Incidents," p. 11.

11. "India's Tragedy: A Warning Heard Round the World," *U.S. News and World Report* (17 December 1984): p.25; and Pushpa S. Mehta et al. "Bhopal Tragedy's Health Effects: A Review of Methyl Isocyanate Toxicity," *Journal of the American Medical Association* (5 December 1990), vol. 264, no. 21, p. 2781.

12. Mehta et al., "Bhopal Tragedy's Health Effects."

13. Kurzman, *A Killing Wind*, p. 41.

14. Union Carbide Corporation, *Bhopal Methyl Isocyanate Incident Investigation Team Report*, Danbury, Connecticut, March, 1985.

15. UCC, *Bhopal Incident Team Report*; Ehrlichs et al., *Ecoscience* (San Francisco: W.H. Freeman, 1977); Kurzman, *A Killing Wind*, p. 22; Weir, *The Bhopal Syndrome*, p. 31.

16. Kurzman, *A Killing Wind*, p. 22.

17. Weir, *The Bhopal Syndrome*, pp. 30–31.

18. Anderson, "Bhopal: What We Learned"; UCC, "Union Carbide Corporation: Bhopal Fact Sheet," distributed by UCC, p. 1.

19. Weir, *The Bhopal Syndrome*, p. 33.

20. *Ibid.*, pp. 41–42.

21. *Ibid.*, p. 35.

22. *Ibid.*, p. 49. See also de Grazia, *Cloud over Bhopal*, p. 44.

23. Kalelkar, "Large-Magnitude Incidents," p. 21.

24. de Grazia, *Cloud over Bhopal*, p. 12. Weir relates a personal interview with M. N. Buch, former planning director for the state of Madhya Pradesh; Buch claimed that old maps of the city showed the existence of these slums before the arrival of the plant; Union Carbide claims that the squatters arrived after the company did. The two accounts are not incompatible (Weir, *The Bhopal Syndrome*, pp. 36–37).

25. "Others accuse the victims of being illegally in the path of the poisonous gases, of being 'illegal squatters,' as if they had no business existing or should have been on holiday at the seashore when the cloud came over Bhopal" (de Grazia, *Cloud over Bhopal*, p. 46).

26. John Rennie, "Trojan Horse: Did a Protective Peptide Exacerbate Bhopal Injuries?" *Scientific American* (March 1992): p. 27.

27. *Ibid.*

28. Mehta et al., "Bhopal Tragedy's Health Effects."

29. Kurzman, *A Killing Wind*, pp. 81–82.

30. Rennie, "Trojan Horse," p. 27.

31. *Ibid.*, p. 184.

32. Kurzman, *A Killing Wind*, p. 47.

33. UCIL's tanks were unusually large for such an operation, which has occasioned criticism in retrospect. The UCIL tank's capacity was 57,120 liters and was almost full. In Germany, the U.S., and Korea, MIC tanks have a capacity of 17,500 liters and are filled only to 50 percent of capacity as a safety precaution (Mehta et. al., "Bhopal Tragedy's Health Effects," p. 2781).

34. Kurzman, especially pp. 37–57.

35. See, for example, de Grazia, *Cloud over Bhopal*, p. 19.

36. UCC document, "Union Carbide Corporation, Bhopal Chronology."

37. Kurzman, *A Killing Wind*, p. 142.

38. Anderson, "Bhopal: What We Learned."

39. UCC document, "Bhopal Chronology."

40. Kurzman, *A Killing Wind*, p. 106.

41. Kalelkar, "Large-Magnitude Incidents," p. 21.

42. *Ibid.*

43. de Grazia, *Cloud over Bhopal*, p. 34.

44. J. Peterson, "After Bhopal: Tracing Causes and Effects," *Science News,* vol. 127 (30 March 1985): p. 196.

45. *Ibid.*, p. 188.

46. Neal Karlan and Peter McKillop, "Sabotage in Bhopal," *Newsweek,* vol. 105, no. 13 (1 April 1985): p. 35.

47. Kalelkar, "Large-Magnitude Incidents," pp. 14 ff.

48. Weir, *The Bhopal Syndrome*, pp. 48–49.

49. Controversy continued on this issue: As late as 1989, when the subject of Bhopal came up at a Business Ethics Conference at Bentley College in Waltham, Massachusetts, some participants disputed Union Carbide Corporation's interpretation of their findings. See Joseph Campbell, "Corporation's Theory About Cause of Disaster Still Subject of Debate," *Hartford Courant* (11 February 1990): p. 9.

50. de Grazia, *Cloud over Bhopal*, p. 116.

51. Kurzman, *A Killing Wind*, p. 157.

52. *Ibid.*, p. 159.

53. *Ibid.*, p. 161 ff. and Chapter 4 generally.

54. de Grazia, *Cloud over Bhopal*, p. 50.

55. Kurzman, *A Killing Wind*, p. 175.

56. *Ibid.*, p. 155.

57. *Ibid.*, p. 195.

58. Wil Lepkowski, "Union Carbide–Bhopal Saga Continues as Criminal Proceedings Begin in India," *Chemical and Engineering News* (16 March 1992): pp. 7–14.

59. Sanjoy Hazarika, "Settlement Slow in India Gas Disaster Claims," *The New York Times* (25 March 1993): p. A6.

60. Lepkowski, "Union Carbide–Bhopal Saga Continues," p. 13.

61. *Ibid.*

62. *Reuters*, "Trial Ordered for Carbide Officials in Bhopal," *The New York Times* (12 April 1993): p. A8.

63. Lepkowski, "Union Carbide–Bhopal Saga Continues," p. 14.

64. *Ibid.*, p. 8.

65. *Ibid.*, p. 173.

66. *Ibid.*, p. 185.

67. Weir, *The Bhopal Syndrome*, p. 24.

68. *Ibid.*, cited from "Union Carbide: A Study in Corporate Power and the Case for Union Power," Oil, Chemical and Atomic Workers International Union, June 1974.

69. *Ibid.*, p. 26.

70. *Ibid.*, p. 62.

71. *Ibid.*, p. 63.

72. Donovan Webster, "Heart of the Delta," A Reporter at Large for *The New Yorker* (8 July 1991): pp. 46–66.

73. Webster, "Heart of the Delta."

74. Carol Kaesuk Yoon, "Nibbled Plants Don't Just Sit There: They Launch Active Attacks," *The New York Times* (23 June 1992): p. C1.

Suggestions for Further Reading

de Grazia, Alfred. *A Cloud over Bhopal.* Bombay, India: Kalos Foundation, 1985. (Kalos Foundation for the India-America Committee for the Bhopal Victims, 55 Mamta-A, Appasaheb Marathe Marg, Prabhadevi, Bombay 400 025 India.)

Kurzman, Dan. *A Killing Wind: Inside Union Carbide and the Bhopal Catastrophe.* New York: McGraw-Hill, 1987.

Weir, David. *The Bhopal Syndrome: Pesticides, Environment and Health.* San Francisco: Sierra Club Books, 1987.

CHAPTER 3

Chernobyl

The Blast Heard 'Round the World

PREFACE: QUESTIONS TO KEEP IN MIND

Nuclear power is a relatively new form of energy. What is it, really, and how does it generate such an enormous amount of heat?

What are the advantages of nuclear power? What kinds of power does it replace? Are we willing to exchange the certain expense, pollution, and vulnerability to Middle East political processes associated with fossil fuels for the risks of nuclear radiation?

What are the disadvantages of nuclear power? Disregarding the danger of explosion, how will we dispose of our radioactive waste? Do we have technical solutions to the problems associated with nuclear energy?

Right now, nuclear power generation is very expensive, partly because of technical problems but largely because of the legal expenses of fighting political opposition. Should those costs be taken into account in any cost/benefit survey of nuclear power use?

We worry about the use of nuclear fission to generate power because of the dangers associated with it—but what can we consider *safe?* William Lowrance comments:

> We are disturbed by what sometimes appear to be haphazard and irresponsible regulatory actions, and we can't help being suspicious of all the assaults on our freedoms and our pocketbooks made in

the name of safety. We hardly know which cries of "Wolf!" to respond to; but we dare not forget that even in the fairy tale, the wolf really did come.[1]

In the realm of nuclear power, Chernobyl was the coming of the wolf. Where do we go from here?

CHERNOBYL: THE EVENT

In the summer of 1986, Soviet investigators prepared a massive report on the accident at Chernobyl. In the revolutionary spirit of *glasnost,* the investigators released their report at an international meeting in Vienna in August of that year. Colin Norman, writing for *Science,* summarized that report:

> A botched experiment and a series of deliberate safety violations, and a reactor that was inherently difficult to operate and control combined to cause the world's worst nuclear accident.[2]

That report was the Soviet account of the explosion and fire that destroyed Reactor Four at the Chernobyl atomic power station and spread some 50 million curies of radiation into the environment—depositing as much as half of the radiation within 30 kilometers of the plant. Somehow, the world's second-to-worst nightmare had come true, and immeasurable injury was dealt to the immediate inhabitants (especially children), to the population of Europe in the path of the plume of radioactivity, and to the food chain of the entire region for decades to come.

What had happened? Let us review the event:

The purpose of a nuclear reaction in a nuclear reactor, as you probably know, is to produce heat, lots of it, that converts water into steam that turns turbines that produce electricity. Thus, the nuclear plant, like most power plants, is simply a teakettle, differing from other power plants only in the type of stove that creates the heat.

The nuclear stove is composed of rods containing nuclear fuel, pellets of enriched uranium, whose unstable molecules spontaneously "decay" or release neutrons, which in turn can strike other uranium molecules, causing them to fission (split apart), thus releasing enormous amounts of energy in the form of heat—and more neutrons to continue the chain reaction. Uranium exists in nature primarily as U-238, also radioactive and capable of fission but not "fissile," which means it does not release enough subatomic particles over time to maintain a chain reaction.

The U-235 isotope is only about 0.7 percent of naturally occurring uranium and not concentrated enough to maintain the chain reactions; therefore, the uranium must be "enriched" to about 3 percent U-235 to be used as a nuclear fuel. Meanwhile, U-238 can be fissioned itself, and it can also absorb neutrons and undergo a transformation to Plutonium-239, which *is* fissile and will thus contribute to the action in the teakettle.[3]

Putting the enriched fuel in place, however, is only the beginning of boiling the water. The reaction will not happen properly (that is, produce power) unless it is governed by a "moderator," a substance that will slow the neutrons released by the decaying uranium below their normal speed and reflect them back into the fuel. Slowing the neutrons increases the intensity of the reaction and the power produced by it, for it raises the chances that the neutrons will hit other unstable atoms of U-235 and split them. The temperature must also be carefully regulated, hot enough to boil the water but not so hot as to create a danger of explosion. Water is usually used as a coolant, so the temperature of the reaction can be raised or lowered by reducing or increasing the flow of water. "Control rods," containing boron or another material that will absorb (rather than reflect) the flying neutrons, are used to slow the reaction, as needed; the intensity of the reaction can be controlled by lowering the control rods into the reactor to slow it down and raising them out of the reactor to allow the reaction to speed up.

With the "light-water" reactors favored in the United States, water is used as both moderator and coolant, circulating constantly among the reactor fuel rods. With the RBMK, the Soviet model that was in operation at Chernobyl, by contrast, water is used as a coolant but the moderator is graphite; the fuel rods and control rods run through chunks of this graphite. The difference in moderator becomes important under the conditions that triggered the Chernobyl accident: In a water-moderated reactor, steam forming in the water will simply slow the reaction by decreasing the moderating activity of the water, but "steam in the cooling water can increase reactivity in a graphite-moderated reactor. As the cooling water turns to steam, it absorbs fewer neutrons. This means that more neutrons will pass to the graphite, which will slow them down and reflect them back, increasing fission. This causes the power level to rise, which in turn increases steam formation, and the process can quickly escalate."[4] This feature of the RBMK reactor—the propensity of steam formation and reaction intensity to reinforce each other in lethal positive interaction, under certain circumstances—is called a "positive void coefficient" (occasionally, "positive reactivity coefficient" or "positive-void effect").[5]

The boiling water, the steam, the turning turbines, and the electricity are the heart of the endeavor. Compared to other stoves, the nuclear stove is clean (no smoke), safe to mine and assemble, and (other things being equal) fairly inexpensive. The downside of this particular stove is, of course, the risk of injury from the radiation.

Exposure to radioactivity hurts living things, sometimes very badly, and enough exposure will kill them; radioactive substances are toxic to all life forms. All those subatomic particles penetrate the cells of the body and, depending upon the dose, either injure or kill them. A less-than-lethal dose will change some molecules in the cells, thus disposing them to problems in the future: If the changed molecule is DNA (which governs the cell and determines when it will divide), the resultant mutation can lead to cancer. Birth defects can also be produced from such mutations. The cells most vulnerable to destruction by radiation are those that divide rapidly (fetal cells, hair follicle cells, and the cells that line the intestinal tract and make up the bone marrow). Death by radiation overdose is debilitating, exhausting, painful, and for those who have been significantly exposed, very quick.

To protect nuclear workers and people in the vicinity of nuclear accidents against injury or death, the U.S. Nuclear Regulatory Commission (NRC) has determined the "maximum permissible concentration" (mpc) of radioactivity in the environment before people have to be removed from the affected area. A *rad* (radiation absorbed dose) is a dosage of radiation absorbed, as measured by the amount of energy, in ergs, per gram of absorbing material. A *rem* (roentgen equivalent man) is the amount of rads absorbed, multiplied by the relative biological impact of the type of radiation. (Heavy particles cause greater biological effects than rads from gamma or beta radiation.) The mpc is the equivalent of a 500-millirem dose (0.005 rem). A *curie,* the measure of actual radioactivity in the region, is equal to the radioactivity of one gram of Radium-226, or 37 billion nuclear transformations per second. (For instance, the mpc for Iodine-131 in air is 0.0001 microcuries/meter^3.)[6]

The products of nuclear fission are inevitably dangerous. Plutonium, one of these products, is notorious for being one of the most toxic of substances, when inhaled, and for its long half-life of 24,500 years. (The *half-life* is the amount of time it takes a radioactive substance to lose one half of its radioactivity.) Plutonium's long half-life makes that substance a very large part of the concern over the disposal of nuclear waste. Uranium's heavy atoms split into two or more pieces; each piece is an element that, when added to the other pieces, will almost equal the mass (weight) of the original atom. Herein lies the major concern about nuclear accidents: These fission products include dangerously radioactive isotopes, such as Cesium-137, Strontium-90, and Iodine-131, all of which could be deadly to local humans (and other living things) if released into the environment.

These elements account for the paradox that "spent fuel," fuel with not enough U-235 to continue the chain reaction at sufficient levels, is much more dangerously radioactive than the fuel that originally went into the reactor, and that nuclear waste is more hazardous than the original fuel pellets. The bombardment from these radioactive elements threatens living bodies, but that is not all: Because these elements continue to be radioactive, they continue to give off the heat associated with radioactive decay even long after the normal U-235 fission has been shut down. You cannot safely walk away when you have turned off the nuclear stove: The spent fuel of shutdown produces about 6–7 percent of the power that the working reactor produces and can cause a meltdown all by itself, unless cooling is maintained.

THE EXPERIMENT

The problems with Reactor Four began shortly after midnight on April 25, 1986. The reactor was scheduled for shutdown for routine maintenance; accordingly, at 1:00 AM the operators began to reduce the power output from its normal operating level of 3,200 megawatts.[7] That night, the engineers were running a potentially dangerous experiment: They planned to test one of the emergency safety systems while the reactor was still running at low power. On the hypothesis that power outages loomed as a real risk in that area, they wanted to find out how long one of the generators, disconnected from the power grid, could continue to power some reactor systems from its own mechanical inertia as it coasted to a stop; this leftover rotational kinetic energy might be used to run the cooling pumps in an emergency.

The experiment was not unreasonable; similar experiments had apparently been conducted before. The danger was that all the safety systems, which were programmed to shut everything down at once when the power failed, had to be disabled to conduct the experiment, so if anything went wrong there would be no way to stop the ensuing reaction. As we all know now, something went very wrong.

The experiment was scheduled to begin when the power output from Reactor Four was reduced to between 700 and 1,000 MW. By 1:05 PM, 12 hours after shutdown had begun, the output had dropped to half capacity; at 2:00 PM, the operators shut down the emergency cooling system to prevent it from activating during the tests. An automatic control system was also disengaged, probably by mistake. Over the next several hours, there were serious instabilities in the operation of the reactor; at one point, the power dipped below 30 MW. Part of the problem, apparently, was a buildup of Xenon in the reactor, which slowed down the reaction and cut the power too low for the experiment to be run. To compensate for this unforeseen slowing of the reaction, the operators withdrew many of the control rods.[8]

By 1:00 AM on April 26, the power was back up to 200 MW in the reactor, but at that output the operators had little control over the reactor; all the control rods had been withdrawn, and the emergency cooling system had been disabled for almost 12 hours. As the operators finally began their experiment, the pumps they rigged to the reactor put in too much cooling water and cooled the reactor so quickly that another emergency shutdown system might have kicked in and turned off the reactor before the experiment had been completed. So, the operators disabled that system, too, and removed the manually operated control rods to make sure that the power stayed high enough. Then, at 1:23 AM, they shut off the steam supply to the generator they were testing, to see how long it could run on mechanical momentum alone. The first result was that the cooling pumps, which were being powered by that generator, started to run down. Now, there was too little, rather than too much, coolant in the reactor. The water began to boil out of control; then, because of the positive void coefficient, the power surged.

The operators spotted the surge and reacted immediately by lowering the control rods into the core of the reactor to shut down the reaction. (The record indicates that corrective action was taken less than a minute from the initiation of the experimental procedure.) It was already too late, however. The drive mechanism was slow, for lack of power; when the rods were released to fall of their own weight, the meltdown was already in progress and they never reached the heart of the reaction.

As the intensely hot fuel melted the reactor and dropped in great pieces into the cooling water, it caused a thermal explosion (possibly two—a steam explosion followed by a hydrogen explosion)[9] that destroyed what was left of the reactor and most of the building.

> The blast(s) knocked aside a thousand-ton lid atop the reactor core and ripped open the building's side and roof. Reactor innards were flung into the night. These included several tons of the uranium dioxide fuel and fission products such as cesium 137 and iodine 131, as well as tons of burning graphite. Explosion and heat sent up a five-kilometer (three-mile) plume laden with contaminants.[10]

With the reactor lid gone, no barrier stood between the sky and the intensely radioactive core of the reactor; the area was showered with radioactive material, and fires started everywhere (some estimate more than 30).

The damage done by the explosions was, quite literally, unbelievable. When the power surge went off the dials in the control room and the mechanism that was supposed to lower the control rods failed, two young engineers were sent to the reactor to lower the rods by hand. They returned to report that the operation could not be done because the reactor was gone—destroyed—its lid blown off, its fuel fused with the graphite in twisted lumps at the base of the building. No one could, or would, believe the report. The plant's director, Viktor Bryukhanov, and the chief engineer, Nikolai Fomin, were told that an accident had happened but that the reactor was still intact. A later report of the real extent of the destruction, from another engineer who had gone to see for himself what had happened, was similarly ignored. All three of these witnesses, incidentally, died of radiation poisoning within days of the accident—the first victims, along with two plant maintenance workers who had been in the reactor building at the time of the explosion; 31 people would shortly die from the accident and its immediate sequelae.[11]

Disbelief slowed measures to minimize or remedy the effects of the blast. The fires clearly needed attention; the local fire department was called, and the fires had been extinguished by morning, allowing the safe shutdown of Reactor Three. (The others were shut down in a few days.) But evacuation orders, even for nearby Pripyat, a city in the direct path of the plume, did not go out until the next day, and the evacuees were badly misinformed (by accident or on purpose) concerning the true scope of the tragedy. The citizens of Pripyat left town in light clothing, expecting to be home soon, leaving their pets behind, and were never permitted to go back; eventually, the army had to be called in to shoot the radiation-sickened animals.[12]

THE CAUSES AND THE BLAME

What caused the accident? For that matter, what is the *cause* of any event? The chronicle of the engineers' actions on that fatal night, presented very briefly in the foregoing,[13] is clear enough. For most purposes, those actions constitute the *cause* of the accident, but actions do not take place in a void. When a disaster occurs, those who are responsible for designing the environment in which the events took place must bear responsibility for the design flaws in that environment. So, the *cause* of an automobile accident might include the sleepy or careless driver who plowed across the intersection into the truck—but it might also include the bad signage that gave him little warning of the approaching intersection, the inferior asphalt that provided no traction for his tires in the light rain, or the inadequate shoulders that gave him no place to dodge the oncoming vehicle. For that matter, the cause of the accident might include the faulty tires that failed to grip the road—either because they were inferior to begin with or because the owner of the car forgot to replace them when they were worn out, and so on. Without for an instant taking responsibility, in the sense of *culpability*, from the sleepy or careless driver, we must remain conscious of functional responsibility, in the sense of *accountability*, that holds every human participant, from designer to builder to manager to operator, partially responsible for every human injury at the site where an incident occurs.

We hold everyone responsible, not from a vindictive desire to blame everyone in sight, but from an acute consciousness that we need better and safer cars and power plants and that the way to get them is to take very careful, and very public, note of the way things fail. An important balancing act is required at this point in any investigation: We must *spread responsibility as widely as it goes* and not ignore any contributor to the event. People must not be led to believe that, since they played such a small part in the project, the shoddiness of their performance is really too small to matter.

On the other hand, we must *attribute full responsibility to those who were really responsible:* We must not let this radiation of blame diffuse all accountability so broadly that no individual is *really* to blame for anything. Responsibility for the accident at Chernobyl can be spread very widely indeed, yet all who failed in their tasks can be held morally accountable.

First, the *design* of Reactor Four failed dismally, at least in the sense that, in a water-moderated reactor, without the positive void coefficient, *that* accident could not have happened.[14] Also, as Gordon Thompson understated, the "containment system at Chernobyl was manifestly inadequate."[15] Then, there was the *construction* of the plant: Viktor Bryukhanov, the plant director, pointed out that the plant had never been in conformity with accepted construction practices. Others echoed his sentiments: "Without rule breaking, the Chernobyl station would have never been completed. Electric cables, for example, should have had fire-resistant claddings, but none were available and ordinary cables were used instead."[16]

These were not the only corners that were cut: *Management* also failed. Robert Lockwood, writing in *TIME* magazine in 1988, concluded that "...sloppy workmanship, mismanagement and lax safety standards [were] the very conditions blamed for causing the accident..."[17] That criticism can be generalized: Valerii Legasov, the Chief Deputy Director of the Kurchatov Nuclear Energy Institute said that the Chernobyl disaster was simply the "peak of the economic mismanagement" that had plagued the Soviet Union for decades.[18] Legasov and the Institute were not the only ones that claimed to have issued warnings about conditions at the reactor, warnings that went unheeded by the management of the plant.

What about the engineers themselves? The difficulties attending the setup of the experiment over the preceding 24 hours should have clued them in to the unmanageable problems in controlling the reactor at low power. "A nuclear engineer at the NRC [the Nuclear Regulatory Commission] said the accident shows the danger of 'people mucking around in a nuclear reactor, but not knowing the what and the why of safety systems and the limits of the reactor.'"[19] Rushworth Kidder, president of the Institute for Global Ethics based in Maine, sees the whole experiment as the sheerest recklessness, motivated by no more than the playful curiosity of bored engineers: "What they lacked, apparently, was the sense of responsibility, the moral understanding, the sense of conscience, the understanding of ethics—however you want to put it—that somehow would have prevented them from going forward."[20] This interpretation seems to put too much blame on the engineers, though. Were they under pressure from management to do whatever it took to get the experiment done? After all, the test could only be run during the yearly shutdown of the reactor.

There is, in short, enough blame to go around. The failure of all the human systems in place to protect the reactor caused the accident, we could say, and did us all a favor, in the final analysis: They woke up the world once more to the perils of the peaceful atom. If this technology is to provide any part of our energy supply in the years to come, we must be willing to reassess our designs and do a much better job on the nuclear reactors of the future.

AFTERWARD:
THE RADIOACTIVE AFTERMATH

Days after the accident, emergency workers were still trying to control the temperature in the devastated core of Reactor Four. Flooding it with water did not work; military helicopters dropped almost 5,000 tons of lead, boron, limestone, sand, and clay (not always accurately) to smother the reaction; soldiers were called out to shovel dirt on the glowing core from what was left of the roof.[21] When the fire was finally out, though, the troubles had just begun.

Some 50 million curies of radioactivity had been released into the air in the explosion and the ten days following it. On the first day alone, radiation levels in the vicinity of the plant increased from 180–600 millirems per hour in the early morning (up to 50,000 times the normal background level for the region) to 720–1,000 millirems per hour by late afternoon.[22] By September, 1986, 31 people had died; many of the operators and firemen who had dealt directly with the explosion and the resulting fires died of radiation burns and poisoning, and the soldiers and volunteers who labored valiantly to cover the exposed core made up the rest of the casualties. There were perhaps 1,000 immediate injuries, and 135,000 persons living within a radius of 30 kilometers of the plant had to be evacuated from their homes in the Ukraine (45,000 of them from Pripyat). Environmental radiation continued to increase, for weeks, from the decay of the melted core.

Ultimately, about 7,000 kilograms of radioactive materials from the core of Reactor Four were released into the environment: 50 to 100 million curies of radioactive isotopes.[23] The city of Kiev, home to 2.4 million people, came out better than could be expected, because the winds blew away from the city during the worst period. "But several wind shifts brought the nuclear cloud over virtually all of Europe—extending as far north as the Arctic Circle, as far south as Greece, and as far west as the British Isles. Potentially health-threatening levels of radioactive materials were deposited more than 2,000 kilometers from the plant and in at least 20 countries."[24] As it happens, the accident first came to light in Sweden, on April 28, when technicians noticed atmospheric traces of radioactive gases, mostly Xenon and Krypton, that could not have come from anyplace but the Soviet Union.[25] Shortly thereafter, radiation was found in scattered regions throughout Europe.

What consequences could have been expected from this contamination? First among the worries, of course, was the health of all those who were exposed to the radiation. After the immediate deaths, about 500 people had to be hospitalized with some form of radiation poisoning; this included some of the bus drivers who evacuated residents from the area. Possibly 24,000 of the evacuees received serious doses of radiation. Disorders caused by radiation, including cancer, have been documented in this population; 40 cases of pediatric thyroid cancer, ordinarily very rare in that population, have been diagnosed among children from the contaminated villages near Chernobyl.[26] Yet, the best prediction for total morbidity among those 24,000 people is 100 to 200 cancer deaths—"not even a blip on the cancer tables."[27] For the region outside the nearest direct exposure, there are few reliable predictions over the long term.

There are three major health threats from exposure to radioactive materials: The first is direct exposure, resulting in burns and massive internal injuries, especially to all areas where cells divide rapidly; this type of radiation poisoning killed the operators and rescue workers around the reactor. Second, damage can result from inhaling radioactive dust; many of the citizens of Pripyat were probably injured by such inhalation. Third, radioisotopes come to rest in the drinking water and the food supply, entering the food chain through rain and grass. This is potentially the most worrisome health threat. Iodine-131, entering the body through food or water, was the major threat immediately after the accident; this element becomes concentrated in the thyroid and was certainly responsible for the cases of rare thyroid cancer among the children. But Iodine-131 has a half-life of eight days and was largely gone from the area in a month or so. Strontium-90, also released in the explosion, has a half-life of 27 years, but it was not present in large quantities; Strontium-90 settles in bones and is thus a leukemia threat.

The worst danger was from Cesium. Cesium-137, with a half-life of 30 years, binds to the soil, concentrates in food chains, and emits gamma radiation for years. "By far the largest area of persistent contamination was made by cesium 137, one of the longest lived radioactive elements ... It was carried on wind high above the ground, and fell where the rain did, along a broad swath of territory from the central Ukraine north across eastern Byelorussia ... Altogether, some 13,100 square miles of agricultural land, dotted with small cities, are contaminated with radioactivity at levels of five or more curies per square kilometer. Cesium contamination forced farmers to destroy produce as far away as Lapland, in northern Sweden, and Italy and Wales."[28] There is no telling how much health damage can result from trace contamination with this element. Estimates run between 5,000 and 50,000 cancer deaths attributable to Cesium-137 from Chernobyl,[29] and the wide discrepancy in the estimates does not inspire confidence. Meanwhile, one computer model yields a prediction of "between 15,500 and 135,000 extra cancer cases"[30] and "a maximum of 35,000 extra deaths" from exposure to Cesium.[31] (What is an "extra death"—the death of someone who would not otherwise have died?)

THE CONTINUING STRUGGLE

Five years after the accident, radioactive Cesium persisted in the air and in the food. The problem turned out to be far greater than anyone had anticipated and beyond anyone's ability to solve it. By that time, up to 600,000 workers had been involved in the cleanup, and many of these workers had been exposed to high doses of radiation. Up to 200,000 people had been evacuated from areas that were determined to have been contaminated; many of these people had received nonlethal doses of radiation, which presumably increase the risk of developing cancer. As Felicity Barringer documented in *The New York Times Magazine,* there were an "additional 2000 still occupy[ing] areas where the contamination measures, on average, 40 curies per square kilometer—up to 300 times the background levels in Byelorussia..."[32] Why did these people continue to live there under these conditions? According to Barringer, they had no place else to go.

At this writing (September 1992), the Ukraine is still struggling with the aftermath of the Chernobyl disaster. Vladimir Yavorivsky, a deputy to the Ukrainian Parliament and head of a committee on Chernobyl, has documented the difficulties of coping with a health crisis of undetermined dimensions, environmental degradation, and the continuing danger of new explosions in "an economically exhausted Ukraine fighting for its sovereignty."[33] Yavorivsky believes that the million people still living in the 30-kilometer zone around the accident site should be moved, but this year the parliament has only about $800,000 to spend on Chernobyl.[34] The sarcophagus built to contain the destroyed reactor is cracked, leaking, and sinking; the fuel that remains within is difficult to monitor (Yavorivsky believes that the heat of decaying fuel actually started a new chain reaction at one point); and the Ukrainian government has decided, apparently for economic reasons, to leave two of the original four Chernobyl reactors, identical in design to the one that blew up, operating until the end of 1993, continuing the danger.

How will we ever assess the total damage caused by the explosion of Reactor Four at Chernobyl? We do not know, but the ways in which we do not know are instructive:

+ In some areas, we do not know *what* will happen: We do not know how long environmental radiation will linger at significant levels or how far (into the water supply, for instance) the radiation will spread.

+ In other areas, we do not know *how to quantify* what has happened. We know, for instance, that the survivors still residing in the area will eventually die and that they have about one chance in three of dying of cancer—but whether *their* cancer will be due to the Chernobyl accident and whether they will die sooner than they would otherwise have, had Chernobyl not exploded, only a very careful statistical analysis after the fact will be able to tell us, and probably not with certainty.

+ In some areas, we do not know how to weight the values: For instance, the value of continuing power production by keeping the remaining reactors in production versus the value of risk reduction for the area or the value of allowing people to stay in their own familiar homes and workplaces versus the value of safely relocating them.

+ In other areas, the whole system of values is in dispute: Chernobyl brought to an end the rapid development of nuclear power as a source for the world's electricity. In a world that is consuming ever more energy, is that perhaps the worst part of the disaster? Or, in a world increasingly dominated by environmentally dubious technology, was that the one positive outcome of the accident?

Ultimately, we will not be able to put the Chernobyl disaster in perspective until we have made the next set of decisions about the world's energy: to rely on other sources of energy, at the price of pollution (nuclear energy is relatively clean); to conserve energy, imposing the most stringent controls on consumption in order to live in ways more friendly to the environment; or to accept the Faustian bargain and put nuclear power back on line.

THE POLITICAL FALLOUT

For the Soviet Union, the fallout from Chernobyl was instant and devastating: This might well have been the incident that consolidated nationalism among the Ukrainians and Byelorussians and eventually brought down the central government of the vast country that had opposed us in a cold war since 1947—but the nuclear industry, and its effects on health and the environment, is our more pressing concern.

The Chernobyl disaster presented the nuclear utility industry with an unprecedented challenge. Since the inception of the nuclear power industry in the 1950s, the industry has been ensnared in a running debate about safety: Do the clear benefits of nuclear power outweigh the dangers of nuclear accident or explosion? Up to now, the proponents of nuclear power had been able to point to a fairly good safety record. There had been accidents before, of course. The Windscale plant, north of Liverpool, England, had caught fire in 1957, spreading radioactive materials over 200 square miles. That same year, a monstrous explosion had shaken the city of Kyshtym, in the southern part of the Ural mountains (but no one knew about it until 1989!). The Brown's Ferry reactor, near Decatur, Alabama, suffered a series of minor accidents over the years, all caused by human error.

In the most serious previous nuclear event, a reactor at a nuclear plant at Three Mile Island, near Harrisburg, Pennsylvania, lost all its coolant, on March 29, 1979, and partially melted. Citizens were advised to evacuate from the immediate vicinity of the plant. Metropolitan Edison, which owned the plant, issued partial and confusing descriptions and explanations of the accident. Groups supporting and opposing the use of nuclear power adopted positions on the implications for energy policy. When it was all over, though (for the rest of us—the plant itself has still not been cleaned out), the containment vessel had held, there had been no deaths, and although many people had been very frightened, there was not one case of any kind of sickness attributable to the accident. So the forces pro and con reached a stalemate on Three Mile Island: On the one hand, there *had* been an accident, caused by an absurd series of human errors; on the other hand, the backup systems had worked and no one had been hurt. Chernobyl, however, led to no such standoff. This technology is dangerous.

THE DEBATE PROCEEDS

Is nuclear power so dangerous that we ought to forswear using it in the world's continuing search for better, cheaper, and cleaner sources of energy? This is the ongoing debate, between those who claim that the clean, safe, and silent operation of the nuclear plant is far superior to the pollution dirt of the fossil fuel plants—especially given the personal and political costs of resource extraction in the case of coal and oil and the limited types of jobs they make possible—and those who plead that the evils they know, from black lung disease to acid rain, are more acceptable than the nuclear evils they do not know.

Chernobyl definitely fueled the debate. Less than a month after the reactor exploded into the night, *Business Week* documented "Battling the Backlash Against Nuclear Energy": The industry's first reaction had been to control the damage, "emphasize the U.S. industry commitment to safety," and, in general, "sing the industry's praises."[35]

In August, 1986, Valerii Legasov presented the official Soviet report on Chernobyl at a conference in Vienna sponsored by the International Atomic Energy Agency (IAEA) and attended by nuclear industry and government delegates from all nations using nuclear power. The report was presented, with accompanying videotapes, on August 25; it was thorough, stark, and terrifying. Journalists present noted that the mood of the conference became "bleak and tense."[36] Yet, by August 29, the mood had lifted noticeably, and whatever long-term pessimism the press had foreseen four days earlier had failed to materialize. The delegates had apparently been persuaded by a variety of considerations that all was not lost for the industry.

First, the health effects needed to be put in perspective: As mentioned earlier, "extra deaths," even extra cases of cancer (beyond the rare pediatric thyroid cancers, all too obviously a product of the Chernobyl disaster), will be difficult to demonstrate; even the 31 radiation deaths must be compared to other sorts of disasters (more people would die in an ordinary airplane crash); and above all, no other nuclear power plants use the RBMK reactor with the fatal flaw in its design. So our reactors are safe, and the future of the industry is entirely safe. This, at least, the delegates concluded.

Meanwhile, the initial harsh criticisms of Soviet technology were muted in light of the evidence of heroic (and effective) measures to bottle up the damage and treat the victims. At the end, "the final plenary saw a comradely closing of the nuclear ranks, amid an outpouring of mutual congratulations on the week's efforts."[37]

Still, the realistic mood of the aftermath is worried and uncertain: "Concerns about the possibility of a serious reactor accident in the United States have increased, mainly because of the widespread contamination from the Chernobyl accident...Most experts...do not believe that a Chernobyl-type accident could happen in U.S. commercial reactors... Most experts interviewed for this article pointed out that it is too early to draw specific lessons for the U.S. nuclear program..."[38]

This article is several years old, but little has crystallized since. The confidence of the nuclear power industry is unchanged since before the Chernobyl disaster, but the weight of the public's fear has slowly ground down the industry to a shadow of its former self. Nuclear reactors are being dismantled, some even before going into production (such as the Shoreham plant on Long Island in New York). No one now expects that nuclear energy is the way of the future.[39]

THE FAUSTIAN BARGAIN

This fear is worth exploring. In all the events that surround the Chernobyl disaster, there is a recurring image of fear: A "Faustian bargain" (accepting danger to gain power) was made by the industrialized nations when they started down the nuclear energy path.[40] Is that danger really acceptable to the great majority of us, however? Nuclear radiation kills, but not like a tiger, nor like cyanide, nor even like a pneumococcus—"radiation is a secret thing."[41]

The first sign of deadly radiation sickness might be simple nausea, yet "weeks or months without apparent sign of injury are no guarantee of health...It's the secrecy of injury that stirs the anxiety."[42] Radioactive wastes from the operation of nuclear power plants must be stored somewhere, yet sites for storage are now nearly impossible to locate, largely because of the popular fear of having such wastes in the area ("Not In My Back Yard!") and because of the tremendous time periods over which such fear can be expected to extend:

> The Department of Energy is currently trying to identify two underground sites in stable geological structures where such wastes, accumulated over a projected 35-year period, may be stored safely for 10,000 years—guarded by warnings that must make sense to passers-by when the markers are twice as old as writing is now. The Great Sphinx at Giza, by way of comparison, is only 3,500 years old, and no one knows why it was built.[43]

It will be necessary to store the worst nuclear waste for 15,000 years to bring radioactivity down to the level of raw uranium ore. On the other hand, most of the most immediately harmful waste (Cesium-137 and Strontium-90) would be reasonably safe after about 300 years.[44] Of course, burial of radioactive contamination will not put an end to our fears: The substances could migrate, find their way into aquifers, surface years later in unsuspected pastures, concentrate in the food chain, and finally threaten us when we have ceased to worry about safety. We wanted the cheap, clean power that we were promised by the nuclear age, but do we really want to pay the price of limitless, comfortless fear?

One perspective was articulated at the Vienna conference:

> The Faustian bargain of nuclear energy has been lost. It is high time to leave the path pursued in the use of nuclear energy in the past, to develop new alternative and clean sources of energy supply and, during the transition period, devote all efforts to ensure maximum safety. This is the price to pay to enable life to continue on this planet.[45]

So concluded Peter Jankowitsch, foreign minister of Austria, speaking to the delegates of the IAEA.

The nuclear enterprise has not turned out the way we had hoped, and the disillusionment is widespread. Christopher Flavin, of the Worldwatch Institute, gleefully documented the negative reaction to Chernobyl: All but a few nations of the nuclear club have undertaken at least a serious reevaluation of the technology, with utter rejection looming in the near future.[46]

Alvin Weinberg emphasizes the point:

> Chernobyl [and other incidents] are revealing some of the social
> costs of nuclear accidents, costs that can hardly be estimated by
> probabilistic risk assessment, especially since the costs depend very
> much upon the cultural and political environment of the country in
> which the accident occurs...An important social cost of Chernobyl
> is the possible abandonment of nuclear power in several West Euro-
> pean countries. Austria, Denmark, and Norway had already
> rejected nuclear power even before Chernobyl...In the United
> States, an ABC poll suggested that 78 percent of the public is now
> opposed to nuclear power.[47]

The few nations who have not abandoned nuclear power include Poland
and, most notably, France.

HOPE FOR THE FUTURE

If there is a hopeful note for the industry, it is sounded by France. France
decided to go nuclear long ago, in light of a lack of natural resources.
When the French found a reactor design that they liked, they stuck with
it; they trained the plant operators to a fare-thee-well, with refresher
courses and strict supervision to make sure that they adhered to guidelines. The result is a single reactor design without the flaws that are associated with Chernobyl or, indeed, even the rest of the reactors of the
world. Possibly, if we act quickly enough, we can buy that solution and
reform the nuclear power industry in the United States. If not, we might
be doomed to a good many more Shorehams, if not Chernobyls:

> The ultimate question is whether we can accept a technology whose
> safety is measured probabilistically...This has traditionally been
> society's attitude toward technological hazards:...if a technology
> confers an important benefit, society has accepted both the technol-
> ogy and the risk.[48]

Will we choose to accept the risk? It is certainly possible to build a safe
reactor. The Swedish Process Inherent Ultimately Safe Reactor (PIUS) has
received a good deal of attention and seems to be safe from all disabling
accidents (with the possible exception of a nuclear bomb explosion).[49]

Proponents of nuclear power are quick to point out that the advantages
of nuclear energy—that it is clean, quiet, and nonreliant on the fossil fuels
that are so environmentally devastating to mine or so politically humiliat-
ing to import—will surely compel a continuation of research on the subject:

> Should nuclear energy founder in the wake of Chernobyl—as it may

in several countries—I cannot believe that the world will forever forswear fission. The possibility of an inherently safe reactor, having been demonstrated theoretically, will tantalize future nuclear technologists. Eventually, some inherently safe reactors will be built and their inherent safety demonstrated. At that time we shall better know whether such devices can produce electricity economically, and whether their use will forever exorcise from the minds of a skeptical public the fear of having to pay for its Faustian bargain...

Nuclear power could then be part of the solution to the problems of acid rain and the atmospheric accumulation of carbon dioxide rather than a festering source of political conflict.[50]

Right now, 15 percent of American electricity is produced by nuclear power. The next generation, with Chernobyl as an object lesson, will decide whether that figure increases dramatically or disappears completely.

SINCE CHERNOBYL

At this writing, there is no permanent solution to the problems posed by the use of nuclear power. We still have no place in the world to put our nuclear waste. Our newspapers are full of tales of nuclear waste dumped illegally in the ocean by the Soviet Union and of vast site contaminations from nuclear weapons plants in the U.S. and in Eastern Europe. Nor are we safe from accidents: Nuclear plants of Soviet design are still in operation in Central and Eastern Europe—other Chernobyls waiting to happen.[50]

Despite these discouraging conditions, nuclear energy advocates continue to press for wider adoption of nuclear power as an energy source. They cite on their behalf the known problems of the use of fossil fuels: the political fragility of the Middle East oil trade, the danger of tanker accidents and spills (see Chapter 4 on the Exxon Valdez disaster), the contribution of hydrocarbon emissions to global warming (see Chapter 8 on the Greenhouse Effect), and the health threat from toxic smog.[51]

Meanwhile, the people around Chernobyl continue to suffer the fear and damage from radiation poisoning, joined by the millions of Russians now discovering their exposure to nuclear waste from the Soviet Union's nuclear weapons facilities.[52] One 1992 account of the extent of that damage estimates that 300,000 people in Eastern Europe are currently being treated for radiation sickness.[53]

There are no safe choices: There is only a choice of risks. We have abundant evidence that all practical sources of energy are irretrievably dangerous; the clean sources—wind, solar energy, geothermal energy, the tides, and maybe others—have not even been under serious investigation

in the U.S. during political administrations that placed their priorities elsewhere. Even as we speak, the energy demands of the world are skyrock-
eting. The time has come for some very concentrated thinking and very
bold action, in a direction that must be determined very soon.

QUESTIONS FOR DISCUSSION AND REFLECTION

+ How many times per generation do we make "Faustian bargains"?
  Chernobyl underlines the difficulty of one of them. Can the other incidents in this volume be seen as telltale signs of other such bargains?

+ How safe can our lives be made, and how important is it to us to make
  them safe? Where do we rank safety on our list of life values—compared,
  say, with prosperity, individual freedom, and self-fulfillment?

+ Whither our nuclear energy policy? What does the world's uranium
  supply amount to? Is it worthwhile to press ahead with the technology
  to consume it? Or is the supply really too small to matter? What
  weight shall we give to the protests of the antinuclear faction? Does it
  matter (does it ever matter, in the democratic process?) how good their
  information is, as long as their positions are freely adopted? How shall
  we bring good science to our policymaking?

Notes

1. William W. Lowrance, *Of Acceptable Risk: Science and the Determination of Safety* (Los Altos, Calif.: William Kaufmann, Inc., 1976).

2. Colin Norman, "Chernobyl: Errors and Design Flaws," *Science* 233:1029
(5 September 1986).

3. Paul Ehrlich et al., *Ecoscience: Population, Resources, Environment* (San
Francisco: W. H. Freeman, 1977): p. 432 ff.

4. *Ibid.,* p. 444; see also p. 581.

5. Gordon Thompson, "What Happened at Reactor Four," *Bulletin of the
Atomic Scientists* (Aug.–Sept. 1986): p. 28.

6. *Ibid.* See also William Sweet, "Chernobyl: What Really Happened," *Technology Review* (July 1989): p. 45.

7. *Ibid.*

8. *Ibid.*

9. *Ibid.,* p. 1,030.

10. Mike Edwards, "Chernobyl: One Year After," *National Geographic*
(April 1987): p. 634.

11. Felicity Barringer, "Chernobyl: Five Years Later, the Danger Persists,"
The New York Times Magazine (14 April 1991): p. 34 (following Medvedev,
"Chernobyl Notebook," 1989).

12. *Ibid.,* p. 30.

13. For a superb account of that causal chain, see Grigori Medvedev, *The Truth About Chernobyl,* Evelyn Rossiter, trans. (from the 1989 original, "Chernobyl Notebook") (New York: Basic Books, 1991). Medvedev devotes 40 pages to the last 20 seconds before the explosion.

14. Norman, "Chernobyl: Errors and Design Flaws."

15. Thompson, "Reactor Four," p. 31.

16. Vera Rich, "Lax Standards Confirmed," *Nature* (2 November 1989): p. 10.

17. Robert P. Lockwood, "More Heat at Chernobyl," *TIME* (9 May 1988): p. 59.

18. Steven Dickman, "IAEA's Verdict on Chernobyl," *Nature* (26 May 1988): p. 285.

19. David Albright, "Chernobyl and the U.S. Nuclear Industry," *Bulletin of the Atomic Scientists* (November 1986): p. 38.

20. Rushworth Kidder, "Ethics: A Matter of Survival," *The Futurist* (March–April 1992): p. 10.

21. "Suicide Mission to Chernobyl," (Boston: WGBH Educational Foundation, 1991).

22. *Ibid.,* p. 1,031.

23. Christopher Flavin, "Reassessing Nuclear Power," *State of the World—1987* (Washington, D.C.: Worldwatch Institute, 1987): p. 58.

24. Flavin, "Reassessing Nuclear Power," p. 59.

25. Thomas Powers, "Chernobyl as a Paradigm of a Faustian Bargain," *Discover* (June 1986): p. 33.

26. Barringer, "Chernobyl: Five Years Later," p. 28. See also Gina Kolata, "A Cancer Legacy from Chernobyl," *The New York Times* (3 September 1992): p. A9.

27. Edwards, "Chernobyl: One Year After," p. 641.

28. Barringer, "Chernobyl: Five Years Later," p. 36.

29. Flavin, "Reassessing Nuclear Power."

30. *Ibid.*

31. An excellent brief discussion of the estimates of morbidity and mortality from the incident, and the complexities of the enterprise of estimating, is found in Albright, "Chernobyl and the U.S. Nuclear Industry," p. 39.

32. Barringer, "Chernobyl: Five Years Later," pp. 31–32.

33. Cited in Nancy Myers, "Coping with Chernobyl," *Bulletin of the Atomic Scientists* (September 1992): p. 8.

34. *Ibid.*

35. Barbara Starr and Richard Hoppe, "Battling the Backlash Against Nuclear Energy," *Business Week* (19 May 1986): p. 46.

36. Walter C. Patterson, "Chernobyl—the Official Story," *Bulletin of the Atomic Scientists* (November 1986): p. 35.

37. *Ibid.,* p. 36.

38. Albright, "Chernobyl and the U.S. Nuclear Industry," p. 40.

39. See Christopher Flavin and Nicholas Lenssen, "Nuclear Power at Standstill," *Vital Signs,* Worldwatch Institute. New York: Norton & Co., 1992.

40. Alvin Weinberg, former director of the Institute for Energy Analysis at the Oak Ridge Associated Universities, Oak Ridge, Tennessee, claims original authorship of the phrase, "Faustian bargain." Alvin M. Weinberg, "A Nuclear Power Advocate Reflects on Chernobyl," *Bulletin of the Atomic Scientists* (Aug.–Sept. 1986): p. 57.

41. Powers, "Chernobyl as a Paradigm," p. 34.

42. *Ibid.*

43. *Ibid.*

44. John Jagger, *The Nuclear Lion: What Every Citizen Should Know About Nuclear Power and Nuclear War* (New York: Plenum Press, 1991): p. 147.

45. Christopher Flavin, "Nuclear Power's Burdened Future," *Bulletin of the Atomic Scientists* (July–Aug. 1987): p. 26.

46. Flavin, "Reassessing Nuclear Power," pp. 64–67. He does a nice job of tracking the extent of nuclear commitment throughout the Third World, also.

47. Weinberg, "Nuclear Power Advocate."

48. *Ibid.*, pp. 58–59.

49. *Ibid.*, p. 59.

50. Malcolm Browne, "Russians Planning to Continue Using Faulted Reactors," *The New York Times* (8 November 1992); Flavin and Lenssen, p. 48.

51. John Greenward, "Time to Choose," *TIME* (29 April 1991): p. 52.

52. Mike Moore, "First Puzzlement, Then Action," *Bulletin of the Atomic Scientists* (March 1993): p. 24.

53. Flavin and Lenssen, p. 48.

Suggestions for Further Reading

Albright, David. "Chernobyl and the U.S. Nuclear Industry." *Bulletin of the Atomic Scientists* (November 1986): pp. 38–40.

Barringer, Felicity. "Chernobyl: Five Years Later, the Danger Persists." *The New York Times Magazine* (14 April 1991): pp. 28–39 & 74.

Edwards, Mike. "Chernobyl: One Year After." *National Geographic* (April 1987): pp. 632–653.

Ehrlich, Paul, et al. *Ecoscience: Population, Resources, Environment.* San Francisco: W. H. Freeman, 1977.

Flavin, Christopher. "Nuclear Power's Burdened Future." *Bulletin of the Atomic Scientists* (July–Aug. 1987): pp. 26–31.

———. "Reassessing Nuclear Power: The Fallout from Chernobyl." *Worldwatch Paper 75.* Washington, D.C.: Worldwatch Institute, 1987.

———. "Reassessing Nuclear Power." *State of the World—1987.* Washington, D.C.: Worldwatch Institute, 1987.

Jagger, John. *The Nuclear Lion: What Every Citizen Should Know About Nuclear Power and Nuclear War.* New York: Plenum Press, 1991.

Lilienthal, David E. *Atomic Energy: A New Start.* New York: Harper and Row, 1980.

Lowrance, William W. *Of Acceptable Risk: Science and the Determination of Safety.* Los Altos, Calif.: William Kaufmann, 1976.

Medvedev, Grigori. *The Truth About Chernobyl* (1989). trans. Evelyn Rossiter. New York: Basic Books, 1991.

Munson, Richard. *The Power Maker.* Emmaus, Penn.: Rodale Press, 1985.

Nader, Ralph, and John Abbotts. *The Menace of Atomic Energy.* New York: W. W. Norton, 1977.

Patterson, Walter C. "Chernobyl—the Official Story." *Bulletin of the Atomic Scientists* (November 1986): pp. 34–36.

Powers, Thomas. "Chernobyl as a Paradigm of a Faustian Bargain." *Discover* (June 1986): pp. 33–35.

Thompson, Gordon. "What Happened at Reactor Four." *Bulletin of the Atomic Scientists* (Aug.–Sept. 1986): pp. 26–31.

Weaver, Kenneth F. "The Promise and Peril of Nuclear Energy." *National Geographic,* vol. 155, no. 4 (April 1979): pp. 459–493.

Weinberg, Alvin M. "A Nuclear Power Advocate Reflects on Chernobyl." *Bulletin of the Atomic Scientists* (Aug.–Sept. 1986): pp. 57–60.

CHAPTER 4

Oil in Troubled Waters

The Wreck of the Exxon Valdez

PREFACE: QUESTIONS TO KEEP IN MIND

How much should corporations do to ensure the safety of their operations? Were Exxon's safety rules sufficient? Was the problem in the rules or in their implementation?

According to the agreements, Exxon was not responsible for cleaning up after spills—Alyeska was. What role did Alyeska play in cleaning up the spill? What, if anything, does this tell us about business consortiums in general?

Once Exxon became responsible for the cleanup, how should *they* have reacted to the spill? What went wrong with the cleanup operation?

One of the most publicized aspects of the accident was the effort to save the otters, grebes, and other wildlife trapped by the oil. On the whole, did the effort do any good? Would we want to mount such an effort again, even if it does not save very many animals?

Why do we need so much oil? Is there something else we could use to fuel our lives—a renewable energy source perhaps—something less damaging to the environment?

INTRODUCTORY NOTE ON RESPONSIBILITY

In the aftermath of the wreck of the Exxon Valdez, it became crucial to place responsibility for the disaster somewhere, to hold someone accountable, if only to save our own sanity in the face of all the ugliness and environmental destruction. Once the terms of the discussion had become clear, three levels of responsibility had surfaced: At the first and most obvious level was Exxon's corporate responsibility for the negligent seamanship that caused the oil spill, and Exxon/Alyeska's corporate responsibility for the lack of preparation ashore that failed to contain its spread within a matter of hours. At the second level, there is citizen complicity in the whole "Alyeska Syndrome," the willing participation in the exploitation of oil resources, for monetary gain, at the peril of the pristine Alaskan environment. At the third level, we can all be held accountable, for our cars and our heated houses, because the developed nations use so much oil, despite our knowledge that the environment would be better off if we ceased—or at least, reduced—our use of this and all other fossil fuels.

This chapter examines responsibility: individual, corporate, national, and environmental. At the end of our discussion, we will raise the ultimate question arising from this incident: Is it imperative that all our energy demands be fulfilled? If our demands must be met with fossil fuels, are there safer ways to extract and transport them? If our energy demands are not to be met, how shall we live? What kind of society might we create that could have room for a decent life for us and the sea otters, too?

THE EVENT: SHIP MEETS REEF

We can reconstruct the incidents of late in the night of March 23 and early in the morning of March 24 (Good Friday), 1989, from various accounts, including Art Davidson's book-length treatment of the incident, *In the Wake of the Exxon Valdez*. At 9:30 PM on March 23, the Exxon Valdez, a 987-foot oil tanker owned by the Exxon Shipping Company (subsidiary of Exxon U.S.A., which is part of the Exxon Corporation) left the dock at the port of Valdez, Alaska, with a cargo of 1.26 million barrels of North Slope oil brought in from Prudhoe Bay to the terminal at Valdez through the Alaskan Pipeline. The tanker headed out—through Valdez Harbor for Prince William Sound, the Gulf of Alaska, and onward to the open ocean—under the command of Captain Ed Murphy, an independent harbor pilot.[1] Captain Murphy took the ship safely through the Valdez Narrows, where the harbor ends, and out into Prince William Sound. At 11:24 PM, he left ship, returning control to the master of the vessel, Captain Joseph J. Hazelwood. One minute later, Captain Hazelwood called the

Coast Guard to tell them that he was leaving the outbound shipping lane and steering a course 180 degrees south into the inbound lanes, which were empty at the time, to avoid ice floes that had broken off the Columbia Glacier to the north.

Then, Hazelwood gave a series of unusual orders: He told the lookout, Maureen Jones, to stand her watch from the bridge, instead of 800 feet in front of it; he told the helmsman, Harry Claar, to accelerate to sea speed, although they were about to start maneuvering around icebergs of unknown dimension, and to put the ship on automatic pilot, which would complicate any course changes. Next, in direct contradiction to company policy, Hazelwood went below, leaving command in the hands of Third Mate Gregory T. Cousins, with orders to continue southerly to the lighted buoy off Busby Island and then return to the shipping lanes. When Cousins discovered that the ship was on autopilot, he put it back into manual mode. Then, he turned to the radar to concentrate on avoiding the ice.

Why was Hazelwood acting so strangely? He was probably under the influence of alcohol. Four days after the accident, Coast Guard Lieutenant Thomas Falkenstein, the first to reach the Exxon Valdez after the grounding, and harbor pilot Captain Murphy had both told a federal investigating team (headed by William Woody of the National Traffic Safety Board) that they had smelled alcohol on Hazelwood's breath just before and after the accident.[2] When the blood tests were finally made, nine hours after the accident, Hazelwood was still legally drunk (0.061 percent alcohol in the blood).[3] This was not some recent deviance, and the record was not difficult to find.

By March 29, an unsigned article had appeared in *The New York Times,* datelined Hauppauge, Long Island (Joseph Hazelwood's hometown), tracking Hazelwood's drinking history. During the five years preceding the accident, he was twice convicted on drunk-driving charges; his driver's license had been suspended or revoked three times and was suspended at the time of the accident.[4]

Exxon company policy specifically prohibits consumption of alcohol on its ships, of course. How could the company claim not to have known about Hazelwood's predilection? Well, they *had* known, and Captain Hazelwood had been treated for alcoholism four years previously and was then released as rehabilitated.

Later testimony of officers who had visited the ship a month before the accident described Hazelwood openly pouring drinks in the lounge among his officers.[5] The drinking was simply ignored, on board and also ashore. Hazelwood had been drinking beer in the local taverns, again contrary to company policy, within four hours before sailing. When all this became known, Exxon fired Hazelwood and the Alaskan Attorney General's office prepared to bring charges against him. This was all a bit too late for Prince William Sound, however.

The condition of those left to pilot the ship might not have been much better than Hazelwood's. The crew was exhausted. Exxon had cut back the crews on their ships to save money, so there were only 20 crew members aboard the Exxon Valdez. That left each member of the crew with an average of 140 hours of overtime per month. Further, Third Mate Gregory Cousins was not licensed to navigate the ship in Prince William Sound.

Did the Mate's inexperience cause the accident, then? On the one hand, the channel presents no difficulties for navigation, as marked and as normally traveled. Paul Yost, Commandant of the Coast Guard, commented on the accident a week after it happened: "Remember, we've got 10 miles of open water there, and for that vessel to have come over and hit a reef is almost unbelievable," he told reporters. "This was not a treacherous area, as you people in the press have called it. It is not treacherous in the area they went aground. It's 10 miles wide. Your children could drive a tanker up through it."[6]

On the other hand, Hazelwood had planned a course that would skirt the southern edge of that ten-mile opening in order to avoid the ice: "A well-timed right turn would be necessary to avoid Bligh Reef, which lay six miles ahead in the darkness. There would be little room for error. The vessel needed at least six-tenths of a mile to make the turn, and the gap between the ice and Bligh Reef was only nine-tenths of a mile wide. The tanker itself was nearly two-tenths of a mile long. The tanker would have to start its turn well before the gap between the ice and the reef if it was to make it through."[7]

Cousins became absorbed in his computations and missed the Busby Island light, where he was supposed to have started his turn. He had no idea how far off course he was until lookout Jones called his attention to the flashing red light off Bligh Island off his *starboard* side, where it should not have been if he was headed out to sea.

Cousins knew for certain he was in trouble when the Exxon Valdez hit the first rock. He apparently tried very hard to make the turn back into the shipping lanes at that point (about 12:04 AM), but the ship's momentum kept her going south to the reef where she ran aground 15 minutes later. The reef punched eight holes in the ship's hull, spilling a quarter of a million barrels of oil (about 11 million gallons) into the clear waters of Prince William Sound. Cousins called Captain Hazelwood to the bridge immediately, and Hazelwood spent 15 or 20 minutes trying to dislodge the ship from the reef, but to no avail. Meanwhile, Chief Mate James Kunkel had arrived on the bridge and had begun to calculate the Exxon Valdez's stability; she was listing four to five degrees to starboard, and he was mightily afraid of being capsized. Had Hazelwood succeeded in getting the ship in motion, that is exactly what might have happened.

At 12:27 AM, Hazelwood radioed the Coast Guard and told them that he had fetched up north of Goose Island, at Bligh Reef. Coast Guard

Commander Stephen McCall promptly warned off all ships, sent a pilot boat out to investigate (manned by Lieutenant Falkenstein and Dan Lawn of Alaska's Department of Environmental Conservation [DEC]), told incoming tankers to drop anchor, and closed the port of Valdez. Fearing capsize, the crew made no further efforts to get the giant ship off the reef; all efforts turned to restraining the spread of the spill with portable booms, keeping the ship stable, and "lightering" her (transferring her remaining million barrels of oil to another tanker) as soon as possible. The rest of the cast of players were then brought on stage: At 12:35 AM, the Alyeska superintendent and marine supervisor were alerted to the accident; the supervisor, Larry Shier, went to the Coast Guard to survey the situation. About an hour later, Frank Iarossi, president of the Exxon Shipping Company (based in Houston, Texas) was notified; he called the Alyeska people, who were busy assuring the Coast Guard and the DEC that "Alyeska was implementing its contingency plan" for oil spills.[8] By 6:00 AM, Valdez Mayor John Devens was attempting, unsuccessfully, to contact Alyeska and Exxon. By 7:00, Jack Lamb of the Cordova District Fishermen United (the fishermen's union) had summoned biologist Dr. Fredericka (Riki) Ott to survey the scene. By midafternoon, Alaska Governor Steve Cowper and DEC Commissioner Dennis Kelso had flown into Valdez from Fairbanks and Juneau. Still notably absent was the Alyeska "contingency plan."

What went wrong? As with many environmental disasters, including others in this volume, there were more than enough predisposing factors to cause the accident, and by foul chance they all converged on one hapless third mate and one beautiful ecosystem, sending death and destruction into the animal communities of Prince William Sound and anger and confusion into the human communities that were affected by the oil spill. To understand the full impact of the spill, however, we need to know something about the environmental background of the Sound and the kind of damage that oil can do in those waters.

PRINCE WILLIAM SOUND: THE END OF INNOCENCE

Every account of the monster spill includes a reference to the *pristine* beauty of the Sound before the accident, in its wealth of birds, fish, wildlife, kelp, and living things of all sorts and the complex web of interdependence that makes a threat to any of those species a threat to them all.

"Pristine" is not an often-used word, mainly because it designates a very rare condition: something left in its original state, according to *Webster's Ninth New Collegiate Dictionary*—pure, untouched, unspoiled, uncorrupted. Prince William Sound had never been fouled, polluted, cut over, industrialized, or settled by environmentally intrusive human groups. The Sound had been the home of Chugach Eskimos and Aleut Indians; Captain James Cook recorded it for the West in 1778 and named it for the British Crown. Spanish explorers had christened Valdez and the nearby town of Cordova; Russian fur trappers had set up bases on Hinchinbrook Island; but none of these incursions had any impact on the stunningly beautiful natural setting. Before the construction of the Alaskan Pipeline, the Sound had been immune to normal twentieth-century depredations.

Prince William Sound is roughly 70 miles long and 30 miles wide, with many bays, inlets, and islands to break up its shoreline. There are approximately 2,500 square miles of open water, 1,800 miles of mainland shoreline, and 1,200 miles of shoreline on islands and rocks. The depth of the Sound ranges from 2,850 feet at its deepest, averaging 480 feet in the shipping channel, to extremely shallow over Bligh Reef at low tide. The Sound is bounded by rocky peninsulas and towering mountains, most prominently the glacier-covered Chugach Mountains to the north.

The wildlife is diverse and abundant: *Audubon* magazine listed "ten species of marine mammals, including sea lions, whales, seals, porpoises, and 10,000–12,000 sea otters; more than 30 species of land mammals, including black bear, mountain goat, fox, wolf, lynx, deer, beaver, mink, marten, porcupine; more than 200 species of birds, including swans, cormorants, kittiwakes, terns, geese, scoters and other ducks, owls, loons, pelagic birds, many alcids (puffins, murres, murrelets, guillemots), more than 15 million shorebirds, and 3,000 bald eagles."[9] All of these species were at risk. "The sound is one of the worst locations imaginable for a major oil spill," wrote Ken Wells and Marilyn Chase in *The Wall Street Journal* a week after the collision. "It is the crossroads for huge migrations of fish and birds, much of which will begin in a week or two. More than 200 species of birds have been reported here, of which 111 are water-related. The Copper River delta at the east end of the sound, 75 miles from the Exxon Valdez, is home to an estimated 20 million migratory birds in late April and early May, including one-fifth of the world's trumpeter swans."[10]

The animals that inhabit the area year-round are just as impressive. "One bay in the sound is home to the largest concentrations of orcas, or killer whales, in the world; its sea otters make up perhaps one fourth of the total U.S. sea-otter population; marshes and estuaries near Cordova on the eastern side of the sound support the entire nesting U.S. population of the rare dusky Canada goose."[11]

The risk from the spilled oil was that much greater because the Sound was enclosed, and the oil slick was therefore continuous; the oil could not break up as it would have in the open ocean. So the benzene and other volatile components of the spill, instead of evaporating, soon dissolved in the water, and now "they are being consumed by cephalopods and other zooplankton at the bottom of the food web," according to Dr. Jacqueline Michel, one of the chief marine chemists of the National Oceaographic and Atmospheric Administration (NOAA).[12] The lack of exit for the oil also increased the time of exposure. "Although other spills have been larger than this one, none occurred in a body of water ringed by islands and relatively isolated from the open sea. The island enclosure has delayed dissipation of the spill, exposing animals to oil for a long period of time and allowing oil to soak deeply into beaches and sediments."[13]

THE DEADLY INVASION OF OIL

How does oil kill an animal? Diving birds and sea otters are most at risk. The birds catch their food by plunging into the water after a fish, coming to the surface and then flying off to their nest. Any extra weight on their feathers will make their flight impossible. If they can get to shore, they will try to clean the oil off their feathers with their beaks (by preening), thereby ingesting the oil, which is fatal. Because oil makes their insulation (the inner layer of down feathers) matted and useless, though, most of these birds will freeze to death before they have time to die of poisoning.

Of particular concern in this case were two species of rare birds, the yellow-billed loon and the merlet, which might be very badly affected. We will probably never know just how bad the damage was: To skip a bit ahead in the story, when the Exxon Corporation applied for permission "to dispose of oil-soaked wastes" some weeks after the spill, its list of throwaway items included twenty *tons* of dead birds.[14] A wildlife photographer counted 650 dead birds on a half-mile of beach on Barren Island. David Cline, the National Audubon Society's regional vice president for Alaska, pointed out, however, "You see only the birds that have managed to struggle to shore, where they shiver to death. And you find only a fraction of them. The majority of the dead you never see. Their oil-sodden plumage weighs them down and they drown." He estimated that as many as 90 percent of oil-soaked birds sink to the bottom of the sea.[15]

Equally at risk were the sea otters. Unlike the other marine mammals of the area (seals and sea lions), otters have no blubber to keep them warm but instead insulate themselves with the air trapped inside their thick, soft undercoat. Oil destroys this insulation, and only a little bit of oil will quickly cause them to freeze to death in the frigid water. The oil also destroys their eyes, lungs, and intestines when they ingest it while attempting to lick their coats clean.

The diving birds and otters, the most immediately and seriously exposed to the oil spill, were only the first of those to die. When birds and otters die on the beaches, bald eagles and golden eagles eat their carcasses and they die too; the oil coats their intestines so they can no longer metabolize food and water, and they die of starvation or dehydration.[16] The Sitka black-tailed deer, who live on kelp and tidal vegetation, eat the oil-soaked seaweed and die the same way—with oil in their digestive tracts. Bears, too, scavenge the oily corpses; they are not expected to incur as much damage as the water-dwelling species, though, for they have alternative food sources inland.

Then there are the fish. The fishing industry earns $100 million annually in Prince William Sound (out of $2 billion for all of Alaska). Herring and salmon are the mainstays, but those fish "are just the start of a rich web of major species, including crab, shrimp, Pacific cod, Alaska pollack, rockfishes, halibut, flounder and sharks ... [17] In 1988, salmon fishermen earned $70 million in Prince William Sound from a harvest of 14.9 million salmon, 15 percent of the state's harvest. King crabs (48,422 pounds were harvested in 1988) and shrimp (178,000 pounds) were the species most endangered by dissolved benzene.[18] The herring roe industry does a $13-million business annually. (Herring roe sells for up to $80 per pound in Japan.) The herring need clean kelp to lay their spawn, but after the spill, the kelp was certain to be covered with oil.

Most of the towns and most of the independent businessmen on the Sound make their living one way or another in the fishing industry, which employs 6,000 people all by itself. It is a growth industry (the average American consumption of seafood has nearly doubled in the last 20 years) and the fishermen were looking forward to a good year.

The fish are not just a means to make a living; the fishermen are united in love for their way of life (which is why they accept without protest the complex web of restrictions on fishing licenses, gear, and seasons, to preserve the fish runs for the future) and for their spectacularly beautiful home. If the spread of the oil could not be stopped soon, the fishing seasons would have to be canceled and a year's income lost—and the fishermen would be at the mercy of Exxon for compensation. Homes might well be lost or their value destroyed. So the fishermen had a tremendous amount at stake in stopping the oil. Would the Alyeska contingency plan work well enough and quickly enough to save the year's fishing?

THE RESPONSE: A STUDY IN DYSFUNCTION

There is no way to characterize the Alyeska/Exxon response to the situation except as a dismal failure. The causes of this failure are instructive, so we shall survey them briefly: They include unpreparedness; the dysfunctionality of large size, where human tasks are concerned; the incentives for ineffectiveness that are built into the system, especially those that cloud the boundary between appearance and reality (between public relations and environmental remediation); and the distractions of the law. Since these failure factors recur in all such environmental disasters (by themselves or generously mixed with human villainy), they are worth examining.

UNPREPAREDNESS

Alyeska Pipeline Service Company, the consortium of seven oil companies (including Exxon) that actually owns the oil pumped out of the North Slope, had promised, when they were seeking approval for the pipeline, that the operations in Prince William Sound would be "the safest in the world."[19] Alyeska's plan, approved by the Alaska Department of Environmental Conservation (DEC), had specified that containment booms and skimming equipment (machinery for mechanically lifting the thick oil off the top of the water into transfer barges, which would then take the oil to shore and off-load it) would be on the scene of any spill within five hours, with backup equipment (chemical dispersants, lasers for burning off patches of oil) available if the booms and skimmers were inadequate for the job. There was no doubt that speed was of the essence when containing a big spill. From Alyeska's containment plan: "Speed in deploying booms is essential in order to contain the maximum amount spilled oil"; the plan promised that "the necessary equipment is available and operable to meet oil spill response needs."[20] That equipment was supposed to be available at the dock.

Unfortunately, Alyeska had estimated that a spill of this size could happen only once every 241 years, which made it seem pointless to keep all that equipment around and all those experts on the payroll. "Alyeska fought steadily to cut back safety measures. The oil-spill contingency plan was trimmed and weakened. A twenty-man oil spill emergency squad was disbanded [in 1981]. Instead of the twelve miles of boom materials that the state wanted Alyeska to have on hand, Alyeska insisted that a fourth that much was sufficient."[21]

The pattern of cost-cutting and crew reduction that perhaps had contributed to the spill in the first place now crippled the response. Barges were supposed to be available for transporting oil and equipment; Alyeska's only barge was in dry dock on the morning of the spill. Skimmers and booms had to be retrieved from a local warehouse. The Alaska DEC, which had jurisdiction over such preparations, had disagreed with Aleyska's decisions to cut preparedness but apparently had no choice but to go along with them. Then the oil companies lobbied to have the state legislature cut funding for the DEC, to hamper the monitoring. Many full-time DEC workers became half-time workers, and found it that much harder to carry on inspections that the oil companies made as difficult as possible anyway.[22]

The DEC was not the only government agency whose preparedness was hindered by cost-cutting measures: One reason that the Coast Guard was out of contact with the Exxon Valdez at the time of the spill was that an "additional radar site strongly advocated in 1981...was never installed near Bligh Reef, and at the time of the accident a cost-saving 50,000-watt radar system had replaced the old 100,000-watt system."[23]

So even at the outset, when Alyeska's obligations were well understood and the weather was calm—ideal for containing and skimming the oil—the "Great Promise" (as Art Davidson calls it in *In the Wake of the Exxon Valdez*) was simply broken. A barge carrying 25 tons of cleanup equipment did not arrive at the accident site until 14 hours after the spill, following an agonizing effort to find the equipment, load it, and make it operational. Even then, there were not enough containment booms available at that time to encircle the oil spill.

Naturally, the Alaskans were seriously disappointed at such a poor showing. But their feelings went considerably beyond disappointment to a very keen sense of betrayal—because Alyeska's cleanup plan had been crucial to the authorization of the Pipeline to begin with. In 1971, when the right-of-way permit had been in doubt, "British Petroleum's top pollution specialist, L. R. Beynon, testified at Department of Interior hearings that Alyeska's contingency plan

> will detail methods for dealing promptly and effectively with any oil spill which may occur, so that its effects on the environment will be minimal. We have adequate knowledge for dealing with oil spills...The best equipment, materials and expertise—which will be made available as part of the oil spill contingency plan—will make operations in Port of Valdez and Prince William Sound the safest in the world.[24]

Dennis Kelso, the DEC commissioner, later labeled that plan "the biggest piece of maritime fiction since Moby Dick." "Yet, it was Mr. Kelso's office that approved of the contingency documents. He said later he placed too much trust in industry to live up to its paper promises."[25] Too much trust? Should we not be able to rely on citizens to live up to promises this specific and detailed—promises that leave no room for the possibility that there might have been some misunderstanding? What most contributed to the Alaskans' sense of betrayal was the value of the quantity at risk—the incredibly fertile beauty of Prince William Sound— and the clear fact that, without such promises, no Pipeline would have been approved.

THE PHANTOM CONSORTIUM

Now that the spill had spread across the Sound, where *was* Alyeska anyway? As the DEC's Dan Lawn phrased it so succinctly, "The people of the United States didn't want 4,700 different oil companies coming in here with 47,000 different cleanup contractors. They wanted one. That was Alyeska. And Alyeska was going to take care of everything. We've got a plan that says that. Where the hell were they?"[26] Why was Exxon suddenly the responsible party, and why was Frank Iarossi of Exxon Shipping Company suddenly in charge? In all the discussion after the accident and still to this day, there has never been a good explanation for the sudden disappearance of Valdez-based Alyeska and the ascendance of the Houston-based Exxon Shipping Company as responsible for the accident and charged with the cleanup operation.

Meanwhile, the weather, which had been balmy for two days after the spill, then turned rough, and skimming would have been very difficult. Exxon thought that it might be possible to use dispersants (detergents that break up the oil), which are made more effective by wave action. Dispersants have problems of their own, however: They do not really remove the oil from the water; they just sink it a few feet below the surface in an emulsion of oil and detergent, killing all marine life in the area just below the surface. The resulting emulsion ultimately diffuses in the ocean. It kills young fish, and it would undoubtedly hurt the otters and birds even more, because the detergent would dissolve the natural oils that insulate fur and feathers. The only real good that dispersants do is make the oil spill seem to disappear and, in sufficient quantities, keep it off the shores.

To the fishermen, Exxon's insistence on the use of dispersants sounded like a cosmetic solution: "It's pretty obvious that the oil company strategy on a spill like this is 'Out of sight, out of mind,'" one fisherman was quoted as saying, "'Sink it' is all they've thought of, since they knew right away that they wouldn't be able to handle it."[27] But expert opinion was divided: The concentrated emulsion created by the dispersant immediately after spraying would indeed be just as harmful as the untreated oil—but, in time, with enough square miles and depth of water to dilute it, the oil would break up and become much less harmful. Dispersants work very well in the open ocean; the issue then turned on whether they would do more good than harm in the confined waters of Prince William Sound.[28]

The question was moot on the practical level, because Exxon had only 69 barrels of dispersant on hand in Alaska.[29] Exxon's Iarossi flew in dispersant from around the world at great expense, but it would have taken nearly 10,000 barrels of dispersant to treat the spill, and there was not that much of it in the world. The question of using a dispersant continued to thrive as a legal issue, though, because Lawrence Rawl, CEO of the Exxon Corporation, blamed the Alaska DEC and the Coast Guard for adding to the seriousness of the spill by preventing the company from using the dispersants. The Coast Guard and Kelso (the DEC commissioner) claimed that there had been prior approval to use dispersants and that Exxon was claiming that it could not get approval only to mask the fact that it did not have enough dispersants on hand to treat the spill effectively. Meanwhile, Exxon set to work with lasers, to burn off portions of the oil, but burning only works when the oil is confined, and the lasers were less effective after the storms.

THE AWKWARDNESS OF SIZE

Very well, the damage was done. For whatever reason, Alyeska did not have the supplies that they were supposed to have on hand, they had no rational plan for deployment of what supplies they did have, and, as soon as Iarossi showed up on the scene, Alyeska simply disappeared. A crucial 48 to 72 hours of calm weather had passed without either booms being deployed or oil skimmed from the water onto barges. The transfer of the remaining million barrels of oil from the stricken Exxon Valdez had begun and continued through the winter storm that tore through the area on the fourth day after the spill and spread the oil from an area of 100 square miles to 500 square miles. Now, forced to improvise, how would the agencies faced with this massive disaster respond? The record is depressing.

The first major problem was one of authority. Davidson described it like this:

> Alyeska, which the state had relied on for spill response, had disappeared. Exxon was trying to respond but needed authorization. Most of Exxon's people, having flown up from other parts of the country, had little knowledge of Alaska and virtually no connection to the land and to Prince William Sound. They didn't know Alaska's weather, Alaska's waters, Alaska's shorelines, or Alaska's people. But the state and the Coast Guard, which could have provided the needed direction, strained against the limits placed on their own authority.[30]

The rules specified that the spiller had to disclaim any responsibility for the spill or egregiously fail to clean it up before anyone could move to take over the operation. Taking over the cleanup would not automatically solve the problems either: At one point, Iarossi actually encouraged Admiral Nelson of the Coast Guard to take over the work, but Nelson pointed out that the procedure for government contracting was so cumbersome that nothing would get done for weeks if he assumed command. Eventually, they settled on government by committee, a troika made up of the Coast Guard, the DEC (Dennis Kelso), and Exxon (Iarossi), plus representatives of any interested community groups; this worked amicably enough but about as inefficiently as committees usually do. Meetings sometimes lasted five hours a day, sometimes longer, and still the oil was not being cleaned up.

The only real work was being done by the fishermen. They had very little to do, after all: On April 3, 1989, Alaska officials canceled the herring fishing season. That was good news for the herring fishermen, for it meant that they would surely get restitution for the season from Exxon. But as the oil continued to advance, it became clear that the precious salmon hatcheries on which their livelihoods depended were in danger, and nothing was being done to protect them.

The salmon hatcheries had been built in the early 1970s, when over-fishing had reduced the pink salmon run so low that the season had to be closed. The fishermen borrowed $18 million from the state to build the Sawmill Bay and Esther Island hatcheries. "By 1989, the Koernig Hatchery, once an abandoned cannery on Sawmill Bay, was producing more than $20 million worth of salmon each year. The Esther had become the world's largest salmon hatchery, releasing 200 million pinks, 100 million chum, 4 million kings, and 2 million silvers."[31] Ironically, the loan granted to build the hatcheries was funded by oil revenues; now, oil again entered the picture as a lethal threat. Oil can sicken, confuse, or kill young salmon, even as it destroys their food supply, the rich spring bloom of phytoplankton. The fishermen were afraid that even a few gallons of that oil sweeping through the rearing pens could wipe out an entire generation of pink salmon.

So, on Monday night, four days after the spill, Jack Lamb, head of the fishermen's union, called for five fishing boats to be deployed to each of the threatened hatcheries to do what they could to protect them. "Ten minutes later, four boats were under way. By 2:00 AM Tuesday morning, another fourteen fishing boats streamed out of the Cordova harbor. The 'Mosquito Fleet,' a makeshift armada of seiners, bow-pickers, long-liners and skiffs, was on its way."[32]

The efficiency of the fleet was impressive, compared to the efforts of the committee officially authorized to coordinate the cleanup efforts. The speed with which the fleet got under way (compared, say, with Alyeska's barge) is symbolic of their performance. Exxon had not been able to produce a skimmer that could collect more than 1,200 gallons of spilled crude per day; Tom Copeland, a bearded fisherman with a searing sense of responsibility, "spent $5,000 of his own money on a pump, gas, and 5-gallon buckets. Then he went looking for oil. When he and his crew reached the slick near Knight Island, they just started dipping buckets and pulling out oil, five gallons at a time, until their arms felt ready to fall off. The first day of work they scooped up 1,500 gallons of oil, and on their best day 2,500 gallons."[33]

The boats that had been sent to the hatcheries, meanwhile, did their best to deploy and hold together the fair-weather harbor boom that Exxon had sent out, while constructing their own booms from logs and other materials. Difficulties attended every attempt to get better supplies from Exxon: "There were so many people in the chain of command that if one link goofed, nothing got done. Some of the Exxon people were trying their damnedest, but there simply wasn't enough equipment available."[34]

The fishermen's heroic efforts staved off the oil until a more solid containment boom was available; the hatcheries were saved. They were saved by people acting on their own, with no chain of command, no formal plan, cooperating with each other only informally. The proper authorities—the huge state, the corporation, and the Coast Guard, acting together—found themselves locked into one vast unworkable gridlock.

HOW BUREAUCRACY AFFECTED THE ANIMALS

Much the same observation could be made about other phases of the cleanup. The animal rescue efforts, for instance, recruited some of the best people available to clean, cure, and release wild birds and sea otters (especially); volunteers worked tirelessly to save the lives of oil-slicked creatures. Yet this effort continually ran afoul of the U.S. Fish and Wildlife Service, which ordinarily catches oiled birds and animals and brings them to veterinarians. In this incident, however, the FWS instructed the experts that had been brought up from the Berkeley-based International Bird Rescue Research Center (IBRRC) that they would get no cooperation from the FWS and they would also have to convince Exxon to pay for their efforts; the role of the FWS was to "monitor" the operations. At every turn—deploying volunteers, setting up labs and pens for the birds and animals, getting equipment—the rescuers found themselves stymied by obstructions from the organizations charged with helping them. "We started calling this the 'oil spill from hell,'" said Jessica Porter of the IBRRC, "not because of the dying birds, the long hours of cleaning, the rugged geography, or even the amount of oil, but because of the attitudes of Fish and Wildlife and Exxon. Why weren't they helping? It seemed as if birds were not important to anybody."[35]

Eventually, the IBRRC decided, just as the fisherman had, that they would have to run the entire operation themselves without help from the government bureaucrats that had authority over such decisions, at least on paper. They found Kelly Weaverling, a Cordova bookseller who knew the Sound well, to take them to the beaches to gather the birds. Weaverling put out a call for birdcatching equipment and got it, free, from volunteers; six days after the spill and one day after making contact with Weaverling, the IBRRC was in business. The operation, working against considerable odds, staffed entirely with volunteers on the beaches, saved birds and then otters and, significantly, healed the participants at the same time.

Emotional accounts of the damage, the work, and the healing, coupled with an appreciation of the overwhelming beauty of Prince William Sound and its environs, flowed from the pens of area residents and visiting volunteers who toured the Sound and helped with the cleanup.[36] Residents and fishermen gave the rescuers solid support and boats to work from. The volunteers only ran into trouble when they had to deal with Exxon's regional managers, who had been sent from Houston to run things for a while: "They come up here in cowboy boots with names like Skeeter and Bubba, and work here for a week or two, and then they're gone." As for the FWS, their major contribution to the rescue effort was to issue a cease and desist order to Kelly Weaverling's fleet, to stop it from capturing otters to be cleaned: "They said we were unauthorized, untrained, and not inspected by the Fish and Wildlife Service."[37]

Things of large size are obstructive by nature. Kelly Weaverling commented in the early stages of the otter rescue,

> I might be more effective than some agency. Bureaucracies can't move with much speed. Too many people have to be consulted. They have to fill out purchase orders and requisition forms, go through committees, do studies and tests. I'm one individual, totally non-aligned. I don't belong to a single organization. I can just walk next door and say, "I need some lumber and this many guys with hammers. Let's meet two hours from now and start pounding nails."[38]

That is how the new otter center in Cordova was built.

Things of large size, on the other hand, have to protect themselves and their cumbersome structures before they can allow any action to go forward. Hence the reflexive attempts, by the large entities involved, to pick off the leadership and the creative individuals of the rescue operation. This explains Exxon's attempts to fire Linda Herrington, coordinator of the fleet, and FWS's disablement of Kelly Weaverling.

The otter enterprise, incidentally, the most visible and appealing part of the cleanup, might have been the least cost-effective. Otters are as vulnerable to stress as to oil, so the process of cleaning them could have injured them as much as the original oil damage. Not many survived the rescue attempts: Of the 357 otters who entered the treatment centers, only 197 lived to be released into the wild. Among those who did survive, there was an alarming incidence of a type of pneumonia, raising fears that these otters might be carrying the disease with them to infect the untreated population of otters outside the oiled areas. Meanwhile, the operation of the rescue centers cost about $18 million, or $50,420 for each of the 357 otters treated. The biologists involved in the rescue have thus concluded that some serious planning will have to precede any such operation in the future.[39]

SYSTEMIC DISINCENTIVES

There might possibly have been more involved than simple bureaucratic bungling in Exxon's handling of the extended cleanup effort. In the complex job of managing human interactions with nature (and with each other), we are challenged to make sure that the incentives are in the right place: that it is in the perceived best interest of any agents to do what it is that we want them to do. Where the territory is familiar, the incentive patterns are known, well-used, and generally reliable. One of the best analyses of such patterns, for instance, is the treatment of voluntary economic exchanges in Adam Smith's *The Wealth of Nations;* he proves that, given the normal incentives to acquire personal wealth, government management of the market is unnecessary to protect justice and counterproductive to the accumulation of national wealth.

Where the territory is unfamiliar, though, we grope and sometimes we fail. With oil spills, for example, European nations will immediately assume public responsibility for the spill, clean it up, and then send the offending oil company the bill for the damage. That approach has drawbacks, because the government workers have no incentive to be frugal and to minimize the cost of the cleanup. So, with Alyeska, a different approach (the contingency plan) was adopted: Alyeska and the spiller would assume responsibility for the cleanup if they could and would. The federal government would not step in and start running the operation (federalizing the cleanup) unless the spiller disclaimed responsibility or admitted inability to continue to handle the cleanup. Exxon never did that. At the beginning of the operations, as mentioned earlier, there was no doubt that the Exxon officers, especially Frank Iarossi, were doing their best to help the cleanup efforts. As the oil spread across the Sound, however, to more and more remote islands and to the Katmai National Park, 400 miles southwest of Bligh Reef, the faltering of the cleanup began to seem systematic.

By this time, the support from Washington, for starters, was beginning to fade. Much of the fading seemed to be emanating from Vern Wiggins, a Reagan appointee at the Department of the Interior (deputy undersecretary for Alaska) who honestly believed that oil development was essential to the state of Alaska and that it was therefore essential to underplay the effect of this spill and the dangers of oil spills in general; Wiggins' influence was very broad, extending to the Coast Guard and the entire U.S. National Park Service.[40]

Meanwhile, strong signals were being received from Exxon that it was time to wind down the cleanup. For example, at Kachemak Bay, near Homer, volunteers set themselves to the job of cleaning up the oil—shoveling oily gunk, globs, tar, and debris into boats that would transfer it to containment vessels and bring it back to Valdez—but there were not enough containment vessels, so oil and debris kept piling up. When transport boats did materialize, the Exxon employees did not want to transport the oil because it contained oil-soaked sand, pebbles, and kelp; Exxon took the position that it was committed to transport *oil*, not substances that the oil had penetrated.

There were several reports about Exxon issuing shovels to workers to clean up a beach, then confiscating the shovels and issuing trowels instead, because the shovels were bringing in too much oil-soaked sand, and then confiscating the trowels and having workers collect the oil with their gloved hands, because even the trowels picked up pebbles. "Oil's hard to pick up just in gloves," commented one of the workers. "It goes through your fingers."[41] After a while, workers sincerely began to doubt Exxon's commitment to getting oil off the beaches. The doubt was reinforced by days of sitting on the beaches with no assignments and reinforced again by the observation that those who worked hardest, especially those who came up with better ways to remove oil from the beaches, tended to get fired.[42]

APPEARANCE AND REALITY

What were the incentives? Clearly, Exxon had a major incentive not to let the spill be federalized, for then they would lose control of the cleanup expenditures. So they wanted to keep up the appearance of an active cleanup operation, at all costs. Two weeks after the accident Exxon workers were spotted by the cameras working furiously to clear the shores of Naked Island: "Forty employees, working amid the drone of the diesel-powered pumps on two ships that fill the crew's hoses with sea water, are irrigating a cobblestone beach, washing the oil down to the shore, where it is contained in booms and picked up by a skimmer. It is here that the company has brought reporters, and it was here that the Coast Guard brought the Interior Secretary and three members of Congress earlier this week."[43]

An incentive to keep up an appearance of doing something, however, is not the same as an incentive to do it. And the greatest incentives that Exxon had, of course, were to have the spill be gone, to have it not be as serious as people thought, and to have the cleanup over and done with. To preserve the appearance that the spill was not very serious, it was necessary not to appear to find very much oil damage. The best way to preserve *that* appearance was to make sure that, one way or another, not very much oil was recovered and brought back to town for the news media to see and measure. So the citizens and volunteers began to detect a pattern in the way that Exxon conducted the cleanup in the later beaches: no vessels available to cart the oil back to Valdez; haggling reminiscent of Shylock and Portia over whether the oil contained sand or other oiled debris; all hard work and all useful initiatives punished by termination. Beaches were not to be cleaned, they were to be "treated" and then left.

Following the chronicle of the Exxon Valdez, the problem still remains: How shall we allot the tasks of cleanup after a major oil spill if our objective is to get the oil cleaned up as quickly and as frugally as possible? How can we allot the tasks of cleanup authority and responsibility to command people and equipment so that the responsible parties will have an incentive to do the cleanup and not be satisfied with the mere appearance that the job is being done?

THE EFFECT OF THE LAW

Further disincentives to real remedy flowed from the operations of the law. We are familiar with the kind of legal wrangling that occurs when people are injured by the actions of a large corporation. Exxon was acutely aware of this sort of wrangling, so they swiftly promised to recompense anyone injured by the spill (the fishermen, for instance). That did not stop the lawsuits. Exxon and the state of Alaska competed for the best law firms. At a preliminary hearing on some 150 lawsuits (58 of them were class-action suits) in Anchorage, 65 law firms were represented. "So the newspaper article about Alaska covered by a slick of lawyers," said Exxon president William Stevens, "is certainly true."[44]

Even when Exxon promised to pay, it was extremely difficult to calculate damages. It is simple enough to pay a fisherman for a missed season, given solid figures on last season's catch, but the damage to the species, especially genetic damage, and the damage to wildlife habitat and microscopic life was incalculable. "We're really up against something unprecedented," said Sheila Nickerson of the Alaska Department of Fish and Game, "and we can't guess what the damage will be based on data from other spills, because there have been no comparable spills."[45]

In the aftermath of the Amoco Cadiz spill off the coast of France in 1978, it was shown that the ultimate liability of the parties to disputes of this nature will depend on a judge's perceptions of the relative contributions of the oil company and the government agencies. Judge McGarr had found, in that case, that the French government's refusal (on environmental grounds) to authorize the use of dispersants in water less than 50 meters deep was "without scientific justification," and "seriously interfered with the success of the dispersant method." Thus, Amoco was relieved of much of the financial liability for damage to the victims of that spill.

Accordingly, Exxon immediately claimed that authorization for use of dispersants had been refused by the Alaskan government. Secretary of the

Interior Manuel Lujan backed them up, asserting that "Alaska has to share the blame" for the inadequate response in the first few days. Alaskan officials, especially Dennis Kelso, hotly denied the allegations.[46] Similar considerations were likely involved in the decision to hold off federalization of the spill, even when strong evidence of foot-dragging began to come in toward the end of the cleanup effort, down the coast:

> Many involved in the spill response can recall when they first sensed that good press and damage-assessment dollars were becoming more important than actually cleaning the beaches. For [Coast Guard] Admiral Nelson, who had been dealing one-on-one with Frank Iarossi, whom he trusted, that moment came when he saw that every suggestion, every move, would have to be processed through a firm of faceless, liability-conscious attorneys thousands of miles away.[47]

This wrangling undoubtedly drained energy from the cleanup,

> ...as the state and Exxon fought each other for moral high ground in the press and for billions of dollars in court...The protagonists, entrenched with their lawyers and press agents, became increasingly isolated from each other. The result in many instances was that the battles took precedence over the problem. Too often the oil cleanup effort appeared to be driven more by legal and public relations strategies than by scientific considerations. And the common goal of restoring the coastal environment frequently seemed to get lost in the shuffle.[48]

THE BLAME

While Exxon and the state of Alaska remained locked in a public relations battle about financial liability, the citizens of Alaska had an opportunity to reflect on their own complicity in the spill. "We're not victims of Exxon," said Tom Copeland, the fisherman whose bucket brigade outskimmed Exxon's best. "We're reluctant participants. Basically, Alaskans are addicted to that oil money. We've got that needle in our arms...We don't deserve another dollar from that pipeline."[49]

The oil companies had paid enough royalties in 1988 that each citizen of the state got a royalty check in excess of $800. (There is no record that any sent back their checks.) When Exxon offered to hire the fishing boats to fight the oil spill, at the rate of $4,000 or $5,000 per day, most fishermen took them up on the offer. Somehow, it seemed in the historic spirit of Alaska to do it: "I've heard people say it's dirty money," said Jay Holcomb of the IBRRC, "but you have to understand that people *want* to be bought off sometimes. People love that money...I've really learned a lot about greed up here, and it's been a rude awakening for me. I think this is probably how Alaska was built—they call it being opportunistic. This oil spill is just another gold rush."[50]

Ray Bane of the Katmai Park Service summed up the feelings of many residents:

> Exxon caused this mess, but it had plenty of assistance. I think all of us who have benefited from that oil have a responsibility to bear. Alaskans take too much for granted. It's a big land—good fishing, lots of animals, wild rivers. We take it all so damn much for granted. The oil spill is only a symptom of all of us closing our minds to the fact that there is always a price to pay when you develop oil, or cut down some trees, or build a road.[51]

The Alaskans were not the only complacent ones. Shortly after the spill, the environmental organization Greenpeace placed an ad in newspapers nationwide, showing Joseph Hazelwood's face with the caption: "It wasn't his driving that caused the Alaskan oil spill. It was yours." Because the truth is, the ad continued, "the spill was caused by a nation drunk on oil. And a government asleep at the wheel."[52] "And ultimately," Cordova fisherman Ed Monkiewicz concluded, "we're all at fault, every single one of us. We've got to have our cars. We use the fossil fuels. Maybe if we put more value on our environment, this wouldn't have happened."[53]

Exxon offered to settle the whole case two years later, submitting guilty pleas in an agreement that would have taken care of criminal charges and civil claims by the federal government and the Alaska state government arising from the spill. Under that agreement, Exxon would have paid $100 million in criminal fines and as much as $1 billion for civil claims. (That was actually not very much money: An editorial in *The New York Times* pointed out that, by mid-April, Exxon had already shelled out an estimated $2 billion for the cleanup.)[54] On April 24, 1991, Judge Russel Holland ruled that $100 million in fines was insufficient, and the legislature of Alaska subsequently voted that the civil settlement was also not enough.[55]

LESSONS ABOUT OIL

Hazelwood Was Not Alone

As the Exxon Valdez was heading for its rendezvous with the reef, Alyeska officials were holding a self-congratulatory victory dinner celebrating the cleanup of a spill a few days before in Valdez harbor. As

Frank Iarossi reached for the ringing telephone in the wee hours of the morning of March 24, 1989, he was still winding down from the Hawaiian spill of March 2: The Exxon Houston had broken loose from her moorings in a storm off Barber's Point, about 15 miles from Waikiki Beach, and went aground on a coral reef about 2,000 feet off the west coast of the island of Oahu.[56]

Three months later, the nation watched in fascination as three major oil spills happened within a 12-hour period: On June 23, at 4:40 PM, the World Prodigy struck a reef in Narragansett Bay, Rhode Island, apparently because the ship had blundered into unfamiliar waters without waiting for a pilot and then repeated the error of the Exxon Valdez, straying to the wrong side of the red channel buoys; 420,000 gallons of number 2 fuel oil flowed into the waters of the bay. At 6:20 PM on the same day, an oil barge collided with a tanker in the Houston ship channel, spilling 250,000 gallons of crude oil; four days later, about half of the oil had been cleaned up. At 4:00 the next morning, the Uruguayan tanker Presidente Rivera managed to stray from its channel in the Delaware River and hit a rock, spilling 800,000 gallons of number 6 fuel; rather little of the fuel was recovered.

> The three spills reopened many of the questions that maritime lawyers, environmentalists and lawmakers had debated after the Exxon Valdez spill. Some environmentalists were asking whether the spills were a coincidence or an indication that something was so wrong that long-established maritime rules need to be changed.

A little investigation showed that these incidents were not at all unusual. Captain Gerard Barton, chief of the Coast Guard's investigations division, told a House Subcommittee that, in 1988, "there were 5,000 to 6,000 spills involving oil and other toxic substances along the coasts and in other navigable waters." Of these spills, 12 were major (more than 100,000 gallons), but this figure is "down sharply from about 13,000 a year a decade ago." The House was unimpressed by the improvement and called for changes in the oil transport system.[57]

Tanker and barge accidents account for only two-thirds of the oil that spills into the waterways each year (an estimated 91 million gallons, for instance, in the period from 1980–1986). The rest of the spilled oil comes from pipe ruptures, such as the rupture of an Exxon pipe that covered the Arthur Kill, off Staten Island, with oil in January, 1990. Operators had simply ignored the warnings of a detection system that had been malfunctioning for a year.[58] That spill cost Exxon up to $15 million, and there was no chance of restoring the environment.[59]

Opinions upon the ultimate significance of these oil spills will differ, of course. Part of the difference is a disagreement on the facts, since the effect of oil on a fragile environment is often completely unknown. There is also a difference of perspective: In Philip Revzin's reassuring article, "Years Temper Damage of Worst Oil Spill" (about the sinking of the Amoco Cadiz, off the coast of France), we are told that "for a year after the gooey oil washed up … business [fishing, oyster-growing, tourism] all but stopped. For five to eight years the aquatic food chain was disrupted, costing crab fishers three generations of their most prized catches." Oil still remained, in pockets. "But generally, it's finished, all is back to normal," says Lucien Laubler, chief scientific advisor to a French oceanic research institute. Back to *normal?* Eleven years after the spill, the French government was suing Amoco for $600 million.[60] *The New York Times* angrily editorialized that it was time to stop the self-deceptions and make rational plans for safety and cleanup for the next spill.[61]

The Political Impact on the Oil Industry

Were these pleas heard? Even as the Exxon Valdez collided with its reef, Congress was debating whether to authorize further drilling for oil in Alaska. Evidence of existing environmental practices confirmed the negative impression left by the accident. A letter to the editor of *The New York Times,* dated April 4, 1989, for instance, described an area at the heart of the existing North Slope drilling complex at Deadhorse: hundreds of vehicles, many of them abandoned; stacks of discarded oil drums; small ponds of oil or ponds of water with floating oil slicks; and general debris. Alaska simply does not have the authority or the resources to enforce antipollution laws.

What happens when the oil is gone? "Judging from the state of Prudhoe Bay, it would be nearly impossible to restore the region to its pristine state when the oil is depleted, as it will be in the near future. Merely to remove the accumulated vehicles, buildings and drilling equipment from this distant place, not to mention detoxifying the polluted tundra and dismantling the roads, airstrips and pipelines, would take years and hundreds of millions of dollars. Who will pay?"[62] Later in the month, a *New York Times* series by Matthew Wald followed up on the damage.[63] The North Slope is tundra, with very little rainfall but with permanent ice below the surface of the soil (permafrost); the effect of all this industrial residue on the native animal populations can only be guessed. Not surprisingly, the first political casualty of the spill was that the proposal to drill for oil in the Arctic National Wildlife Reserve was shelved. Proponents of this bill, like Senator Frank H. Murkowski, a Republican from Alaska, argued that no connection could be drawn between the Valdez incident and the oil drilling but conceded that the two were very much connected, in the popular perception.

Within two weeks of the Exxon Valdez spill, reports drew public attention to the political repercussions of the accident: The spill pointed up the complacency of corporate America and of a Republican administration that had backed off from environmental promises. "Some see the accident," remarked E. J. Dionne in *The New York Times*, "as a watershed for the environmental movement."[64]

"This may be one of those defining moments that we have heard about," said then–Senator Al Gore, Jr., "A huge spill like this focuses media coverage and political attention, not only on the [Prince William Sound] environment itself, but also on the larger problems for which it is a metaphor: we are spilling chemicals in massive quantities into our ground water, surface water, atmosphere and stratosphere."[65]

The spill undoubtedly raised environmental consciousness generally throughout the country: According to a *New York Times* poll taken three months after the event, "eighty percent of the 1497 people interviewed by telephone from June 20 through 25 said they agreed with this statement: 'Protecting the environment is so important that requirements and standards cannot be too high, and continuing environmental improvements must be made regardless of cost.'" That 80-percent figure had increased from a low of 45 percent when President Reagan took office.[66]

But did this environmental consciousness last? Did the national attention span keep the problems in focus long enough to result in environmentally protective action? Not, certainly, on the government level. There was some attempt at responsible action in the business community, with the publication of the "Valdez Principles," by the Coalition for Environmentally Responsible Economies (CERES) Project of the Social Investment Forum. The Valdez Principles (appended to this chapter) are modeled on the Sullivan Principles for investors in South Africa and are designed to guide business investment and provide "sticks and financial carrots" for good environmental citizenship. "They are structured to reward responsible corporate actions with significant investment dollars, and potentially to withdraw dollars from irresponsible corporations."[67]

According to an unsigned report in *Business Ethics*, two years later, there are not many signatories and no rush for big corporations to sign up. The major problems, according to CERES Executive Director Alix Sabin, involve the requirement that an environmental manager be appointed and compensatory damages pledged for any damage to the environment.[68] For all the outrage at the time the oil began to spread and all the calls for tightening the Clean Water Act and turning up the heat on offenders,[69] business went on as usual—the Exxon Valdez floated off the reef to be repaired some weeks after the accident, Joseph Hazelwood was appointed to the State of New York Maritime Academy as an instructor, and the oil floated into history, leaving only the fishermen and the sea otters to remember the Sound the way it once was.

SO THAT IT WILL
NEVER HAPPEN AGAIN

Ultimately, the big story is one of oil and energy—not about Hazelwood's driving, but about ours. From the renewed public discussion that followed the oil spill, three sets of imperatives emerged, to set the agenda for the effort to avoid "another Exxon Valdez":

First, there were imperatives to enforce the law, monitor compliance to existing policies, and implement known technology for the safe transport of oil. There are sufficient laws on the books, and clauses in the contracts, to enforce the safe operation of the oil industry. Complacency, carelessness, and criminal negligence produce oil spills. Tankers can be required to have double hulls, more effective containment booms can be developed (the ones in use in Prince William Sound broke repeatedly), and we can develop new technology for the containment of oil spills. (One interesting suggestion involves using fly ash—a pollutant removed from the chimneys of many industrial plants—fused with titanium dioxide into tiny glass beads, which will absorb the spill, permit burning it off, and incidentally, get rid of the fly ash.)[70] More importantly, if the penalties are sure enough and severe enough, it will be to the advantage of the oil industry to monitor the state of preparedness of its cleanup crews and equipment, not to mention the state of inebriation of its employees.

This set of imperatives is not controversial: If we pass a law or set a policy, we presumably have no objection to carrying it out, but more effort will be required. Even after the disaster and after Exxon spent three billion dollars to make minimally acceptable repairs, the industry is still well below standard. As 1993 began, British Petroleum inspectors found 73 deficiencies in a 550-foot Maltese tanker: "Many of the navigation charts aboard the Greek-owned vessel...hadn't been updated for 20 years. Two of its engineers were unlicensed. Its anticollision radar was out of whack. The crew was Greek and Filipino, but the ship's safety and mechanical manuals were written in Serbo-Croatian."[71]

Also, the fire-control plan was inadequate, the crew regularly ignored the no-smoking regulations, and there were 22,000 tons of gasoline in the hold. The Institute of London Underwriters, a marine-insurance consortium intensely interested in raising shipping safety standards, notes "a continued deterioration" of worldwide ship accident rates. The United Nations is powerless to enforce the standards and safety regulations it promulgates, but the United States is pioneering perhaps the most effective approach to oil transport safety. With the 1990 Oil Pollution Act, the United States raised the liability for owners of an average-sized supertanker operating in U.S. waters to around $100 million from about $14 million under U.N. standards. "In addition, [the act] authorizes unlimited liability of the spill results from a violation of federal law—operation of a ship while intoxicated, for example."[72]

Advances in technology also offer hope for safer oceans. U.S. law will soon require double hulls on all oil tankers, which will surely provide a measure of protection, although ship designers argue that other solutions might be better in the long run. There is a great deal of room for technological advance; but public interest tends to flag as disasters fade into the past, and without that there will be no motivation for change.[73]

PRESERVATION OF THE LAND

The second set of imperatives aims to protect forever the last remaining tracts of unspoiled land in the world, to the extent that it is in our power to do so. Whatever we thought we would gain by building the Alaskan Pipeline from Prudhoe Bay to Valdez—and we certainly had our doubts about it at the time (1973), when then–Vice President Spiro Agnew's vote was required to break the tie in the Senate—photos of the beaches mired with oil changed our minds, at least some of our minds. Everything else in this world besides land—energy, money, production, recreation—is ultimately fungible; we can always find a substitute that will do just as well. The land alone is unique and, once polluted, can never be fully restored to its previous state.

Exxon Corporation now insists that, ultimately, not very much damage was done to Prince William Sound.[74] Not all observers are convinced of that, given Exxon's interest in finding no long-term damage (clauses in the legal settlements of claims from the spill permit reopening the lawsuits for an additional $100 million if long-term damage is found). Whatever the merits of Exxon's new claims, most participants acknowledge that protecting the land means setting it aside from human use and exploitation. It can mean leaving oil underground forever in the Arctic National Wildlife Refuge, the Bristol Bay fishery, the Florida Keys, and New England's Georges Bank fishery. It will surely mean protecting the land from all mining, logging, and other exploitation of natural resources. In an increasingly crowded world, we must also consider to what extent we can afford to give preference to the interests of the land—land that only a handful of people will ever see—over the present economic interests.

ENERGY

The third set of imperatives involves our use of energy, specifically energy supplied by fossil fuels. Conservation of fuel can, realistically, relieve the pressure on some of the lands proposed for future exploration:

> Merely improving the efficiency of existing oil and gas furnaces and water heaters to the fullest cost-efficient extent would save the equivalent of 4.5 billion barrels of oil. This is roughly the same amount of oil that is believed to underlie the most sensitive areas.

Moreover, aggressive weatherization programs for America's 53 million oil- and gas-heated homes would save twice the oil believed to be in these areas.[75]

There are certainly limits to what can be accomplished by conservation measures, like those above just mentioned, that entail no change in lifestyle. Beyond this, we know that we must scale back tremendously on our use of the automobile, on long-distance travel, on the scattering of residences and shopping malls across the land. How can we persuade the people of the world—and that means the people of the United States to begin with—that we require drastic changes in our lifestyle expectations and practices?

One excellent proposal is the imposition of a significant federal tax on sales of gasoline (50 cents or a dollar per gallon) and a modest tax on heating oil. In the absence of other changes or laws, the advantage of a tax—simply raising the cost of a gallon of oil or gasoline—is that it conscripts the infinite ingenuity of the consumer to the work of conservation. If the law tells me to conserve, I will try to get around the law; on the other hand, if it is to my immediate material advantage to conserve, I will discover ways of conserving that I would previously have found impossibly burdensome (such as carpooling, keeping the speed of my car at 50 mph, or heating my home to 65 degrees in the winter).

This proposal has been around for a very long time: It received renewed currency after the Exxon Valdez debacle and again when our embroilment in the Persian Gulf reminded us of the real costs of imported oil,[76] and the idea was mentioned again during the 1992 presidential election campaign. We can begin to hope that the gas tax has acquired the patina of inevitability and might actually happen someday soon.

Of course there are limits to expectable lifestyle changes, too. Suggestions that we go back to some pre–fossil fuel civilization are not only unrealistic but antienvironmental; the use of wood for fuel and animals for transport had all but turned Connecticut into a desert before the discovery of fossil fuels, and the rest of the country could not have been far behind. Renewable resources work only when the population is low enough to give the resources time to renew, and ours has long outstripped that point. Fossil fuels actually saved the environment once; we need a new fuel breakthrough to save it this time.

QUESTIONS FOR DISCUSSION AND REFLECTION

✦ Until we find a way to do without oil, we will have to transport it over long distances, sometimes through dangerous passages. How can we make that transport as safe as possible?

✦ Above all, we must learn to conserve energy. What form should conservation take? Are we prepared to change our lifestyles—to band together in apartment houses to save oil, to abandon our shopping malls and do all our marketing at stores within walking distance of our homes?

✦ As mentioned earlier, for the development of a non-fossil fuel economy, we will need a technological breakthrough. What sort of breakthrough are we looking for? Should we build more nuclear power plants? The current political opposition to nuclear plants makes the prospect of economical nuclear power a pipe dream at this juncture.

✦ Could the production of clean, economical hydroelectric power be expanded? Hydroelectric power cannot be further developed without destroying valuable parks and wilderness areas. We have experimented with geothermal, wind, and tidal energy and found that they are not yet economical. Are there better ways to work with these?

✦ One clear imperative is to develop better batteries, to store electrical energy generated by wind and waves more efficiently, so we can use these clean sources of energy. Where would we begin to look for better batteries?

✦ Of course, we also need to find out how to use solar energy. What kind of photoelectric cell will most efficiently turn solar energy into electricity? Just as important, how can we use the power of all that solar heat to make our lives better? What direction should solar energy research take right now?

✦ What kind of commitment do we need to pursue the development of the necessary practical technologies for alternative sources of energy? Would an international project be feasible? All that we know for certain is that massive efforts to reeducate a population addicted to fossil fuels will have to be part of any real reform of our patterns of energy consumption. What would make a massive reeducation project successful? Are there any precedents for this?

Notes

1. This account is taken from Art Davidson, *In the Wake of the Exxon Valdez* (San Francisco: Sierra Club Books, 1990), and from contemporary newspaper accounts, as noted.

2. Philip Shabecoff, "Captain of Tanker Had Been Drinking, Blood Tests Show; Illegal Alcohol Level; Coast Guard Opens Effort to Bring Charge of Operating Ship While Intoxicated," *The New York Times* (13 March 1989): pp. A1 & A12.

3. *Ibid.*

4. "Captain Has History of Drinking and Driving," special to *The New York Times* (28 March 1989): p. B7; Timothy Egan, "Elements of Tanker Disaster: Drinking, Fatigue, Complacency," *The New York Times* (22 May 1989): p. B7.

5. *Ibid.*

6. Shabecoff, "Captain of Tanker Had Been Drinking," p. A12.

7. Davidson, "In the Wake," p. 16.

8. Davidson, *Ibid.*, p. 22.

9. Catherine A. Dold and Gary Soucie, "Just the Facts: Prince William Sound," insert in George Laycock, "The Baptism of Prince William Sound," *Audubon* (September 1989): pp. 74–111.

10. Ken Wells and Marilyn Chase, "Paradise Lost: Heartbreaking Scenes of Beauty Disfigured Follow Alaska Oil Spill," *The Wall Street Journal* (31 March 1989): pp. A1 & A4.

11. *Ibid.*

12. Malcolm W. Browne, "Spill Could Pose a Threat for Years," *The New York Times* (31 March 1989): p. A12.

13. Malcolm W. Browne, "In Once-Pristine Sound, Wildlife Reels Under Oil's Impact: Biologists Say Spill Could Set Records for Loss of Birds, Fish and Mammals," *The New York Times,* Science Times (4 April 1989): pp. C1 & C5.

14. George Laycock, "The Baptism of Prince William Sound," *Audubon* (September 1989): p. 81; emphasis supplied.

15. *Ibid.*

16. Browne, "Once-Pristine Sound."

17. Wells and Chase, "Paradise Lost," pp. A1 & A4. Other sources for this section include George Laycock, "The Baptism of the Sound," and Michael D. Lemonick, "The Two Alaskas," *TIME* (17 April 1989): pp.56–66.

18. Browne, "Once-Pristine Sound."

19. Laycock, "The Baptism of the Sound," p. 84.

20. Davidson, *In the Wake,* pp. 24–25.

21. Laycock, "The Baptism of the Sound," p. 84.

22. *Ibid.*

23. Davidson, *In the Wake,* p. 73.

24. Statement by L. R. Beynon for Alyeska Pipeline Service Company, Trans-Alaska Pipeline hearing, Department of the Interior, Anchorage, 25 February 1971, exhibit 48, vol. 3; cited in Davidson, *In the Wake,* p. 81.

25. Egan, "Tanker Disaster," p. B7.

26. Cited in Davidson, *In the Wake,* p. 81.

27. Brad Matsen, "Fishermen Battle Pain, Anger and Spilled Oil," *National Fisherman,* no. 95 (June 1989): p. 3.

28. Davidson, *In the Wake,* p. 51.

29. Egan, "Tanker Disaster." Iarossi claimed that Exxon had 365 barrels ready to use; see Davidson, *In the Wake,* p. 53.

30. Davidson, *In the Wake,* p. 58.

31. *Ibid.,* p. 103.

32. *Ibid.,* p. 105.

33. *Ibid.,* p. 109.

34. *Ibid.,* p. 110.

35. *Ibid.,* p. 134.

36. See, for instance, Anne Pacsu Wieland, "Legacy of an Oil Spill: Out of Anguish and Despair, a Challenge to Live More Harmoniously in Our Fragile Environment," *Swarthmore College Bulletin* (November 1991): pp. 10 ff.

37. Davidson, *In the Wake,* p. 157.

38. *Ibid.,* p. 156.

39. Janet Raloff, "An Otter Tragedy," *Science News,* vol. 143 (27 March 1993): pp. 200–201.

40. *Ibid.,* pp. 242–243.

41. *Ibid.,* p. 261.

42. *Ibid.,* p. 262.

43. Matthew L. Wald, "Cleanup of Oily Beaches Moves Slowly," *The New York Times* (23 April 1989): p. 30.

44. From his testimony before the committee on Interior and Insular Affairs, oversight hearing, Washington, D.C., 28 July 1989; cited in Davidson, *In the Wake,* p. 115.

45. Davidson, *In the Wake,* p. 117.

46. This dispute, as rancorous in tone as one is likely to find in public, is documented in Davidson, *In the Wake,* pp. 118–124.

47. Davidson, *In the Wake,* p. 200.

48. *Ibid.,* p. 199.

49. *Ibid.,* p. 109.

50. *Ibid.,* p. 147.

51. *Ibid.,* p. 273.

52. Greenpeace USA; 1436 "U" Street NW, Washington, D.C. 20009.

53. Davidson, *In the Wake,* p. 277.

54. Editorial, "Dolphins and Double Hulls," *The New York Times* (14 April 1990): editorial page.

55. Charles McCoy and Allanna Sullivan, "Exxon's Withdrawal of Valdez Pleas Will Maintain Pressure to Settle Case," *The Wall Street Journal* (28 May 1991): pp. A3 & A6.

56. "Tanker Spills Oil off Hawaiian Coast," *The New York Times* (4 March 1989): p. 6.

57. Philip Shabecoff, "The Rash of Tanker Spills Is Part of a Pattern of Thousands a Year," *The New York Times* (29 June 1989): p. A20.

58. Craig Wolff, "Exxon Admits a Year of Breakdowns in S.I. Oil Spill," *The New York Times* (10 January 1990): pp. A1 & B3; Craig Wolff, "Leaking Exxon Pipe Ran Through Regulatory Limbo," *The New York Times* (11 January 1990): B1 & B7; Tim Golden, "Oil in Arthur Kill: Publicity and Peril for Urban Marsh," *The New York Times* (18 January 1990): pp. B1 & B4.

59. Allan R. Gold, "Exxon to Pay up to $15 Million for Spill," *The New York Times* (15 March 1991): p. B1.

60. Philip Revzin, "Years Temper Damage of Worst Oil Spill: Starkest Fears of 1978 Amoco Disaster Weren't Realized," *The Wall Street Journal,* p. A10.

61. Editorial, "On Oil Spills: Trust Turns Into Anger," *The New York Times* (28 June 1989): editorial page.

62. Paul Muscat and Michael Gilson, "Oilfields Scar Arctic Wildlife Refuge even Now," Letter to the Editor, *The New York Times* (4 April 1989): editorial page.

63. Matthew L. Wald, "Drilling Plans Point up Questions on Oil and Wilderness in Alaska: Industry Showcase or Environmental Disaster?" *The New York Times* (23 April 1989): pp. A1 & A30.

64. E. J. Dionne, Jr., "Big Oil Spill Leaves Its Mark On Politics of Environment," *The New York Times* (3 April 1989): pp. A1 & A12.

65. *Ibid.*

66. *The New York Times* (2 July 1989): p. E7.

67. Joan Bavaria, Editorial, "Business, Clean up Your Environmental Act! Witholding Investment Can Influence Corporate Actions," *Newsday* (7 September 1989): editorial page. Barnaby J. Feder, "Group Sets Corporate Code on Environmental Conduct," *The New York Times* (8 September 1989): pp. D1 & D5.

68. Unsigned note, "Whatever Happened with the Valdez Principles?" *Business Ethics* (May–June 1991): p. 11.

69. See, for example, "Late and Lame on the Big Spill," lead editorial in *The New York Times* (12 April 1989): p. A24.

70. Malcolm W. Browne, "Experts See Glass Beads as Low-Cost Tool for Oil-Spill Cleanup," *The New York Times* (11 April 1992): p. 12.

71. "Craft Warning: Unsafe Oil Tankers and Ill-Trained Crews Threaten Further Spills," *The Wall Street Journal* (12 February 1993): pp. A1 & A5.

72. *Ibid.*, p. A1.

73. Judith Tegger Kildow, "Keeping the Oceans Oil-Free," *Technology Review* (April 1993): pp. 42–49.

74. Caleb Solomon, "Exxon Attacks Scientific Views of Valdez Spill," *The Wall Street Journal* (15 April 1993): pp. B1 & B12.

75. Sarah Chasis and Lisa Speer, "How to Avoid Another Valdez," *The New York Times* (20 May 1989): p. 27.

76. See, for instance, "Another Wake-up Call: Save Energy," the lead editorial in *The New York Times* (4 September 1990), in response to the war in the Persian Gulf; see also L. H. Newton, cited in Rierdon, "Connecticut Q & A," *The New York Times* (11 December 1988).

Suggestions for Further Reading

Davidson, Art. *In the Wake of the Exxon Valdez.* San Francisco: Sierra Club Books, 1990.

Audubon magazine (September 1989): entire issue.

Keeble, John. "A Parable of Oil and Water." *The Amicus Journal* (Spring 1993): pp. 35–43.

APPENDIX: THE VALDEZ (CERES) PRINCIPLES

1. Protecting the biosphere

2. Sustainable use of natural resources

3. Reduction and disposal of wastes

4. Energy conservation

5. Risk reduction

6. Safe products and services

7. Environmental restoration

8. Informing the public

9. Management commitment to protect the environment

10. Accountability (environmental audits and reports)

CHAPTER 5

Forests of the North Coast

The Owls, the Trees, and the Conflicts

PREFACE: QUESTIONS TO KEEP IN MIND

Who, or what, is the northern spotted owl? Why is this diminutive raptor, uniquely adapted to life in the ancient forests of the Pacific Northwest and nowhere else, so very important? Why should we be concerned by the collapse of the population to an estimated 2,000 breeding pairs of these owls left in the world today?[1]

What are the forests? They are beautiful, yes, and unique in many ways—but human beings have been cutting down trees since the beginning of the human race. Why do the evergreen forests of the Northwest Coast (especially the old groves of northern California redwoods) have a special claim on us?

What are the imperatives of the lumber industry in the United States? Why have lumber companies been shutting down their mills and exporting raw logs? Should lumber companies operate on the same imperatives of short-term profit that drive discount retail chains? Why or why not? Can we use what happened to Pacific Lumber to demonstrate the weaknesses of the present system?

The media have characterized the struggle between the loggers and the environmentalists as essentially a class conflict: the working-class lumbermen against the elite professional class that typifies the environmental movement. How does the United States generally handle white-collar versus blue-collar conflicts? Will the lessons learned elsewhere in that type of conflict help us here?

BACKGROUND: THE TRAGEDY OF TREES

"Save a Life, Kill a Tree?" is an article written by Sallie Tisdale;[2] it describes the most recent "trees vs. people" ammunition, the anticancer drug taxol that is found in the bark of the Pacific Yew of the Northwest old-growth forests. "Save a Logger—Eat a Spotted Owl" is a bumper sticker commonly seen throughout this area. A grocery store in northern California recently displayed boxes of Spotted Owl Helper (a takeoff on Hamburger Helper). A recurring theme in this controversy is that something (usually a tree, but sometimes an owl) has to be killed in order to save something of human value; this gives the whole topic an overtone of tragedy. In tragedy, victory is impossible, and reconciliation comes at terrible cost. Simply because the issue will not yield to politically conscious pragmatism (the peculiarly American version of reason), it invites complications from the political and economic left and right and sanctions violence in defense of endangered values. Our first job, then, is to sort out the complications, so that the intersecting ethical dilemmas can be treated independently. Let us consider the issues:

1. *The owl.* The northern spotted owl is threatened with extinction by logging operations in the Northwest Forest. The owl is protected to some extent by the Endangered Species Act (see Appendix following this chapter), but the issues involved go beyond the law. Why might we have a moral obligation to save an endangered species? On the other hand, why should we care about insignificant faraway birds, anyway? What good is *biodiversity?* And what should we be willing to do to maintain it? Biodiversity will be treated relatively briefly in this chapter, because we discuss it in detail in the chapter on the Amazonian Rainforest.

2. *The trees and the business practices that threaten them.* Ted Gup describes the owl as "a fine bird, yes, but...never really the root cause of this great conflict."[3] It is the trees themselves—great groves of Sequoia and other cone-bearing trees, some of them more than 2,000 years old, spontaneously likened to the great cathedrals of Europe by many who have seen them—it is the trees that really fire the imagination. Do we have an obligation to preserve these trees, just as a singular treasure for the world?

We live with a free-enterprise system that generally serves us well. Do we have an obligation either to protect businesses that operate in environmentally sensitive ways, or to require that all businesses do so? The case of Pacific Lumber Company shows a company that preserved environmental values pitted against hostile financial initiatives that were good for the shareholders but bad for the trees. Does the fiduciary duty of the company extend to the environment? Should the trees have a vote at the annual meeting? Do we have an obligation to protect the workers—the loggers, and their peculiarly specialized way of life?

3. *The varied roles of the government.* Consider the "alphabet soup" in the Appendix: What is the role of the government in protecting owls, trees, business, and ourselves? What do we want the government's role to be? What should government be empowered to do? at what cost?

All these questions turn on one indisputable fact: the Pacific Northwest Rainforests, ecosystems unlike any others in the world, have been logged for a century to the point of threatened extinction, not only of the species housed there but of the forests themselves. These forests are managed and regulated by an incredible mix of national bureaucracies; the actions of these agencies affect the livelihoods of millions of people and the economies of three states. The loggers and lumber companies are in conflict with the environmentalists; both parties are in conflict with the regulators; the politicians are on all sides of the conflict, depending on their constituencies; and everything ends up in court, where the "lawsuits, motions, and appeals... [seem to] have increased faster than the owl population."[4]

THE OWL AND ITS TREES

The currents of the Pacific Ocean provide abundant warmth and moisture to the Northwest Coast of the United States. Through millions of years of evolution, these conditions have allowed the appearance, probably 6,000 years ago, of what we now call "old-growth forests." These are forests with some thousand-year-old stands, forests with trees that are 300 feet tall and ten feet in diameter, trees that are at least twice as massive as those found in tropical rainforests, trees that each contain enough lumber to build two houses. These forests extend from the Alaskan panhandle (Sitka Spruce) south through Washington and Oregon (Douglas Fir, Western Hemlock) to northern California (Redwoods, Ponderosa Pine).

These forests experience rain for six months of the year and, accordingly, affect both the regional and the global climate. Despite the poor volcanic, basaltic soil, the forests contain the largest examples of the 25 species of conifers found in the region. The dead trees (called snags) can remain standing for up to two hundred years, because it takes two to five hundred years for them to decay; nevertheless, the streams and forest floor are littered with decomposing trees that provide nutrients for the living ones and a habitat for thousands of animal species (1,500 invertebrate species were counted on a single tree).

One of the *vertebrate* species is the focus of this controversy, however. The northern spotted owl (hereinafter, called "the owl") is a subspecies of the spotted owl; some are now officially listed as "threatened" under the Endangered Species Act. The northern spotted owl is listed as "endangered." The owl weighs less than two pounds, has a two-foot wingspan, and must eat its weight in food each day to survive. Estimates of the surviving numbers vary. A 1990 source states that a count of the northern spotted owl and its fellow subspecies, the California spotted owl, netted 2,900 pairs;[5] a later estimate suggests 2,000 pairs for the northern cousin alone.[6] For reasons that are not well understood, the owl breeds late (after three years of age) and dies young; both factors militate against survival. Without interference from the loggers, though, the owl had held its own; the major cause of its threatened extinction, as in most cases, is loss of habitat.

The owl is one of those species that requires unique stable conditions to survive: It appears to be totally dependent upon old-growth forest, and hunts there exclusively. To house the owl, the trees must be dense, and some proportion of them must be over 200 years old. Thus, the future of the northern spotted owl is linked with that of the old-growth forest, and the owl is therefore considered an *indicator* species—that is, a species whose condition will indicate the condition of the entire ecosystem (similar to the canary in the coal mine). Not only does the owl require old growth, it requires a lot of it. Studies have shown that, in northern California, each pair ranged among 1,900 acres of old growth; in Oregon, six pairs averaged 2,264 acres as their range; and six pairs studied in Washington had an average range of 3,800 acres.[7]

It is not fully understood why the spotted owl requires old growth, and so much of it, but it has been well documented, at some cost to the documenters. One researcher commented, "Critics who ceaselessly argue that more research is needed before any management decisions are made should spend a year or two tracking these nocturnal birds across the rugged terrain of the northwest."[8] The owl evidently requires such old-growth characteristics as broken branches that provide platforms, debris, and protective thermal cover—characteristics not found in new growth. Also, the owls' prey—squirrels, voles, and rats—share the old-growth habitat and feed upon the fungi that forms on the decaying trees.

Further, competition with other species might be forcing the spotted owl back into the old growth. The younger stands provide habitat for the great horned owls, which feed upon young spotted owls; great horned owls also do well in clearings and on the edges of the old growth. So the spotted owl loses its protection against predators when it is forced from the density of the old growth or flies across clear-cuts from one old-growth stand to another. Too, if the spotted owl survives predation in the clear cuts and second growth, it has to compete for food with the more aggressive barred owl that makes its home there. Finally, the owl's habitat is especially threatened by natural disasters—25,000 acres of habitat were lost with the eruption of Mount Saint Helens—because it requires such a large range and so much of the old growth in that area is already gone.

ENDANGERMENT
AND OBLIGATIONS

The northern spotted owl, then, is clearly endangered. To save it, we must save large numbers of the oldest trees. Given that 90 percent of the forest has been cut down already, virtually all the remaining old growth, whether in private or public hands, must be preserved. Should we do this for the sake of the owl?

Do we have an obligation to preserve endangered species? For starters, what does "preservation" mean in this context? If only the genetic material is in question, we can preserve the spotted owl by capturing a sufficient number of breeding pairs (say, 20), putting them in a climate-controlled zoo, and allowing them to produce baby owls to their hearts' content—and we can do this without gumming up the logging operations. (If no zoos have room for owls right now, we could freeze owl eggs indefinitely and regenerate the species any time it is convenient to do so.) Or does preservation of a wild species always mean preservation in the wild, living as the species has evolved to live, naturally? If this is preservation, then what cost are we expected to absorb to preserve the habitat? Granted that the owl is worth something to us (we would not wish it extinguished, other things being equal), but what is it worth when it affects these other things: jobs, regional economies, and the evolved lifestyle of the North Coast loggers?

The preservation of a species contributes to the biodiversity of the area—this means, literally, the number and variety of species that are living there. For any ecosystem, we assume that the species have evolved as members of a niche and that the destruction of one species, leaving its niche open and its role unfilled, will have an unfavorable impact on the others. For the sake of *all* species, then, we should preserve *each* species. We cannot predict just which of these species will suddenly prove to be dramatically useful to humans—by, say, providing a cure for cancer (see the chapter on the tropical rainforests). This argument was used, but only hypothetically, until the discovery of taxol, a drug that has recently shown better than expected results in treating ovarian and breast cancer; taxol originates in the bark (and perhaps the needles) of the Pacific Yew, which is indigenous to the old growth. The U.S. Forest Service used to consider the Yew a weed, to be removed from a clear-cut and burned; now, of course, there is pressure from many fronts to harvest these trees for the cancer drug. Would we have ever found out about this use for yew trees if the old groves had all been gone? For the sake of the human species, then, we should protect *any* species, no matter how humble, no matter what measures (within the obvious limits of reason) are required to preserve the conditions that species needs to live.

ACTING TO PRESERVE THE SPECIES

Persuaded by such considerations, Congress passed the Endangered Species Act (ESA) in 1973. According to this bill, the National Marine Fishery Service (Department of Commerce) and the Fish and Wildlife Service (Department of the Interior) are empowered to list marine and land species, respectively, as either threatened or endangered; then, these species can no longer be hunted, collected, injured, or killed. The bill also prohibits any federal agency from carrying out or funding any activity that could threaten or endanger said species *or their habitats.* (This latter provision has caused the most controversy with regard to logging in the old-growth forests, but also other projects, such as dams, highways, and other development receiving federal funding.) Therefore, both the Bureau of Land Management (Department of the Interior) and the Forest Service (Department of Agriculture) must consult with the Fish and Wildlife Service before undertaking any action that might threaten a species such as the owl.

This bill is typical of environmental legislation on several counts: (1) It is informed by the best science available, so it is enlightened, far-reaching, and probably the world's most stringent species-protection legislation. To be in noncompliance with the ESA is a criminal act; both civil and criminal penalties are called for, including imprisonment. (2) This bill is also among those most pitifully funded. Until 1988, the yearly funding amounted to about the cost of 12 Army bulldozers.[9] The 1988 amendments doubled the budget, but legislative environmentalists consider that the bill has nowhere near the support it needs to preserve marine and terrestrial species worldwide. (3) Three cabinet-level departments must work harmoniously together for the act to be implemented.

Implementation presents other problems. According to the 1982 amendment of the act, the economic implications of the protection of a species *may not* be considered in determining its status, whether or not it is endangered; that decision must be based "solely on the basis of the best scientific and commercial data."[10] Economic factors *may* be considered after the listing, during the required preparation of a recovery plan for the listed species. (In practice, because of the complexities involved, few plans have been prepared.) The act also calls for a determination of the species' "critical habitat" but allows a year to elapse after the listing for the determination and acknowledges that, because of complications, the habitat might be indeterminable.[11]

When determining the critical habitat, the Fish and Wildlife Service *must* include economic considerations. On two occasions, court-ordered reconsiderations on the basis of economic impact have impelled the FWS to reduce the acreage required to preserve the owl. Additionally, those who feel that their economic interests are damaged by species protection may appeal to the Endangered Species Committee (the "God Squad"). The bureaucratic hurdles to overcome on the way to actual protection of the owl seem daunting even to the most hardened Washington veterans; nevertheless, it *is* legal protection and, as such, the strongest statement that we can make, as a nation, about the value of our most threatened creatures.

THE TALLEST TREES ON EARTH

The owl is not really the central character in the dramatic controversies that plague the timber industry in the Pacific Northwest. Central to it all are the cathedral groves of redwood trees, especially in northern California. The redwoods come in two species, *Sequoia gigantica* and *Sequoia sempervirens*. What's left of *gigantica*, largest of trees, is largely protected now in state and national parks. At issue for this chapter is *sempervirens*, the coastal redwood, to the best of our knowledge the tallest trees that have ever lived.[12] These giants, on the misty Pacific coast of northern California, are the focus of increasingly bitter disputes between environmentalists and the timber industry, its workers and its communities.

Climatically unique conditions are responsible for producing these beautiful trees. Coniferous trees (gymnosperms) dominated the planet before the evolution of flowering, deciduous trees (angiosperms). Angiosperms were more successful than gymnosperms, because the reproductive strategy of a flower becoming a seed-bearing fruit is much more effective than a cone bearing a "naked" seed. Extended areas of coniferous trees are now found only in those northern latitudes and higher altitudes where conditions preclude deciduous vegetation. In the Pacific Northwest, peculiar climatic conditions—winter cold, despite ample water and light, and summer drought, despite ample warmth and light—hinder photosynthesis in deciduous trees and allow the better-adapted conifers to take over. More-

over, regardless of the environment, the rule of nature is change, or suc-
cession. An ecosystem's species change with time, from pioneer species
through more stable species to the most stable, climax species. The climax
species will remain dominant until some cataclysmic event causes the process to start all over again (the Mount Saint Helens volcano eruption is a
good example). When the ecosystem is as immune to natural forces as are
old-growth forests, however, it will remain, grow, and reproduce itself for
centuries; therefore, some individuals are likely to be older than Christen-
dom. To quote Sallie Tisdale, an admirer of old growth, "There is little on
this earth so close to immortal."[13]

Unfortunately for those who hope for the survival of these trees, they
are the most commercially valuable trees in the United States. The
extent of the original forest and of the remaining acreage is very debat-
able and probably depends on one's definition of "old growth," which is
generally described as the largest old trees, living and dead, standing and
fallen, within a multilayered canopy. Estimates of the extent of the original forest range from 20 to 70 million acres (depending on what is considered a large tree); some 70 to 95 percent of this forest has been logged
over the last century, and the rate of logging has increased dramatically
over the last few decades. Estimates are complicated, too, by the frag-
mentation of the forest by clear-cutting, leaving some stands isolated in
a barren landscape.

From the corporate viewpoint, logging just makes good business sense.
The woods, as a popular song would have it, are just trees, and the trees
are just wood. Humans have always cut and processed timber for lumber—for houses, boats, fences, furniture—virtually since our beginnings
on this planet, and the redwoods are eminently suitable for such harvest.
The lumber from redwoods is beautiful, durable, light, strong, has good
nail-holding capacity, and is insect- and fire-resistant. Each tree yields an
average of 12 or 13 thousand board feet—enough to build two houses.[14]
The harvest is very profitable but strictly limited. Once those old-growth
trees are logged, there will be no more: The trees will be gone forever.
The second growth does not share the characteristics of the old growth in
its resistance to insects, disease, fire, and decay, nor is it as dense and massive, of course. We might suppose that the twentieth-century remnants of
a 2,000-year-old forest were composed of the best survivors of all attacks:
The less-resistant trees will have succumbed centuries ago. The old
growth is then an irreplaceable asset: It could be argued that it will
become more valuable every year into the indefinite future and that it
therefore demands careful husbanding and conservative forestry practices.
Wise management would seem to require very sparing cuts of the old
growth while encouraging plantations of new trees to satisfy demands for
ordinary lumber.

PACIFIC LUMBER AND
THE LOGGING BUSINESS

What is "wise management," anyway, where a publicly owned company is concerned? Business theory holds that investors put their money into a company for the sole purpose of making money for themselves; from this it follows that (in the immortal words of Milton Friedman) "the social responsibility of business is to increase its profit."[15] Every first-year economics student knows that existing money is more valuable than future earnings. Business managers fulfill their fiduciary obligation to the shareholders when, and only when, they put profits in the shareholders' pockets as quickly as possible; no other considerations may intrude upon their efforts toward that objective. Because cut timber brings financial returns while uncut timber is nothing but a tax burden, it follows that the quickest and most cost-effective (least expensive) harvest of the old-growth forests would be the best approach. In contrast to the conservative forestry practices demanded by the long-term best interests of both the trees and the corporation, the interests of the current shareholders would be best served by clear-cutting old groves as quickly as possible.

The conservative business approach is oriented toward the long-term maximization of value from assets, the long-term competitive positioning of the company itself, and the continuity of its arrangements with suppliers, customers, and employees. Rarely do we witness a direct face-off of this approach and its radical short-term descendant (known colloquially as "grab the profits and run") made famous during the 1980s. Curiously, the Pacific Northwest gives us just such a confrontation in the story of the Pacific Lumber Company. It will be worthwhile to retrace, very briefly, the adventures of this very American corporation.

The early Pacific Lumber Company (before 1985) was a model of Fezziwig-style enterprise: community service, environmental sensitivity, and scrupulous consideration for its workers. Indeed, Pacific Lumber was so successful as an old-fashioned paternalistic company that a pair of fascinated sociologists (Hugh Wilkerson and John van der Zee) wrote a book about living in its employment in the company-owned town, appropriately titled *Life in the Peace Zone*. From this chronicle emerges a unique story: The company and its headquarters in Scotia, California, were both founded about 1869. After a period of free-cutting (with very primitive equipment, so not much damage was done), in the 1930s, the company adopted a policy of perpetual sustained yield; mature trees were marked for selective cutting, felled, snaked out by the Cat tractor, and milled. The younger trees then matured faster with more light; where bare spots were left, the company reseeded. In theory, such practices should "keep the company supplied with redwood logs from its own lands in perpetuity."[16] This sustained-yield policy is both economically sound and kind to shareholders. Pacific Lumber's financial statements for the years through 1984 show small cyclical adjustments to demand but steady earnings on its outstanding shares.[17]

The company also took very good care of its workers: "After he has put in ninety days on his mill job, [a worker] can get on the list to move into Scotia, where a comfortable one-bedroom company bungalow, with a garden and a lawn on a quiet residential street rents from under sixty dollars a month. Water and sewage and garbage removal are free. Every five to seven years, the company will repaint his house, inside and out, free. As he moves up in the company, or as his family grows, he can move to a larger house in another part of town...He has good accident and health coverage, and a choice of pension plan or an investment program...And, in the remote future, as a Pacific Lumber employee, if his son or daughter qualifies for a four-year college, he or she will receive a thousand-dollar scholarship from the company."[18] Further, Pacific Lumber hired any son of a worker who wanted a job, never laid off anyone, rarely fired anyone, and promoted entirely from within. The pension plan was overfunded and generous; a secure old age was a certainty for Pacific Lumber employees. Thus workers could be forgiven a certain amount of complacency. Corky, one of the workers the sociologists interviewed in some depth, was happy with his job and everything else in his life: "Golly, for the rent, you can't match this." He was twenty-four at the time of the interview. "I got forty-one years to go, and I can't see any reason I'd leave."[19]

The liberal sociologists' conscientious efforts to find something outrageously wrong in this secure lifestyle availed them nothing. One schoolteacher pointed out that the children's conviction of utter security, in some cases buttressed by two or three generations with Pacific Lumber, was based on faith alone: "What they don't know is that PL could fold tomorrow. And then what?" But that seemed so unlikely, even to the authors, that they dismissed the possibility: "Most people,...recognizing that Pacific Lumber with its high-quality line of products and enormous timber holdings is not about to fail overnight, decide to...settle for the obvious rewards of a relatively comfortable and untroubled future."[20] The authors concluded, "What Scotia is really offering those dismayed with the world outside, the tie that pulls men back who vowed to leave, is not the promise of fulfillment but an assurance of moderation, the possibility of living a humane life in a humane community. And for that, there will always be a waiting list."[21]

THE HOSTILE TAKEOVER

And then, in 1986, came a hostile takeover, and Pacific Lumber failed their employees overnight. Charles Hurwitz, financier turned corporate raider, seized control of the company (with $900 million in high-yield, high-risk junk bonds from Drexel Burnham Lambert); he immediately "terminated the pension plan and grabbed the $55 million worth of surplus pension funds to pay down part of his buyout debt."[22] Executive Life Insurance, a company controlled by Hurwitz, bought more than one-third of the bonds and issued the annuities required by federal law to replace pension funds when their managers deplete them. Executive Life collapsed along with the junk-bond market, leaving the workers pensionless.[23]

Repayment of Hurwitz's debt required that he get money off the land as fast as possible, and Pacific Lumber's old-growth forest was certainly available for cutting. Forestry practices immediately changed; the plan became to attack groves that the old Pacific Lumber had been saving for the end of the century, to clear-cut where selective cutting had been the rule, to speed up the pace of logging, and to abandon the costly replanting projects that had ensured a future harvest. The practice of selective cutting and replanting, besides providing for future harvests, had helped to hold the soil in place after logging and to prevent erosion of the steep slopes during the relentless rainfall in the region; under the new management, the soil began to wash into the streams.

However undesirable these results might seem, we should point out here that the only way a company can become prey to a hostile takeover is by offering the shareholders more money for their shares than they could otherwise obtain. Hurwitz certainly did make such an offer, obtaining the cash to do so from the sale of the junk bonds and other loans against the assets of the company. The shareholders of record at the time of the takeover made out very well indeed. (Later in this sort of game, shareholders make out somewhat worse.)[24]

Is the CEO's fiduciary duty not to the shareholders and the shareholders alone? If so, how can we condemn Hurwitz for making the lives of retired Pacific Lumber employees miserable? If it was legal to terminate the pensions under these conditions and very much in the shareholders' interest to do so (because of the high price they received for their stock), it could then be argued that Hurwitz was obligated to do it. As John Boland points out, "the only direct, clear legal obligation of corporate fiduciaries (beyond obeying civil law and contractual constraints in general) is to the corporate owners who pay them."[25] After all, it could be argued, the government will take care of the retired workers; corporations are not in the business of running charities for pensioners.

As for the environmental concerns, those too are beyond the competence of business to resolve. Everything Hurwitz did was arguably within the law (although some lawsuits are still pending). If the American people, through their elected officials, wish to keep more of certain kinds of products (such as trees) in the ground and away from the market, let them pass a law to that effect, and law-abiding businessmen will adhere to the law. But in a publicly held, profit-oriented corporation, how could it be management's obligation, or option, to look after the long-term fate of the trees? Pacific Lumber is in business to make money for the stock-holders, not to act as unpaid trustee for the Northwest Coast forest.

As for the laws to protect the trees, we should add that a good corporate officer would regret, as a citizen, the loss to the economy that any restriction on logging would represent and would feel obliged to notify the citizens of the potential cost in jobs, tax revenues, and so forth. (See references to "the timber interests" in the chronology in the Appendix; the timber interests are always interested in cutting more timber.) In this effort, company presidents, contemplating profits and prices per share, would be joined by the loggers, contemplating their jobs. As a matter of fact, the major initiatives to limit the effect of the Endangered Species Act and to free more acreage of old-growth timber for cutting have come from workers and small businessmen in the affected regions; the major timber companies, Pacific Lumber included, have taken a back seat.

This pattern persists as the most politically advantageous for the timber interests. At the "Timber Summit" called by President Bill Clinton in one of his first months in office (April 2, 1993, in Portland, Oregon), the news media immediately picked up on the testimony of a "typical" logger, Buzz Eades, the sixth generation of his family to ply that trade. He was, he said, "scared" for his job, and in that fear he represents thousands and thousands of "modern Paul Bunyans who are hiding in their cars while their wife buys groceries with food stamps." These loggers easily succeed in capturing the sympathy of the country with their economic fear and threatened pride.[26]

The loggers in this case have very few options: Most of them were raised in the region, either in the Pacific Lumber family or in similar areas with similar expectations. They do not see themselves as having the skills to move elsewhere; in their view, only a job cutting down trees (or milling them or serving those who do) saves them from permanent unemployment. "Jobs or woodpeckers?" their signs demand; their bumper stickers insist that they "Love spotted owls: fried, boiled, barbecued...," or that "loggers, too, are an endangered species." With such strong political alliance, then, the timber companies have little motivation to retrain loggers for other employment.

TREES, THE ENVIRONMENT, AND THE LAW

Aristotle and Adam Smith both proved, in very different ways, that private property (specifically, land and all resources for production) was better off, more likely to be taken care of, than public property. We accept as established fact that a private owner is the best caretaker of property. The centrality of the right to private property in John Locke's writing depends on that presumption, as do our standard defenses of the American business system.

Is this presumption now generally false? Pacific Lumber's redwoods are clearly not safe in Hurwitz's hands. Do we have a legal right, then, to take the land away from him? We know that, under the doctrine of eminent domain, we can seize the redwoods for a new national park—but can we seize all that land just to continue a more conservative logging operation? What are the business imperatives of a company that logs redwoods? Is it a sufficient discharge of our obligations to replace 2,000-year-old groves with young growth that can be harvested in 40 to 80 years?[27]

Another environmental effect of the logging, presently unmeasurable, is its contribution to global warming. The old growth is a veritable storehouse of carbon, a fact of increasingly intense interest, for carbon dioxide is the most important of the "greenhouse gases" credited with causing the projected global warming. While these trees are alive, they absorb huge amounts of carbon dioxide from the atmosphere in the photosynthetic process. Nature's recycling laws require, of course, that the same amount of gas be returned to the atmosphere, through the trees' respiration and eventual decay, but that happens, as we have noted, over a period of hundreds of years.

When the trees are felled, the photosynthetic carbon dioxide absorption stops and, compounding the crime, when the resulting debris is burned, the stored carbon is abruptly added to the atmosphere as carbon dioxide. The timber industry has claimed that, by cutting old growth and planting young trees with a faster photosynthetic rate, they are actually ameliorating the threat of global warming. To be sure, a rapidly growing tree absorbs more carbon dioxide than a mature tree of the same size, but a small seedling does not approach the chemical activity of the enormous trees in the Northwest Forest, trees that are many times as massive as those found anywhere else in the world. The Northwest old growth "stores more carbon…than any other biome—twice as much per unit of area as tropical rainforests."[28]

Incidentally, the claim of the timber companies—that their little plantings are really much better at taking carbon from the air than the mature redwoods—is typical of the self-serving half-truths that tend to harden attitudes in these controversies. This claim, with just enough scientific fact to make it respectable yet clearly in the service of company interests, enrages environmentalists and encourages public cynicism. Should the timber companies be held responsible for global warming—an unintended but predictable, consequence of their operations?

GOVERNMENT AND THE
NATIONAL FORESTS

If the timber companies can no longer be counted on to protect the trees, but instead await laws that force them to stop cutting before they will stop cutting—in short, if they insist on waiting for the government to regulate them—then, by what means, and to what end, shall the government regulate? The entire alphabet soup of government agencies (see the Appendix following this chapter) represents efforts to answer these questions; government response to the problems of managing the trees has been multifold and complex. At various stages in the effort, Congress has opted for (1) preservation of the woods for the people to enjoy forever; (2) conservation of the woods to support the timber industry into the indefinite future; and (3) protection of the right of private owners to cut all the wood they want, subject only to minimum regulation.

Preservation is administered by the Department of the Interior, which supervises the national parks and wilderness areas. Wilderness areas are simply those protected from any invasion at all. National parks are a different matter: The values of *wildness* or the preservation of wilderness and easy access for tourists will never sit easily together, and we as a people will probably never agree on how to treat our parks. In neither area, though, can trees simply be cut for lumber.

The national forests, on the other hand, were established during Teddy Roosevelt's administration by his chief forester, Gifford Pinchot, for the express purpose of making sure that there would always be trees for the timber industry to cut (although, even at the beginning, other recreational and educational purposes were mentioned). Here, in the national forests, is where the trees can be cut, and here is where controversy begins.

The U.S. Forest Service, a division of the Department of Agriculture, is responsible for managing these national forests, federally owned forestland that includes about 36 million acres in the Northwest United States. From its founding in 1904 until World War II, the Forest Service had no problem reconciling its two charges: to promote logging while preserving wilderness for study, watershed protection, recreation, and other uses. During that time, the major timber companies were cutting on private land and were, in fact, discouraging Forest Service timber sales as unwanted competition. With the war, however, came an abrupt increase in timber demand at a time when much of the more accessible privately owned land had already been cut; so began the transformation of the Forest Service from "guardian, to arm of the timber industry."[29] In the postwar years, the Forest Service's reputation as a "federal timber company"[30] grew, as logging on federal land began to exceed their own guidelines, with the warm approval of loggers, pulp and paper companies, lumber interests in general, and the congressional delegation of the Pacific Northwest.

Along with more extensive logging came technological advance, in the form of giant machinery capable of clear-cutting the woods; the economic advantages of clear-cutting were immediately apparent to lumber companies, and the practice became widely adopted. National ambivalence toward the justifiability of such a practice (also felt by the lumber companies and their regulators) is shown by the Forest Service requirement that protects the ordinary citizen from having to view the clear-cut land. "Visual protection corridors," a suitably broad band of trees left in place alongside highways, are mandated by Forest Service regulations; the insiders call them "fool-'em strips."[31]

The national forests tend to be the most inaccessible of forestland; private interests will already have bought up the land that could be more economically logged. To address the problem, the Forest Service built a network of access roads, at taxpayer expense; these roads are now *eight times* the length of the entire interstate highway system. These breaks in the forests, combined with the clear-cut slopes and constant rain, produce conditions where severe erosion is inevitable, with the consequent landslides, stream siltation, habitat destruction for fish and land animals alike, seasonal floods, and deteriorating water quality. Nevertheless, the Forest Service was simply following their mandate: They were protecting the U.S. lumber industry.

Occasionally, the Forest Service's management of the national forests suggests that its role as auxiliary to the lumber industry is increasingly important relative to its role as protector of public assets. The Forest Service is supposed to sell timber to the companies and make a profit for the taxpayer in the bargain, but it does no such thing: It operates at a loss. Some economists estimate that the Forest Service loses up to $200 million a year. The price charged to lumber companies for the right to cut and sell the lumber on forestland has been, historically, notoriously low. Financial horror stories abound: for example, spending $3 million to log $40,000 worth of timber, a loss of 90 to 99 cents on every dollar spent by the Forest Service. The Forest Service has been accused of selling trees so cheaply "that loggers would be foolish to say no. It [the Forest Service] builds roads, pays rangers, absorbs the risks of fires and insects, then sells at a loss."[32] Taxpayers can be expected to dislike this result. The Forest Service makes the situation look better by amortizing the cost of roads over hundreds of years. One critic commented, "It's as if the current Italian government was still paying for the Appian Way."[33]

How else could jobs be preserved? The Forest Service explains its actions primarily in terms of aid to the regional economy: providing jobs and also preserving all the occupations that depend on those jobs and the economic viability of the region itself. The truth of the matter might be that the Forest Service has little choice in the matter but merely reflects the political mood of the administration it serves—and, in the years since the hostile takeover of Pacific Lumber, U.S. administrations have not made saving the forests a high priority.

One sign that the source of the trouble with the Forest Service is higher on the ladder than the rangers themselves is the fate of the individual rangers who have attempted to blow the whistle on the overlogging and bad environmental practices they have observed. One regional director, 51-year-old John Mumma, a Forest Service veteran of 32 years, told Congress that he had been offered a Washington desk job or retirement after he refused to meet timber-cutting targets because of environmental regulations. He testified that the law required him to sell a certain amount of timber but that he was also required to abide by environmental laws, and he could not do both.[34] There is also hostility from the region itself: James Farrell, a Forest Service biologist whose job it is to locate and study the spotted owl, does not advertise his assignment, nor does he disclose exact nest sites. "There have been owls shot...and there have been threats," he said.[35]

Why does the bureaucracy fail so pitifully to protect the trees in its charge, even to the point of persecuting its own junior members? It turns out that a systematic conflict of interest is built into the work of these agencies. The timber industry is, after all, still the best job prospect for an ambitious young man or woman who has spent time in a low-paying job with the California Department of Forestry or the National Forest Service. It would be unwise for a government employee to offend the industry's representatives; this is why it has seemed, at times, that the bureaucrats existed only to serve their industry masters. Thus government regulation has been ineffective even when attempted, which is rare.

CREATIVE ALTERNATIVES

The strongest indication that the Forest Service and its allied agencies in the federal government might not be the true villains, however, lies in the work they do when the law asks them to think creatively about these forests and their future. Pursuant to the 1960 Multiple Use Sustained Yield Act (see the Appendix), the Forest Service, the Bureau of Land Management, and the U.S. Fish and Wildlife Service were asked to describe ways that the owl might be saved and the trees might be put to work for the nation without being cut down. The agencies did a fine job: The combined report of the Forest Service and the BLM, "Actions the Administration May Wish to Consider in Implementing a Conservation Strategy for the Northern Spotted Owl" (May 1, 1990), recommends a drastic cutback in the harvesting of old-growth trees by forbidding export of raw logs, then recommends and describes extensive educational and retraining programs for the loggers who are put out of work by the ban. Technical assistance would make logging and milling more efficient (avoiding the extensive waste entailed by present practices); recreational facilities would make the forests better-known and better-used and create political pressure to conserve the trees. Even more impressive is the FWS report, "Economic Analysis of Designation of Critical Habitat for the Northern Spotted Owl" (August 1991). Going beyond the multiple-use scenario, the report specifically addresses "non-use values," the value to the nation just to have the forests *there:* "Estimates of recreation user demand, benefits of scenic beauty, and benefits of water quality represent only a partial estimate of society's total value for the spotted owl and its associated habitat. The public also is willing to pay for the option of recreation use in the future, the knowledge that the natural ecosystem exists and is protected, and the satisfaction from its bequest to future generations...The average willingness to pay higher taxes and wood product prices reported in a referendum contingent valuation format was $190 per year. The lower limit of the 98 percent confidence range was $117 per household."[36]

These reports place the federal government's environmental services in a new and much better light. Bureaucrats in general, and federal bureaucrats in particular, have been harshly criticized for their role (or lack of same) in the protection of the forests. But these reports on alternate usage of the forests suggest, though, that the idealists who once joined government service to protect the nation's environmental heritage might still be around, waiting only for public opinion to catch up to them. A new agenda for the environment will require a trained corps of experts in science and policy to articulate a national environmental ethic and to frame the plans for implementation. In developing their reports, the Forest Service, the BLM, and the FWS have made an auspicious start.

SUMMARY

The heart of the problem, from an environmental point of view, is the old-growth forest. From the loggers' point of view, the problem is jobs. The owl, the financier, and the government agencies are all bit players in an agonizing twentieth-century drama of loss and conflict. We need not search for villains. Once we all thought that the forests were unlimited. The timber industry's managers watched the old growth disappear before their eyes and did not realize that it could not be restored—that once gone, it would be gone forever; but they were no more ignorant than their regulators, their customers, or their fellow citizens. The environmental movement is not the sole prerogative of Eastern elitists, as the loggers suspect, nor is the timber industry composed of a series of tintypes of Charles Hurwitz, as the environmentalists are convinced.

Protecting the forests will require the abolition of a way of life that has been honored and valued in the immediate past. What, exactly, are we prepared to do to compensate and redirect the people who are stranded by systematic and extensive preservation? On the other hand, are we prepared to spare ourselves that difficult decision by allowing the forests to be destroyed? Once the trees are gone, the industry will die, and the workers will be unemployed anyway, but then it will be *their* problem, not ours. How much are we willing to lose in order to avoid the pain of making this decision now—before it is too late? Our history suggests that we are willing to lose quite a bit.

The most disturbing aspect of our political response to these dilemmas, though, is the hypocrisy of the United States urging Brazil and other Third-World countries to halt the cutting of their tropical rainforests to prevent the worsening of global warming, while we cut our forests about twice as fast. To quote an official with the Oregon Natural Resources Council, "It's interesting that we're telling Third World countries, 'don't cut your forests' [while]...we're wiping out our fish runs, we're wiping out our biotic diversity, we're sending species to extinction...we're not a Third World country. We're not so poor that we have to destroy our ancient forests. And we're not so rich that we can afford to."[37]

THE CURRENT STATE
OF THE CONTROVERSY

During twelve years of unsympathetic administrations, positions have hardened. Defenders of private rights to use public property for private profit—not only in timber, but in mining and grazing, and regardless of damage to the land—have become entrenched. The claims of the unemployed, now ranged in tragic opposition to the environmentalists, find a sympathetic ear in the Clinton administration, which has promised to focus "like a laser" on the economy. In ominous response to these pressures, the administration has, at least for the moment, dropped serious efforts to impose new mining and grazing fees on federally owned lands in the West; President Clinton needs the support of senators from Western states for other parts of his program.[38]

On the other hand, many environmentalists have lost interest in compromise. They point out that 90 percent of old-growth forests are already cut: There is no reason to yield one more tree. "If they want to cut the baby in half, the answer is no," argued Andy Kerr, conservation director of the Oregon Natural Resources Council.[39] To these groups, not even very conservative forestry practices are permissible anymore, since they take at least some trees. Even conscientious timber operations, like Homer McCrary's Big Creek company, find themselves bedeviled by the most extreme of the environmental groups.[40] While less enlightened operations continue, the unfortunate consequence of such action is to force the conscientious operator out of business and turn the trees over to the clear-cutters, who will ruin the land as well as take the trees. Someone ought to remind the environmentalists that the first concern is not the trees but the land; if the soil remains, then the forest can recover over time. Conservative timber operations preserve the soil, and should thus be encouraged.

President Clinton would very much like to negotiate a settlement on the Northwest Forest that will save jobs, trees, and owls all at once, but he has predicted that the outcome of his administration's work will not make anyone "completely happy." The Timber Summit reached no settlement despite his efforts and his presence, along with Vice President Al Gore and Secretary of the Interior Bruce Babbitt.

Meanwhile, many of the most damaging mistakes of the last decades continue in the public literature. An ominous compendium of these mistakes was included as an insert (authored by Gregg Easterbrook) in an April, 1993, *Newsweek* article covering the Timber Summit. It argued, in sum, that there was really no conflict between environmental concerns and economic concerns and based that argument on some very questionable claims.

Thus, "Loggers are green, too…If any resource is endlessly renewable, it is the tree." Therefore, environmentalists ought to encourage people to use wood instead of plastic. "For all the recent blather about 'sustainable development,' anti-logging sentiment is forcing workers and customers out of one of the few industries that is in every sense sustainable." Not every sense, of course. If people used wood now for everything they used wood for at the beginning of the century, all the trees in the country would be gone in a week. Interestingly, one of the regulations he cites as uselessly "driving up the cost of wood" requires planting trees to replace those that have been cut down. Without replanting, it is difficult to see how the industry could be sustainable in *any* sense.

Easterbrook's second claim is that American forests are not in decline. He concedes that "the tall-tree forests of the Pacific Northwest have been hurt in recent decades," but points out that forests nationwide are "thriving," giving as an example that Vermont, 35-percent forested a century ago, is now about 76-percent forest. We wonder how many readers of *Newsweek* will immediately know the difference between old-growth forests of the Northwest and the second-growth trees and scrub now taking over the abandoned farms of New England.

He echoes the claims cited (and contested) earlier in this chapter that all wood is infinitely renewable, that the forests can be replanted whenever we want them to be, and that young trees from plantations take more of the global warming gases out of the air. These claims are, as mentioned earlier, not quite truthful where the massive redwoods are concerned; above all, the claims fail to address the damage done to the soil by abusive timbering practices that could prevent regrowth.

His solution is to log more intensively on private lands, which would "permit higher production of sustainable timber, while reducing the need to log Forest Service lands, which could then increasingly be set aside for strict preservation."[41] This proposal fails completely to address the problems of the ancient groves. Private lands are very much part of the problem; it might make a great deal of difference to Pacific Lumber or to the Forest Service whether an old grove is on private land (and therefore zoned for lumbering) or on public land, but it makes no difference at all to either the owls, to the trees themselves, or to the conservationists, who want very much to save all of them. Another article on the Timber Summit pointed out that the biggest problems "include sky-high lumber prices and heavy logging—often with brutish logging techniques and harsh impacts on wildlife—on private timberlands."[42]

The timber industry's current efforts are directed toward getting the court to lift injunctions banning logging on millions of acres of public forest. This will be difficult; the provisions of the Endangered Species Act leave little wiggle room, and Forest Service biologists have just completed a survey identifying more than 600 species that might be put at risk by logging.

Another interesting suggestion is that the administration restrict raw-log exports, which are high even though millworkers have been cast out of work by the thousands because of log shortages. Here, we might actually obtain agreement between the workers and the environmentalists, but no moves have yet been made in that direction.

On these and other issues, the possibility of consensus leads to cautious hope. At the end of the Timber Summit, President Clinton asked his cabinet to produce a plan within 60 days to end the stalemate. "It wasn't action, but it created a mood of reasonableness," noted one commentator. Clinton himself finished the conference by saying, "I don't pretend that any of this is easy." Possibly not, but the most hopeful part is that people are thinking and talking, and the Clinton administration seems to be listening.[43]

QUESTIONS FOR DISCUSSION AND REFLECTION

+ What is a forest—especially a forest with trees that have been alive for up to two millennia? a resource? a national treasure? a world treasure? How could the citizens of the world express an interest in preserving this forest?

+ Is it time to reexamine the functions of the institution of private property? Could you present an argument that there ought to be no private property in land at all (as there is no private property in the air or on the ocean)? Property *rights* and the *imperatives* of private enterprise are arguably the causes of the destruction of the forests, are they not?

◆ What set of laws or financial practices could we institute to support businesses (like the old Pacific Lumber) that conserve environmental resources? Would these be preferable to the laws and financial practices now in force?

◆ How valuable is the spotted owl? and why? What commitment should we undertake, as a nation, to protect endangered species?

Notes

1. Manuel Velasquez, "Ethics and the Spotted Owl Controversy," *Issues in Ethics* (Santa Clara Ethics Center) vol. 4, no. 1 (Winter/Spring 1991): pp. 1 & 6.

2. *The New York Times* (26 October 1991): Op-Ed section.

3. Ted Gup, "Owl vs. Man," *TIME* (25 June 1990): pp. 56–62.

4. *CRS Issue Brief,* "Spotted Owls and Old Growth Forests," updated 19 August 1991 by M. Lynne Corn, Environment and Natural Resources Policy Division, Congressional Research Service, The Library of Congress, p. 2.

5. David S. Wilcove, "Of Owls and Ancient Forests," *Ancient Forests of the Pacific Northwest* (Washington, D.C.: Island Press, 1990): p. 27.

6. Velasquez, "Ethics and the Spotted Owl."

7. Wilcove, "Of Owls."

8. *Ibid.,* p. 78.

9. G. Tyler Miller, Jr., *Living in the Environment* (Belmont, Calif.: Wadsworth, 1990).

10. *CRS,* "Spotted Owls."

11. That habitat includes "specific areas outside the geographical area occupied by the species,...on which are found...features essential to the conservation of the species, [and] areas outside the geographical area" at the time of listing, later deemed by the Secretary of the Interior "as essential to the conservation of the species." *(ibid.)*

12. Catherine Caulfield, "The Ancient Forest," *The New Yorker* (14 May 1990): p. 46.

13. Sallie Tisdale, "Annals of Place: In the Northwest," *The New Yorker* (26 August 1991): p. 54.

14. Hugh Wilkerson and John van der Zee, *Life in the Peace Zone: An American Company Town* (New York: Macmillan, 1971).

15. Milton Friedman, "The Social Responsibility of Business Is to Increase Its Profit," *The New York Times* magazine, 1970.

16. Wilkerson and van der Zee, "Life in the Peace Zone," pp. 112–113.

17. In the third quarter of 1984, for instance, PL reported that its net earnings rose 50 percent over the previous year ($11,337,000 or 47 cents per share, compared to $7,547,000 or 31 cents per share for the third quarter of the previous year). See Pacific Lumber Company's annual reports, 1981 through 1984.

18. *Ibid.,* p. 45.

19. *Ibid.,* p. 49.

20. *Ibid.,* p. 83.

21. *Ibid.,* p. 106.

22. Gisela Botte and Dan Cray, "Is Your Pension Safe?" *TIME* (3 June 1991): p. 43.

23. *Ibid.;* see also James Castro et al., "A Sizzler Finally Fizzles: In America's Largest Life Insurance Company Collapse, California Officials Seize Control of Shaky Giant Executive Life," *TIME* (22 April 1991). "Nightline" (ABC-TV) presented a program on June 18, 1991, about the dire straits of workers who have lost their pensions in the collapse of insurance companies in general, with special attention to Pacific Lumber. The program featured interviews with aging, bewildered, and frightened retired workers who were demonstrating in the streets and demanding the return of their pension funds.

24. This is because the assets are spent down so quickly. For another account of how Hurwitz's financial dealings and shareholders work in the market, see William Barrett, "Aluminum Cow," *Forbes* (6 January 1992), which details Hurwitz's dealings with Kaiser Aluminum.

25. John Boland, editorial in *The Wall Street Journal* (10 February 1988).

26. Tom Morgenthau et al., "A Lighter Shade of Green," *Newsweek* (12 April 1993): pp. 24–25.

27. Jack Shepard, *The Forest Killers* (New York: Weybright and Tally, 1975): p. 33.

28. Tyler Miller, *Living in the Environment,* seventh edition (Belmont, Calif.: Wadsworth, 1992): p. 275.

29. *Ibid.,* pp. 18 & 19.

30. *Ibid.,* p. 31.

31. Caulfield, "The Ancient Forest," p. 60.

32. *The New York Times* (3 November 1991): p. E.1.

33. "News of the Week in Review," *The New York Times* (3 November 1991): p. 3.

34. *Sierra,* January–February 1992; *The New York Times,* 16 September 1991; *Greenpeace,* January–March 1991.

35. James Farrell, *National Wildlife,* vol. 29, no. 1 (December 1990): p. 28.

36. U.S. Fish and Wildlife Service, Department of the Interior, Washington, D.C., "Economic Analysis of Designation of Critical Habitat for the Northern Spotted Owl" (August 1991).

37. Caulfield, "The Ancient Forest," p. 67.

38. Keith Schneider, "Western Exposure: Clinton the Conservationist Thinks Twice," *The New York Times,* Week in Review (4 April 1993): section 4, pp. 1 & 3.

39. Tom Morgenthau et al., pp. 24–25.

40. Charles McCoy, "Cut Down: Even a Logger Praised as Sensitive to Ecology Faces Bitter Opposition," *The Wall Street Journal* (1 April 1993): pp. A1 & A16.

41. Gregg Easterbrook, "Beyond Owls versus Loggers," insert in *Newsweek* article (12 April 1993): p. 25.

42. Charles McCoy and Rose Gutfeld, "Timber Summit to Attract 30,000 Peacemakers in War Between Loggers and Environmentalists," *The Wall Street Journal* (31 March 1993): p. A16.

43. Easterbrook, "Beyond Owls."

Suggestions for Further Reading

Caulfield, Catherine. "The Ancient Forest." *The New Yorker* (14 May 1990).
Shepard, Jack. *The Forest Killers.* New York: Weybright and Tally, 1975.
Tisdale, Sallie. "Annals of Place: In the Northwest." *The New Yorker* (26 August 1991).
Wilcove, David S. "Of Owls and Ancient Forests." *Ancient Forests of the Pacific Northwest.* Washington, D.C.: Island Press, 1990.

APPENDIX AND APOLOGY:
AN ALPHABET SOUP FOR OUR TIME

We try to avoid the technical jargon of government regulation—the esoteric debate that turns on the uncountable agencies and mystifying fragmentary legislation of federal and state governments. This mass of information, because it dominates the corridors of the U.S. Congress and governs the bureaucrats who actually make the day-to-day decisions, is occasionally crucial, though, to an understanding of the real and major issues in contemporary affairs and the environment in particular. Following is a master list of *only* the most common of the agencies and laws that govern the fate of the Northwest Coast redwoods.

Selected Agencies Affecting Old-Growth Forests and the Spotted Owl

U.S. Fish and Wildlife Service (FWS)—an agency of the U.S. Department of the Interior. This agency administers the Endangered Species Act and the Migratory Bird Treaty Act; all other federal agencies must clear any action related to an endangered species with the FWS.

U.S. Forest Service—an agency of the U.S. Department of Agriculture. This agency manages national forests and has a mandate, under the National Forest Management Act, to ensure viable populations of wildlife in the forests it controls.

U.S. Bureau of Land Management (BLM)—an agency of the U.S. Department of the Interior. This agency manages timberlands, mostly in Oregon, under the Oregon and California Act and the Federal Land Policy and Management Act (see next section).

U.S. National Park Service (NPS)—an agency of the U.S. Department of the Interior that manages national parks.

Interagency Scientific Committee (ISC)—a committee formed in 1988 by all of the above-mentioned agencies, specifically to find ways to save the northern spotted owl.

Selected Legislation Affecting Old-Growth Forests and the Spotted Owl

Migratory Bird Treaty Act (MBTA: 1936)—This treaty protects the spotted owl and other birds. This legislation was passed as a result of the 1936 Convention for the Protection of Migratory Birds and Game Mammals.

Oregon and California Act of 1937 (O&CA: 1937)—This act covers federal land management, mostly in Oregon, and directs the BLM to manage those lands.

Multiple Use Sustained Yield Act (MUSYA: 1960)—This act urges the Forest Service to encourage activities other than lumbering (for example, tourism and camping) on federal lands.

National Environmental Policy Act (NEPA: 1970)—Significantly, this act requires that all federal agencies include in any legislative recommendation or report, or any other federal action, an *Environmental Impact Statement* (EIS), whenever any aspect of the contemplated action might affect the environment.

Endangered Species Act (ESA: 1973)—This requires the FWS to determine which species are threatened or endangered and to guarantee protection for these species and for their habitats.

Federal Land Policy and Management Act (FLPMA: 1976)—This act extends the mandate of the O&CA.

National Forest Management Act (NFMA: 1976)—This act requires the Forest Service to protect indicator species (and, indeed, all vertebrate species) on federal lands that agency manages.

The Evolution of a Conflict: A Chronology (updated 1/12/92)

1905—The U.S. Forest Service is formed.

1936—The Forest Service is authorized to purchase 863,000 acres of timberland in northern California (during the Great Depression when land was inexpensive).

1936—The Convention for the Protection of Migratory Birds and Game Mammals results in the MBTA.

1937—The Oregon and California Act is passed.

1939—The first purchase of lands by the Forest Service. (Buying activity stopped by World War II.)

1945—The last purchase of lands by the Forest Service is 59 acres. (During the postwar period, lumber prices were on the rise.)

Redwood cutting begins on both public and private lands.

1952—Clear-cutting begins near Humboldt State Redwood Park, California.

1955—Flash floods cause the destruction of 300 redwoods and 50 acres of soil in Humboldt State Park (presumably because of clear-cutting).

1960—MUSYA is passed in reaction to the apparent damage to national and state forests; the Forest Service is hereby instructed to consider activities other than lumbering on U.S. land.

1966—The drive for formation of a 90,000-acre Redwood National Park began. (In connection with this campaign, Ronald Reagan, then a candidate for governor of California, opined that "You've seen one redwood, you've seen them all.")

Controversy erupts as the Forest Service supervises the cutting of 17.6 million board feet of lumber in areas that agency conservationists were urging the government to set aside as a park.

1968—The Redwood National Park is formed, containing 58,000 acres; 27,000 acres were former state parks. Of the area that was privately owned, 40 percent had been clear-cut.

1973—The Endangered Species Act is passed (and amended in 1982, 1985, and 1988). This act directed government agencies, for the first time, to pay attention to and protect animals and plants with no economic value.

1976—NFMA is passed, carrying on the initiative to save endangered species by requiring the Forest Service to maintain viable populations of game animals and also all vertebrate species.

1984—The Forest Service institutes a plan to preserve the northern spotted owl, requiring that 1,000 acres of old-growth forest be preserved for each 263 pairs of owls. (This plan was successfully appealed as ineffective by environmentalists; the Forest Service was then required to prepare a supplemental Environmental Impact Statement.)

1986—The controversy intensifies as the Forest Service's draft EIS is challenged by spokesmen for the timber interests.

1987—The BLM announces that it will set aside only 300 acres for the owls and will not reconsider until 1990.

A lawsuit *(Portland Audubon v. Hodel)* is brought by the Audubon Society of Portland, Oregon, against the BLM, to prevent the sale of trees more than 200 years old near the 289 identified owl habitats. An injunction was granted until the BLM could prepare an EIS and comply with FLPMA, O&CA, and MBTA. On appeal, the 9th Circuit Court lifted the injunction and the Supreme Court upheld the Circuit Court's decision.

1988—The FWS rejects a petition to list the spotted owl as threatened under the ESA. The General Accounting Office found that FWS (1) did not allow time for complete analysis, (2) changed the substance of some scientific analysis, and (3) considered factors other than the owl's survival, contrary to the ESA.

August, 1988—The ISC is formed by the Forest Service, FWS, BLM, and NPS to design a plan to save the owl.

1989–1990—Congress, with appropriations acts, calls for limiting the sales of old-growth timber, enlarging the owl's habitat, restricting the export of timber, and assisting logging communities. (Some aspects of this legislation were rescinded by the courts and the rest expired; nothing substantive resulted from these efforts.)

April 2, 1990—Controversy is engendered by an ISC report calling for saving 50 percent of the federal lands outside the owl's range with trees having a diameter of less than 11 inches and a 40-percent canopy.

June, 1990—The Forest Service and BLM respond to the ISC report in a study that warns of the loss of 19,000 jobs in three states by the year 2000, in addition to the 9,000 jobs already lost because of other regulations—for example, NFMA. (A second report, not issued but leaked to the press, said that 6,100 jobs would be created.)

June 22, 1990—The FWS lists the northern spotted owl as threatened throughout its range.

February 26, 1991—In a lawsuit brought by conservationists, *Northern Spotted Owl v. Lujan* (C88-5732 W.D. Wash 1991), the FWS is accused of having "failed to discharge its obligations" under the ESA. The judge orders the FWS to publish the owl's critical habitat by April 29, 1991.

May 6, 1991—The FWS publishes a critical habitat proposal for the owl that sets aside 11.6 million acres of old-growth forest. (This proposal was approved by environmentalists but not by timber interests.)

August 5, 1991—The FWS reduces the acreage of critical habitat to 8.2 million acres. Industry opposition continues; the FWS ruling is challenged (August 31, 1991).

Congressional activity to protect old-growth redwood forest, owls, and timber-related jobs continues through the summer.

September 11, 1991—The "God Squad" is formed: This was a committee convened by Interior Secretary Lujan at the request of the BLM; it was called the "God Squad" because it could reverse a decision to protect a species if it determined that the pressure on the economy was unacceptable.

January 8, 1992—"God Squad" hearings are held to determine whether the BLM will be allowed to go ahead with logging on 4,500 acres of federal land in Oregon that serves as habitat for 50 owls.

May, 1992—The "God Squad" grants exemption from the ESA to the BLM for Oregon timber sales. (This was the first such exemption in the history of the ESA.)

February, 1993—A federal Appeals Court orders an inquiry into the claim made by environmental groups that the Bush administration illegally pressured some of the squad members to vote for the exemption.

April 2, 1993—President Clinton calls a "Timber Summit" in Portland, Oregon, to air the issues surrounding the Northwest Forest. No conclusion is reached, but Clinton assigns his cabinet the task of devising a framework for a solution over the next two months.

CHAPTER 6

The Diversity of Life

Chico Mendes and the Amazonian Rainforest

PREFACE: QUESTIONS TO KEEP IN MIND

What, in general, do we mean by *life?* How do we define *diversity* so that diversity of life is desirable? By *life* we must mean at least biological life or lives, the community of all living things. The drive to preserve biodiversity—the diversity of life among the myriad species of the world—eventually entails an imperative to preserve species of insects that live on only one tree in the Amazonian Rainforest. Why do we want to save the lives of distant insects? What is the role of biodiversity in survival, for humans and other species?

What constitutes *sustainable* use, or sustainable development, of land? We say that ecosystems are being treated *sustainably* when we can continue to do whatever we are doing in that ecosystem indefinitely without hurting or using up the living environment around us. *Sustainability* entails limiting our intrusions into nature to those that the environment can repair in the normal processes of its life. Should we, ideally, be able to live on the land as the hunter-gatherers did before us, so that after hundreds of years of human activity, the nonhuman life would still flourish?

There are isolated and unique tribes of humans living in the rainforests whose existence is threatened as are those of the insects. If their forest is felled, these people will die. Why? What sort of life do they lead that makes them so vulnerable to change?

These tribal groups are not biologically unique (all humans are members of the same species, *Homo sapiens*), but their culture is. What kind of culture do they have that we should value it? Is cultural diversity desirable in itself?

Sometimes, when we use the word *life,* we simply mean lifestyle, occupation, our way of getting on in the world. Are rubber tappers worth preserving, simply as an occupational subset not known elsewhere in the world? We do not protect steelworkers in their lifestyle, but we do protect family farms. What relation do the rubber tappers have with the forest that makes it possible for them to live compatibly with it?

Still, we consider individual human life to be of infinite value. We will start our story with one such human life.

CHICO MENDES: THE MAN AND HIS HERITAGE

Francisco Alves Mendes Filho (Chico Mendes), the president of the Xapuri Rural Workers Union, was murdered on December 22, 1988, as he walked out the back door of his house toward the outbuilding that contained his only source of fresh water.[1] The suspected murderers are the agents of a local cattle rancher who despised the rural rubber tappers, their union, and its president.

Chico Mendes "was to the ranchers of the Amazon what Cesar Chavez was to the citrus kings of California, what Lech Walesa was to the shipyard managers of Gdansk."[2] His funeral was held on Christmas Day and attended by thousands from around the world: labor leaders, academics, celebrities, reporters, environmentalists, and politicians.

The year 1988 had been the hottest year on record; it had seen massive (deliberate) burning in the Amazonian Rainforest and massive (natural) burning in Yellowstone Park in the U.S. Also in 1988, Jim Hansen (see the chapter on global warming) had warned of global warming known to be associated with deforestation. In that year, too, this simple worker, Chico Mendes, had attained world recognition for singlehandedly confronting the powerful cattle barons who were slashing and burning the forests of the Amazon.

In 1925, Chico Mendes' grandfather had moved from the coast of Brazil to Acre in the Amazonian interior, near the borders with Peru and Bolivia. He had moved to escape a lethal drought and to pursue his trade tapping the rubber trees. Mendes' father, Francisco, was 12 years old when his father moved to Acre and he grew up in the rubber-tapping community, enduring its cycles of booms and busts, cycles controlled by the global supply of cheaper Asian rubber. The employment situation was terribly exploitive, one of classic servitude; the tappers were almost always in debt to the bosses who had virtually complete control over their lives. World War II brought a boom to the region; rubber was desperately needed by the Allies but was no longer available from Singapore. The boom, however, did not mean prosperity for the imported and local labor, including Chico's father, whose rewards for their patriotic efforts were malaria and more exploitation.

Mendes was born in 1944 as a child of the Amazon. He developed an intimate knowledge of the forest, helped with the rubber work by the age of nine, and became a full-time tapper by eleven. Shortly thereafter, he met Euclides Fernandez Tavora, a communist-trained tapper who introduced him to the radio, taught him to read and write, and incidentally instilled him with Marxist ideology by regaling him with tales of coups, dictators, class struggles, Brazilian history, and the enormous gap between Brazil's rich and its poor. By 1966, at age 22, Mendes was agitating for better conditions for the tappers, for schools for their children, and for the right to sell the fruits of their labors.

SOME BACKGROUND ON BRAZIL

During the 1960s, Brazil was saddled with a terrible burden of foreign debt and a population of 70 million. Only 3.5 percent of the population lived on 50 percent of the land, the Amazon basin; the rest of the population, mostly landless, crowded the coastal cities. The settlement of the Amazon seemed a logical solution to the debt and urban poverty, following the precedent set by Indonesia's "Transmigration," which called for the relocation of 140 million people from densely populated islands to less-populated ones, from 1950 to 1985.[3] Also, to reduce the debt, Brazil could log the rainforest and sell the logs to Japan, always a ready market for raw wood. So the government developed an elaborate plan to build roads into the Amazon for some 30 million people to travel to the interior and lay claim to practically free land. The authors of the plan expected the land to be not only a source of lumber for foreign exchange but also a useful social safety valve: land reform that would cause no distress whatsoever to the very small number of very wealthy and powerful owners of most of Brazil's arable land.

By 1970, the Trans-Amazon Highway was under way, aiming out into the sparsely populated areas such as Rondonia in the northeast, built by malaria-ridden work crews who were as exploited as the rubber tappers, directed by the usual bosses and middlemen. The death toll during this construction is unknown; there were no roadside graves.[4] By 1972, a 1,200-kilometer section of road was open, and about 70,000 families were on their way from cities and rural areas. One million kilometers were open by 1980 and, eventually, some 100,000 families took advantage of the government's offer of 250-acre wooded lots, free to those who would claim and clear them.

Besides the free land, the people had been lured by promises of schools, churches, and other amenities that never materialized. Most of these would-be homesteaders shortly abandoned their claims, defeated by malaria, the poor soil of the area, and the decrease in the price of coffee, but the government's terms, which included tax breaks and subsidized loans and credits, encouraged wealthier ranchers, who could clear the land, surely and efficiently, to invest in a no-risk situation: The government paid their expenses and they were allowed to keep any profits. The agents of these ranchers followed the hopeful settlers down the highway with every intention of displacing them, along with any Indians or (incidentally) rubber tappers who might be in their way.

The settlers or the cattlemen's crews cut the forest, burned it during the dry season, and used the ash to fertilize any crops or fodder they grew. Here, the limitations of rainforest soil became crucial: The clearing, burning, and planting could provide useful grazing or crops for a few years (estimates range from 2–3 years to 10–12 years, depending on the estimator and the area in question), but then the settlers would be forced to move on to do more slashing and burning elsewhere, for there is no topsoil in the rainforests, so agricultural use is nonsustainable.

One outstanding characteristic of the soil is its nutrient paucity. The rainforests are like "wet deserts," to use Edward Wilson's term, considered to be as fragile as any biome on the planet. The soil is naturally nutrient-poor, partially because of runoff from the drenching rains of the tropics; any topsoil or organic materials added to the soil would not stay and decay but wash away. Additionally, what nutrients are available are locked in the immense biomass of the trees. So when the trees are cut and carted away, the nutrients go with them; when the trees are cut down and burned, the remaining ashes serve as a one-shot-only fertilization. Even when the land is selectively cleared and fertilized by decaying litter, it quickly becomes almost sterile. The problem is that the decay rate is so fast in the hot, humid conditions of the tropics; decaying soil quickly reverts to laterite, a hardpan of inorganic minerals with no supporting organic humus. Consider this: In temperate latitudes, a leaf takes about a year to decompose, and the combination of the decomposing organisms, the products of their metabolism, the partially decomposed organic material, and the soil minerals, all form the humus that builds up topsoil. None of this happens in the tropics; after a few years of farming, the soil is lost forever.

Knowing this then, why do the ranchers slash and burn the rainforests? One or two experiences of watching their ranches turn to desert should teach them the futility of ranching on the rainforests. The answer seems to be that they do not care if the land is wrecked as long as they own the wreckage. All the ranchers want is more land, free of complications such as the rights of native Indians and rubber tappers. As Shoumatoff states in *The World Is Burning,* "The cattle are a smokescreen for land speculation. The forest is not even being converted to hamburgers. Most of it is going up in smoke to augment the holdings of the 1 percent of Brazilians who own most of the country's arable land, the majority of which is not in use."

So the ranchers are engaged, indirectly, in a form of "ecotage," sabotaging the environment for some unrelated purpose. All attempts to convert this magnificent ecosystem to other agricultural uses besides forest are doomed to failure because of the lack of topsoil. Allowing land to be ruined, so that no one else can use it so that you can then buy it inexpensively and hold on to it is perfectly legal in most places in the world—but is it right? If not, why not? Who is being hurt by these practices?

Most of us are being hurt, as it happens. A tropical rainforest is good for only what it is: a genetic gold mine; a biological wonder of the world; a source of fruit, nuts, rubber, and sometimes rare woods; a carbon storehouse; a defense against global warming; a climate maker; and an artist's delight—a farm or ranch it will never be. Chico Mendes died attempting to stop an activity that had no purpose beyond turning forest into desert; like the ranchers, he knew ranches would not work in the rainforest but, unlike them, he knew the value of the forest.

TROPICAL RAINFORESTS

The Amazon system encompasses about 2.7 million square miles—approximately 90 percent of the area of the contiguous United States—and touches areas of eight South American countries besides Brazil. This system is a 2,000-mile-long, continuous, 200-foot-high canopy of growth that has been called a "green cathedral."[5] The Amazon River is 4,000 miles long and dumps 170 billion gallons of water every hour into the Atlantic Ocean. The forest stores seven billion tons of carbon in its biomass; in an area of four square meters (about six square feet) have been found 750 species of trees, 125 species of mammals, 400 species of birds, 100 species of reptiles, and 60 species of amphibians—and, in one tree alone, 400 species of insects. According to Thomas Lovejoy of the Smithsonian Institute, "the Amazon is a library for life sciences, the world's greatest pharmaceutical library and a flywheel of climate. It's a matter of global destiny."[6] The world is at stake here; the wealth of the world is tied up in that enormous mass of life.

The world's tropical rainforests have been evolving for the last 350 million years, and natural selection has been acting on the species within them for 150 million years. Flowering plants began to dominate the land some 100 million years ago, taking over from the conifers, ferns, mosses, and other more primitive plants. Around the time the dinosaurs departed, 60 million years ago, began the immense increase in the biodiversity of the tropical forest. Although only about 1.5 million species have been identified and catalogued worldwide, it is generally agreed that somewhere between 10 and 100 million different species exist on this planet, *half* of them in tropical rainforests: 30 percent of all the world's birds are in the Amazon; another 16 percent in Indonesia. One entomologist saw 429 butterfly species in 12 hours in Brazil; there are 440 butterfly species in the entire eastern United States. In Peru, one hectare (2.5 acres) of land supports 300 species of trees, whereas all of Canada and the United States support 700 tree species.

In a landmark experiment, Terry Erwin of the National Museum of Natural History counted the species of insects in one small section of the rainforest canopy. An estimated two-thirds of all the forest's species live *in* the canopy, where there is abundant sunlight and (thus) photosynthesis, as opposed to the lower levels where less light is available—but reaching the canopy is a problem in logistics, for obvious reasons. So, Erwin devised a bug bomb that reached the treetops, set the bomb off, and then methodically collected and analyzed the thousands of insects that fell out of the canopy. Extrapolating from his data, Erwin estimated that there were 8,150,000 species of beetles living in the tropical canopy and a total of 30 million species of tropical arthropods.[7]

What makes this forest (a mere 6 percent of the world's landmass) the richest ecosystem on the Earth? Some factors that clearly contribute to this biodiversity are the heat of the tropical sun, the large contiguous area of living trees, the stability of the climate, and (of course) the humidity. (Interestingly, the greatest marine biodiversity is found in the same latitude, occupying the coral reefs.) Some marshes might be even more productive than the rainforests in terms of total mass of life, but certainly not in terms of the number of species, presumably because of the impact of seasonal changes. Within the stability of the tropical rainforests, one small piece of the system can provide a large habitat; for instance, the pools of water found in epiphytes ("air plants," plants that anchor on trees but get all their nutrients and water from the air) are the habitat for the damselfly nymphs that would be found in ponds in more temperate latitudes.[8]

THE THREAT TO THE FOREST

Those species are severely threatened, because the rainforests are threatened, which is the very problem that brought these Brazilian provinces to our attention. Extinction is now proceeding at an increasingly rapid rate:

"A fifth or more of the species of plants and animals could vanish or be doomed to early extinction by the year 2020 unless better efforts are made to save them."[9] As Wilson points out, we cannot afford to lose these plants and animals:

> Why should we care? What difference does it make if some species are extinguished, if even half of all the species on earth disappear? Let me count the ways. New sources of scientific information will be lost. Vast potential biological wealth will be destroyed. Still undeveloped medicines, crops, pharmaceuticals, timber, fibers, pulp, soil-restoring vegetation, petroleum substitutes, and other products and amenities will never come to light. It is fashionable in some quarters to wave aside the small and obscure, the bugs and weeds, forgetting that an obscure moth from Latin America saved Australia's pastureland from overgrowth by cactus, that the rosy periwinkle provided the cure for Hodgkin's disease and childhood lymphocytic leukemia, that the bark of the Pacific yew offers hope for victims of ovarian and breast cancer, that a chemical from the saliva of leeches dissolves blood clots during surgery, and so on down a roster already grown long and illustrious despite the limited research addressed to it.[10]

The very specialized evolution of the tropical rainforest, the product of millions of years of climactic stability and ecological integrity, adds to the problem of regeneration after human assault. After the assault, not only is the topsoil gone, but the seeds of the forest's plants have trouble germinating in the new conditions. These tropical species evolved in a very stable environment, so they tend to be less adaptable to changing conditions. The seeds have a short germination time that precludes their being spread by wind or animal to a more suitable location or remaining dormant until favorable conditions return. All this bodes very ill for the recovery or regeneration of the rainforest, once we have cut it down.

Without exception, every scheme to develop tropical rainforests has been a disaster—if not an immediate disaster, certainly a disaster for the well-being of the forests and all species, including our own, that are dependent upon them. When farming and ranching fail (as discussed before), the ranchers simply add the resulting desert to their landholdings. When the settlers left Rondonia, the miners also moved in, seeking iron, tin, and gold; slashing and burning as they went; destroying one-fourth of the trees in the state of Rondonia and causing intolerable water pollution. One immediate result of this assault on the environment was the decline in the area's Indian population from 35,000 in 1965 to 6,000 in 1985, due to disease and the stress of resettlement. These indigenous tribes, like the plants, evolved in conditions of stability unthinkable further north and are just as specialized as the damselflies. As Linden pointed out,

"Move a hunter-gatherer tribe 50 miles and they'll starve to death."[11] The dislocations caused by the miners' assaults were beyond endurance and impossible to hide; finally, in an atmosphere of anarchy, the government closed the area to mining.[12]

THE ROLE OF INTERNATIONAL AGENCIES

The World Bank must take some of the responsibility for this series of debacles. The Grand Carajas Mining Project had been supported by a $3.5 million loan from the World Bank, as an alternative to cutting down the forests, and the project backfired: The miners required loggers to produce the wood from which to produce the charcoal necessary for the iron smelters; the result was extensive deforestation, and serious pollution of air and water. Yet the mining continues, yielding 30 million tons of iron per year and aiming for 50. The Polonoroeste resettlement project, also backed by the World Bank, was equally disastrous; the settlers who survived the malaria epidemic left the unproductive land for the ranchers to exploit, as we have described above.[13]

The debate over deforestation of the Amazon region soon became global. Environmentalists started to take on the multilateral development banks, in response to loans that they had apparently made without any environmental or human considerations whatsoever. Even the dams these banks supported resulted in little power but lots of breeding areas for malaria-carrying mosquitos. Brazilians, stung by international criticism of Amazonian destruction through road-building, became defensive and chauvinistic, pointing out that Americans would certainly not have appreciated outside objections to a road being built from New York to San Francisco.

It is sadly ironic that, as Edward Wilson points out, the poorest countries of the world have the responsibility of caring for its richest resources.[14] Yet one Brazilian environmentalist, Jose Lutzenberger, commented that, "This talk of 'we can do with our land what we want' is not true. If you set your house on fire it will threaten the homes of your neighbors."[15]

World pressure on Brazilian President Collar (exacerbated by pressure from U.S. environmentalists during his visit to the United States) contributed to the eventual creation of a 36,000-square-mile reserve for the Yanomani indians, who had suffered a 15-percent population decline, primarily because of epidemics introduced by the settlers and ranchers.[16]

Other Amazonian tribes also suffered equally: The Yuqui indians of the Bolivian Amazon were resettled to a missionary outpost as a means of resolving the battles between them and the loggers and settlers that had been attracted by land grants. These indians, totally uninitiated in modern ways, were suddenly forced to cope with a ten-thousand-year culture shock. The missionaries, dedicated to the material and spiritual welfare of the indians they served, were prepared to offer food, shelter, medical care, and education in Western ways to the disoriented Yuqui but tended to be insensitive to efforts to preserve their culture. Meanwhile, another road-building project was funded by the Inter-American Development Bank to train the Yuqui tribesmen to farm, but the project's road builders were in conflict with the missionaries over the treatment of the tribe. Finally, the government intervened (by now, there are *three* groups of outsiders telling the indians how to live); this discouraged the missionaries' evangelical approach but allowed them to provide education and medical care to the tribe. The indians were torn from their land, normal occupations, traditional learning, rituals, and recreations and lost virtually all contact with their past.[17]

This loss of Amazonian indian culture, as a result of development, is a major concern for anthropology, beyond the human concern for the suffering of the individual uprooted tribespeople. Since 1900, 90 of Brazil's 270 indian tribes have disappeared. In cultural extinction, the Yuquis will join a growing roster of human groups who maintained an independent and unique culture time out of mind but have now succumbed to the restless forces of modernization. Of the world's approximately 6,000 languages, for instance, it is estimated that 3,000 are "doomed."[18]

A GLOBAL RECAPITULATION

Stepping back from the Amazon for a moment, we note that the problem of tropical deforestation is terribly serious worldwide. Not all of it is happening in Brazil, and not all of it is the result of human inequality, national and individual poverty, or simple shortsightedness. The Sarawak Forest in Borneo, Malaysia, the oldest rainforest on earth, is being depleted solely for profit; it houses the last remaining stands of Philippine mahogany, highly valued by the Japanese, who are involved not only in purchasing the lumber but in the actual logging operation.

The Japanese and the local politicians and lumber merchants are becoming millionaires at the expense of a forest the size of New York state that houses 20,000 plant species, thousands of tree species, and hundreds of species of butterflies. Once again, the indians (in this case, the Penang, comprising half the local population) are the big losers. One tribe of hunter-gatherers, isolated from and ignorant of any other cultures, were driven from their home and habitat by government officials who tagged them as communists. It is estimated that Malaysia, now responsible for two-thirds of the world's export of raw logs, will become a net importer in ten years even though two-thirds of its remaining forest is licensed for logging.[19]

Tropical rainforests once covered 14 percent of the planet's landmass. Less than half remain, and most of the loss has occurred since World War II; an area about the size of Germany is lost every year. The Indian teak forests have become deserts; the Philippines have lost 90 percent of their forests over the last 50 years; and Thailand, which was once 53-percent forested, now has only 14 percent of its land as forest.[20] Rainforests are disappearing at a rate of 2 percent per year, or one football field per second. If we remember that the world's tropical rainforests are roughly equal in area to the lower 48 United States, the annual loss is about equal to the size of Florida.[21]

ALTERNATIVES

It doesn't have to be like this. Alternative development strategies are working in Costa Rica, which has become the paradigm country for the tropical rainforest advocates. Costa Rica is a country with a stable and historically democratic government that has a cultural reverence for its ecological treasures; its three million people have managed to preserve 85 percent of their original rainforests. The movers and shakers in Costa Rica have discovered and tapped the international appeal of conservation and, with the financial help of First-World foundations, have managed to create enough national parks and protected reserves to give guarded assurance to the future of the 5 percent of the world's animal and plant species they house. These reserves also feed the national treasury by attracting crowds of "ecotourists." The nation also has an agreement with the Merck pharmaceutical company to share the profits from any medically useful discoveries that occur within their boundaries.[22]

Similarly, the Ranomafana Forest in Madagascar, which houses some endangered species and others that are unique to the island, has become a national park and has thus been saved from the logging that would have destroyed it by 2025. Once again, enlightened First-World money was involved: In this case, our own U.S. Agency for International Development donated $3.2 million to provide schooling and health care to the peasants affected by the changes and also to train the peasants to become "ecotourist guides."[23]

Other than ecotourism and the gathering and harvesting we have discussed, the highest and best sustainable use of the resources of the rainforest is as a source of medically and industrially useful chemicals, as yet unknown, from its magnificent array of flora and fauna, including all those yet to be identified. Some 80 percent of the world's population uses *traditional* (folk) medicine to tend to their ills. (Given the growth in world population, these must be fairly successful.) Research done in Belize for the New York Botanical Garden and Yale University revealed that the dollars made from medicines gathered on two test plots (0.7 and 0.6 acre) equalled $294 and $1,346, respectively, versus the profit of $137 per acre in Brazilian Amazonian agriculture.[24] The potential profits are thus beyond belief—even setting aside the benefit of acquiring better medicines for the world's health—if we can keep the rainforest alive.

THE PEOPLE AND THE FOREST

Chico Mendes became the symbol of the fight to save the forest, although that had not been his first concern. He was a rubber tapper, and he was fighting for his people and their livelihood. Mendes himself was not comfortable being labeled an environmentalist. At one point when he heard himself so described, he said, "I'm not protecting the forest because I'm worried that in 20 years the world will be affected. I'm worried about it because there are thousands of people living here who depend on the forest—and their lives are in danger every day."[25] The unique feature of this environmental conflict is the unity of interest between the indigenous (aboriginal) hunter-gatherers and those who live off the natural bounty of the forest, such as the rubber tappers. This means that the forests have a real human voice pleading for them, as long as that voice is allowed to live and to be heard.

Chico Mendes' first marriage collapsed for the same reason that his second was being threatened at the time of his death: He was spending most of his time away from home, roaming the forest, and organizing the tappers to fight the incursion of the ranchers. Because Acre was the poorest state in Brazil in 1970, its governor followed the national policy of promoting road-building and ranching, and the battle lines were quickly drawn between the newly arrived ranchers and the tappers who had been there for generations. In 1975, the union of rubber tappers was formed, and Mendes was elected secretary-general. In 1977, Mendes was elected to the local town council. By 1978, there was a statewide association of unions, real political power, and the beginnings of a political strategy, largely due to Mendes' leadership.

The unions' primary tactical weapon was the *empate,* a species of non-violent confrontation developed at the beginning of the battle to save the Amazonian Rainforest. An *empate* is conducted like this: Once the location of future logging was determined, the union leaders would enlist tappers who then marched to the site. There, after a civil conversation with the loggers, which might include an assessment of the loggers' future after the trees were cut, the loggers usually gave up their chain saws peacefully and went home while the tappers destroyed their camp. (The loggers and tappers had a lot in common as victims of bosses.) Each *empate* set back the ranchers' progress and absolutely infuriated them. The rubber tappers actually managed to drive two of Brazil's largest ranchers out of the area.[26]

The Amazon was Brazil's "Wild West," where might (and only might) made right and where there was (in fact if not in theory) no enforceable law or justice. In the late 1970s, there was a slight increase in political freedom and, therefore, more union activity; the rancher-sponsored killings then increased from under 25 deaths per year in the early 1970s to 39 deaths in 1975, 44 in 1976, and 51 in 1977.[27] Since 1980, one thousand people have been killed in arguments over land.[28] In July, 1980, Wilson Pinheiro, the president of the local union, was murdered. The tappers, too incensed to attend to Mendes' pleas for nonviolence, retaliated by killing the rancher (de Oliverea) who was known to have hired the killers. Thus the cycle of increased violence was begun.

In 1981, Mendes replaced Pinheiro as the president of the Xapuri Rural Workers Union; he then organized schools, promoted educational projects, and participated in regional and nationwide rural workers' meetings and demonstrations. In 1984, while 4,000 delegates, including Mendes, attended a national meeting of rural workers, the government was still backing (slash-and-burn) "agrarian reform," and the confrontations between the tappers and ranchers continued. The *empates* continued to be successful and continued to enrage the ranchers. By 1985, Mendes' life was being openly threatened. From January, 1985, to June, 1987, 458 activist rubber tappers (rural workers, priests, union workers, lawyers, and so on) were killed, and 114 of those murders were proven to have been committed by hired killers.[29]

A WORLDWIDE CAUSE

Meanwhile, Mendes was discovered and lionized by international academe; ecologists, anthropologists, and the media began to pay attention to him. Brazilian anthropologist Mary Helene Allogretti signed on for the cause in 1976 and remained for the duration. She helped Mendes plan a national meeting of rubber tappers in 1985. At the meeting, Allogretti, Steve Schwartzman (former free-lance anthropologist and currently with the Environmental Defense Fund), and English photographer Adrian Crowell promoted Mendes as a spokesperson for the Amazon and backed his idea of creating extractive reserves—areas to be protected from chain saws and to be used only sustainably. The group was joined by Bruce Rich, an attorney with the Natural Resources Defense Council (and later with the Environmental Defense Fund), and an expert on the workings of the multilateral development banks (such as the World Bank and the Inter-American Development Bank) that were funding various of destructive projects in the Amazon. This team believed that the outside world would never rally around such a narrow issue as freedom for rubber tappers in Brazil, and so they set out to convince Mendes that the only way he could gain international support was to be seen as a savior of the Amazon.

Meanwhile, they rallied support from other constituencies, especially by demonstrating the value of the intact rainforest. Schwartzman published articles appealing for the protection of the Amazon as no mere "elitist environmentalist" idea but as a means of saving a way of life and a threatened economy. Studies of forest and agricultural output showed that an acre in the jungle, used to raise cattle, would earn $15.05 per year over a 20-year-period; whereas the same land, used to extract rubber, nuts, and other products, would earn $72.79 in the same time period. Another study showed that tappers, when freed from the rule of the bosses, earned twice as much as those living in Brazil's slums, while enjoying a much better standard of living.[30]

In 1987, this group arranged for Mendes to visit the United States and attend a meeting of the Inter-American Development Bank. (Mendes procured the first suit he had ever worn through a friendly nun whose order had received a charitable shipment of clothes from Italy.) The group arranged visits with members of Congress who influenced the development banks, and they promoted Mendes' nomination for several environmental awards, including the United Nations Environment Program's prestigious Global 500 award, which is one of those he did receive.

So behind the "greening" of Chico Mendes was a conscious strategy by environmentalists to save the world's tropical rainforests. By publicizing Mendes' legitimate status as a folk hero, the group focused attention on the forests and the plight of their indigenous citizens and rallied public support for their cause. At the same time, it became apparent that one of the best ways to stop the ecological and human devastation wrought by poorly conceived development projects was to attack their funding, which meant taking on the international development banks. The route to the banks was via those members of Congress responsible for determining the U.S. contribution to the banks' assets. So it was that the Marxist-educated, rural Brazilian rubber tapper, Chico Mendes, who was fighting cattle ranchers, met with Robert W. Kasten, the conservative Republican Senator from Wisconsin, a state dependent on dairy products. Kasten was impressed by Mendes' recitation of the effects of the loans on the Brazilian environment and the peasants, rural workers, and indians; he threatened to withdraw U.S. funding if the banks involved did not start to factor ecological concerns into their loans.[31]

DEATH SENTENCES

With Mendes' considerable notoriety abroad came, predictably, opposition at home. He was blamed for blocking progress in Brazil and even called a "tool of the CIA."[32] Nevertheless, he continued his true life work, recruiting and organizing tappers. His principal enemy was the Alves da Silva family; the family owned a 10,000-acre ranch that they planned to expand to take advantage of the government's generous conditions. This family had a history of violence and killings; its members were known to have killed anyone who dared to cross them. When their attempts to buy out the tappers failed, the inevitable *empate* occurred and brought tensions to a fever pitch.

By now, the government was more sensitive to the potential violence, so they settled the issue, for a time, by buying the land from the Alves da Silva family—land that the family may very well not have legally owned in the first place—and converting it to an extractive reserve. Although, on the surface, this solution was a compromise, the Alves da Silva family members considered it a defeat; their gunmen now openly roamed the streets of Xapuri, brandishing their weapons. By early 1988, the violence was out of control; one friend of Mendes' was shot in cold blood. Although Mendes was enraged by the harassment of his family and friends and had taken to carrying a gun, he continued to counsel nonviolence. In May of that year, some demonstrators were shot by hired guns and, in June, one of Mendes' fellow councilmen was killed. The death *threats* that Mendes had been receiving, implying a probability of death, were replaced by *pronouncements,* implying certainty.

The incident that most likely led to Mendes' death was the discovery of an old indictment against the Alves da Silva family. Mendes and his supporters pursued the issue to the point that family members were forced into hiding. The most prominent son, Darly, was furious, saying, "Chico won't live out the year. No one has ever bested me. And Chico wants to do that."[33] Mendes' friends and family accepted that his death was inevitable, but a local priest, Otavio Destro, said, "Chico had the wisdom of the Indian and the guile of the Indian so it was difficult for a rancher to catch him in the forest."[34] His murderers did find him at home, however, and killed him.

In December, 1990, Darly Alves da Silva and his son, Darci Alves Pereira, were convicted of the murder and jailed in a "maximum-security" prison that actually had no security—no searchlights, towers, or high walls. On February 15, 1993, the two escaped, to no one's surprise. Mendes' widow said that warnings about the jail's lax security had been ignored, and the acting security secretary admitted that "the only people who don't escape from our jail are those who don't want to."

The senior Alves da Silva's conviction had actually been overturned in March, 1992. Evidently, an impending trial in another Brazilian locale for a 20-year murder charge[35] had prompted the escape: The prison to which he would have been moved was *truly* a maximum-security facility.

Nevertheless, Chico Mendes' legacy lives on. Forest reserves, parks, and streets have been named after him, and his U.S. environmentalist friends continue to exert pressure on the Brazilian government to mete out justice.[36]

PRESERVING BIODIVERSITY

We must start to save the forest by at least attempting to map the biosphere—to find out what species are out there before they disappear forever. We know that, in the tremendous undiscovered chemistry of the tropical rainforests, we will find benefits for our species; we can learn from the plants of the forest. As Diane Ackerman pointed out in her *New Yorker* article on the golden monkeys of the rainforest, those jungle plants are no wimps. The survival mechanisms that have evolved over geologic time include all sorts of strategies to attract the proper pollinating insects and to turn away possible predators. Colors, fragrances, and poisons abound in the rainforest and all of these could contain formulas useful to us. This is the currency of *coevolution,* the development of unique relationships among specific species (for example, plants and pollinators).[37] Wilson has mentioned one example out of thousands, the rosy periwinkle of Madagascar; it has given us two alkaloids that are involved in curing Hodgkin's disease (a once-lethal cancer of the lymph nodes) and acute lymphocytic leukemia, formerly a notorious child killer. From the economic viewpoint, these drugs are estimated to net their manufacturers $188 million per year.[38] As Wilson says, though, "useful products cannot be harvested from an extinct species."

The results of the loss of our tropical rainforests are probably well beyond estimation. In fact, it has to be, because we have only an inkling of what we are losing. Beyond the rainforest's biodiversity, its role as carbon storehouse and thus shield from global warming, and its role as the home of ancient human cultures and as global climate maker, there are other, perhaps more subtle, considerations worth our attention: For instance, the part of the Brazilian Amazon that has suffered the most deforestation lies in western Brazil, away from the coast. We know that the Amazon system produces at least half of its own rain through transpiration and evaporation, but if the forest becomes denuded and is away from coastal humidity, some predict it will start to destroy itself by drying out—another example of positive feedback with very negative results.[39]

There are so many unknowns here. We know that symbiotic relationships exist, for example, between plants and insects, as we have mentioned. What we do *not* know is what happens to a whole food web when an integral part of it, a relationship developed over thousands of years, falls apart. Does the whole web and all the life that depends on it then fall apart as well?

A less esoteric and more topical consideration, perhaps, is one described by Richard Preston in *The New Yorker*: "The emergence of AIDS appears a natural consequence of the ruin of the tropical biosphere." He continues to explain that, because these tropical ecosystems contain the most species, they therefore contain the most viruses, given that each species hosts viruses. As man intrudes, destroys, and stresses these ecosystems, very adaptable viruses that lose indigenous hosts might happily jump to *Homo sapiens*. There is a list of very virulent viruses that have already done this. Perhaps the most frightening pronouncement in Preston's article (which, after all, was written about viruses, not tropical rainforests) is that HIV is considered "an emerger...since its penetration of the human race is incomplete and is still happening explosively with no end in sight."[40]

It stands to reason that this one small area of the planet, which houses half its treasures and dangers, deserves special consideration. We had better pay attention.

QUESTIONS FOR DISCUSSION AND REFLECTION

◆ What sorts of living things are meaningful or significant? How likely is it that a chemical squeezed from an insect's body will somehow, someday, be useful to us? Should we work to preserve that insect—especially when preserving it entails some immediate economic sacrifice? Apart from any utilitarian purpose, is it worth our while to take the preservation of species seriously at all? In the end, are insects—even those unique in the entire history of the world—worth our concern and political effort?

◆ What moral principle underlies our commitment to save endangered species? Is it purely utilitarian—that we might be able to use, for example, an esoteric secretion of an obscure species to solve a medical mystery someday? Is it aesthetic—the variety of life contributes to the beauty and wonder of the world and should be preserved? Is it metaphysical or religious—that each species is a unique creation, placed on Earth not by any labor of ours, and that we are therefore obligated to maintain it in being, to save it from extinction as Noah once did at God's command?

◆ Human lives are certainly significant, but what about human lifestyles? Should the forest be preserved for indigenous peoples, simply because indians (unlike you and me) will die if their forest is felled around them? Why should nonadaptive groups of humans be protected? What value is there in preserving remote and unfamiliar languages, cultures, occupations, and ways of living?

✦ Edward Wilson, a nationally known biologist and champion of biodiversity who has been cited frequently in the foregoing, argues that tremendous economic benefits could be reaped from developing sustainable uses of the rainforest, but he goes on to say that "I do not mean to suggest that every ecosystem now be viewed as a factory of useful products. Wilderness has virtue unto itself and needs no extraneous justification."[41] That "virtue unto itself" is the cutting edge of the inquiry for environmental ethics: How can we capture, in language and theory adequately respectful of human rights, our nagging sensation that the magnificent rainforest deserves our protection just because it is *there* and just for its role in the life of the planet?

✦ How can we save the rainforest and still respect the national sovereignty of tropical nations? Policy problems surface at several levels. Can we, and should we, influence the utilization of Third-World resources? Why not just *buy* all the land we want and hold on to it? Would the land thus be safe from depredation? Would the United States inherit the opprobrium of the colonizing nations, who once held land in foreign countries to serve their own purposes?

✦ Finally, will we fail at compromise? Will we eventually be forced to abandon our attachment to individual rights and national sovereignty and declare the rainforest a global resource, with its protection enforced by the United Nations? Is such a course feasible? Is it desirable?

Notes

1. Unless otherwise noted, all biographical material on Chico Mendes is taken either from Andrew Revkin, *The Burning Season* (Boston: Houghton Mifflin, 1990); or Alex Shoumatoff, *The World Is Burning* (Boston: Little, Brown, 1990).

2. Revkin, *The Burning Season,* p. 8.

3. Shoumatoff, *The World Is Burning,* p. 48.

4. *Ibid.,* p. 51.

5. Edward O. Wilson, *The Diversity of Life* (Cambridge: Harvard University Press, 1992): p. 196.

6. Eugene Linden, "Playing with Fire," *TIME* (18 September 1989).

7. Phylum Arthropoda includes the crustaceans that we are familiar with, such as lobsters and shrimps, millipedes, centipedes, and spiders (arachnids), as well as insects, but insects comprise well over 90 percent of the species within this phylum.

8. Wilson, *The Diversity of Life,* pp. 190–206; and Erik Eckholm, "Secrets of the Rain Forest," *The New York Times* (17 November 1988): p. 20.

9. Wilson, *The Diversity of Life.*

10. *Ibid.*

11. Linden, "Playing with Fire."

12. James Brooke, "Plan to Develop Amazon a Failure," *The New York Times* (12 November 1991).

13. *Ibid.*

14. Wilson, *The Diversity of Life,* pp. 272 ff.

15. Linden, "Playing with Fire," p. 82.

16. *EDF Letter,* "Brazil Creates Rainforest Reserve for Yanomamis," Environmental Defense Fund (April 1992).

17. Sandy Tolan and Nancy Postero, "Accidents of History," *The New York Times* magazine (23 February 1992): p. 38.

18. Eugene Linden, "Lost Tribes, Lost Knowledge," *TIME,* vol. 138, no. 12 (23 September 1991): p. 46.

19. Stan Sesser, "A Reporter at Large: Logging the Rain Forest," *The New Yorker* (27 May 1991): p. 42.

20. *Ibid.*

21. Wilson, *The Diversity of Life.*

22. Shirley Christian, "There's a Bonanza in Nature for Costa Rica, but Its Forests Too Are Besieged," *The New York Times* (29 May 1992): p. A6.

23. Jane Perlez, "Whose Forest Is It, The Peasants' or the Lemurs'?" *The New York Times* (7 September 1991): p. 2.

24. Catherine Dold, "Tropical Forests Found More Valuable for Medicine than Other Uses," *The New York Times* (28 April 1992).

25. Revkin, *The Burning Season,* p. 261.

26. *Ibid.,* p. 8.

27. *Ibid.,* p. 154.

28. *Ibid.,* p. 10.

29. *Ibid.,* p. 224.

30. *Ibid.,* p. 219.

31. The *greening* of these banks has been a very slow process, but that's a topic for another volume.

32. Revkin, *The Burning Season,* p. 227.

33. *Ibid.,* p. 266.

34. *Ibid.,* p. 149.

35. Presumably, this is the murder charge that Mendes had brought to light.

36. James Brooke, "Brazilian Sequel: A Jailbreak, a Bitter Widow," *The New York Times* (17 February 1993).

37. Diane Ackerman, "A Reporter at Large: Golden Monkeys," *The New Yorker* (24 June 1991): p. 36.

38. Wilson, *The Diversity of Life,* p. 285.

39. Linden, "Playing with Fire."

40. Richard Preston, "A Reporter at Large: Crisis in the Hot Zone," *The New Yorker* (26 October 1992): p. 58.

41. Wilson, *The Diversity of Life,* pp. 282 & 303.

Suggestions for Further Reading

Eckholm, Erik. "Secrets of the Rainforest." *The New York Times* magazine (17 November 1988): p. 20.

Myers, Norman. *The Primary Source.* New York: Norton, 1984.

―――. *The Sinking Ark.* Oxford: Pergamon Press, 1979.

Revkin, Andrew. *The Burning Season.* Boston: Houghton Mifflin, 1990.

Ryan, John C. *Life Support: Conserving Biological Diversity.* Worldwatch Paper 108. Washington, D.C.: Worldwatch Institute, 1992.

Sesser, Stan. "A Reporter at Large: Logging the Rain Forest." *The New Yorker* (27 May 1991).

Shoumatoff, Alex. *The World Is Burning.* Boston: Little, Brown, 1990.

Wilson, Edward O. *The Diversity of Life.* Cambridge: Harvard University Press, 1992.

CHAPTER 7

The Hole in the Middle of the Air

The Depletion of the Ozone Layer

PREFACE: QUESTIONS TO KEEP IN MIND

The news that the ozone layer was in danger—threatened by aerosol cans of hair spray and deodorant!—was for many of us the first time that we had heard of such a thing as the ozone layer. Before we worry about protecting it, what *is* the ozone layer? How did it get there and what does it do? Why, in short, should we care about it?

Next, how can chlorofluorocarbons, from spray cans or from elsewhere, damage the ozone layer? What transpires between these chemically inert and useful molecules and that distant layer of air between us and the sun's ultraviolet rays? Above all, are we sure that all this is really happening at the alarming rate claimed by some scientists?

For that matter, how *do* we put together our data about the physical world, especially those parts that are distant, invisible, and mysterious?

Having decided that the loss of the ozone layer is a real and terrible danger, how much are we justified in restraining otherwise beneficial economic activity to protect it? Even if we have the right to decide for ourselves (for the United States) that we must find substitutes for CFCs and must not manufacture or use them anymore, can we make that decision for others? The primary use of CFCs is for refrigeration; there do not seem to be cheap and effective alternatives that are easily available for this purpose. Can we deny this technology to the Third World, which has no hope of entering the global consumer economy without refrigeration?

BACKGROUND

The evolution of the ozone layer in the stratosphere is the most important precondition for the evolution of life-forms from water to land about two billion years ago.[1] This makes that evolutionary event very important to us terrestrial animals; if the ozone layer is now being threatened, it is worth our while to find out why and to consider the relative merits of the options before us.

This is the scenario: The earliest life-forms consisted of heterotrophs, cells able to obtain energy (albeit inefficiently) from nutrients without the presence of oxygen. Evolution eventually brought forth photosynthetic, single-celled, marine bacteria and algae. With photosynthesis came the gradual buildup of oxygen in an atmosphere that had been virtually without it.[2] As the oxygen concentration increased, some of the oxygen molecules (O_2) were broken into two atoms ($2[O]$) by the energy from solar ultraviolet (henceforth called u.v.) radiation. A single oxygen atom will immediately combine with an oxygen *molecule* to form a molecule of ozone (O_3). Because ozone is chemically unstable, the action is reversible. After another billion years or so, a dynamic equilibrium between the two oxygen compounds was reached; the conversion from one to the other being fueled by u.v. radiation. As a result, much of the radiation that had reached the Earth's surface was "used up" in the ozone layer, its energy spent in bringing about the conversions. Before the evolution of the ozone layer, the protection of water had been necessary for living things to survive the radiation; now, life was possible on land. To say it another way: "Without the protective ozone veil, u.v.B [the most dangerous u.v. radiation] would scrub the earth clean of life."[3]

The ozone layer is located in the lower stratosphere about 11 to 20 miles above the Earth. (The troposphere is the lowest part of the atmosphere, where virtually all of the weather happens; the stratosphere, which extends to about 30 miles above the Earth, is comparatively devoid of activity.) The ozone layer is thinning, however, by as much as 50 percent in the Antarctic spring and 8 percent in the northern U.S. winter. With every 1-percent decrease in ozone there is a 2-percent increase in u.v. radiation that can reach the surface of the Earth, accompanied by an increase in the incidence of skin cancer, other human health effects, and numerous ecosystem disruptions.

CHLOROFLUOROCARBONS (CFCs)

The main culprit in the destruction of ozone is a group of man-made chemicals called chlorofluorocarbons (CFCs). There are other ozone-destroying chemicals, but they are relatively insignificant. CFCs were developed in 1928 by a team led by Thomas Midgley for DuPont and/or Frigidaire (then a subsidiary of General Motors).[4] Until then, refrigerators worked by removing heat through vaporization of liquefied gases such as ammonia (which is poisonous), sulfur dioxide (likewise), and methyl chloride (which is toxic). The CFC group consists of chlorine and/or fluorine atoms connected to a carbon atom; these chemicals were given the trade name Freon. Under pressure, at room temperature, they liquefy, and then vaporize instantly upon the release of the pressure, gobbling up heat in the process, thus being an ideal refrigerant. They are nonflammable, nontoxic, efficient, and inexpensive. They are also (and this is the interesting part) extremely stable.

CFCs do not react readily with other chemicals; chemically, they are virtually inert. This made them ideal as a propellant in spray cans for everything from deodorants to insecticides, because they do not react with, or change, the payload; but their stability is the undoing of the atmosphere, for they do not react with the chemicals in the troposphere either. Most chemicals that are released into the air "wash out" in the rich soup of chemical reactions in the atmosphere near the Earth, only reaching the stratosphere in minute amounts; CFCs simply do not wash out. Instead, they slowly (this can take up to a decade) migrate to the nearly barren stratosphere, where they encounter u.v. radiation, a greater energy than heretofore experienced. This energy does cause the chemicals to react, releasing chlorine, which is capable of destroying ozone.

HISTORY AND DISCOVERY OF THE HOLE IN THE OZONE LAYER

The existence of the ozone layer has long been known. Early predictions of ozone concentrations at various altitudes, however, were not borne out by experimental results: The predictions were significantly higher than the observed values. As a result, some scientists speculated that a portion of the ozone that theoretically *should* have been there was being catalytically destroyed by chemicals that were able to reach the stratosphere. (A catalyst is a substance that is involved in, but not changed by, a chemical reaction and is thus able to cause this reaction to repeat over and over at an accelerated rate.) One possibility considered was that the OH⁻ radical (a chemical component of water) might be acting as a catalyst; other theories held that water vapor and/or nitrogen oxides were involved. In fact, the suspicion that the latter two substances would cause ozone depletion is credited as a factor in the defeat of the U.S. Supersonic Transport program, since both substances are emitted into the stratosphere by supersonic planes. (Economic considerations left the Concorde as the sole survivor of that project.)[5]

Meanwhile, Jim Lovelock—a creative British chemist and author of the *Gaia* theory, the theory that the biosphere as a whole is one living organism—reasoned that all the CFCs we were putting into the atmosphere must still be there. When he started looking for them in 1971, he found them. In 1973, chemists Mario J. Molina and F. Sherry Rowland, aware of Lovelock's work, started to investigate the fate of CFCs in the stratosphere. They theorized that u.v. radiation would break a chlorine atom loose from a CFC molecule, that the chlorine would combine with oxygen to form chlorine monoxide, which in turn would catalyze the destruction of ozone. They predicted that each molecule of CFC would be capable of causing the demise of 100,000 molecules of ozone—and they were right.

Molina and Rowland published their calculations in *Nature* in June, 1974, and described them at a meeting of the American Chemical Society in September; during the meeting, Rowland posited that, if CFC production continued at the current rate, there would be a 10-percent increase per year in CFCs that would cause a 5- to 7-percent decrease in ozone by 1995 and a 30- to 50-percent decrease by 2050, and every 5-percent decrease in ozone would cause an increase of 40,000 skin cancers in the United States.[6] The immediate recommendation was to cease all production of CFCs, but CFCs were very profitable and useful, so neither consumers nor manufacturers were willing to have them discontinued. The battle lines were drawn.

Over the next four years, as recounted by David Fisher,[7] the battle raged:

- The news of Molina and Rowland's calculations appeared on the front page of *The New York Times*, and a Harvard research team confirmed their work.

- DuPont, the major CFC manufacturer, countered with a suggestion for a three-year study of the effects of CFCs and, as a first installment of that research, published a study that reported (correctly) that CFCs were benign in the troposphere. (After all, CFCs are dangerous in the stratosphere, precisely *because* they do not react with anything in the troposphere).

- Research showed an ominous 200-percent increase in CFCs in the atmosphere from 1968 to 1975. Even though some CFC production and use was voluntarily halted (in some types of spray cans, for instance), CFC production increased overall.

- Meanwhile, new research challenged the Molina/Rowland estimates as too high (claiming that not as much ozone was being destroyed), and observations were put forth that made CFCs look much less dangerous. For instance, nitrogen oxides were found to react with chlorine, thus theoretically blocking its action on the ozone layer.

- The National Academy of Sciences pronounced that CFCs were indeed deleterious to the ozone layer and then recommended two more years of study.

- The CFC industry claimed that there was not a shred of hard evidence that CFCs caused ozone damage; environmentalists said that using CFCs in spray cans was absolutely unthinkable. They were both right.

✦ The National Research Council finally recommended banning CFCs from spray cans by 1978.

In 1976, the Food and Drug Administration (FDA) came out against CFCs in aerosol cans, and in 1977, the Environmental Protection Agency (EPA), the FDA, and the Consumer Product Safety Commission prohibited nonessential use of CFCs in aerosol cans. This action was particularly notable because it was the first time in the United States that a substance had been banned without having been *proven* harmful. By 1982, 20 other countries had joined the United States in banning CFCs in aerosol cans.[8] In the United States, the issue lost its audience in the early 1980s; the Reagan administration was not enthusiastic about environmental issues (or any issues requiring extension of regulation), and the general public thought that the problem had been solved when CFCs were banned from spray cans. In fact, worldwide CFC production continued apace, at a rate of a 5- to 7-percent increase per year.[9]

THE HOLE IN THE OZONE LAYER

As early as 1956, G. M. B. Dobson of Oxford University reported a temporary drop of ozone over Antarctica; in the 1970s and early 1980s, a British team in Halley Bay, Antarctica, began to notice minor, but consistent, ozone declines during the Antarctic spring. Around the time they were measuring the ozone layer from the ground, the United States was measuring it from a Nimbus satellite with a "Total Ozone Mapping Spectrometer" and "Solar Backscatter Ultra-Violet Measurer" and found no depletion. The British team did not trust their own data because their instruments were outdated, the U.S. results contradicted their findings, and they were unable to explain the temporary, seasonal nature of the ozone loss. In 1982, the team measured a 20-percent depletion, but still hesitated to publish their findings. By October, 1983, they had newer instruments that detected a 30-percent depletion of ozone; this time they announced it.

The news sent U.S. scientists scurrying back to their instruments. To their embarrassment and dismay, they realized that they had programmed their computers to ignore any large deviation from expected results, assuming such deviation would be an error. Thirty-percent depletion was well beyond what they had expected to find, so that measurement was not recorded. (There's a lesson here!) By October, 1985, after a bit of catch-up, it was acknowledged that half of the ozone layer in the stratosphere over Antarctica was gone, and the *ozone hole* was born.[10]

World reaction to this discovery was characterized by confusion and disagreement. Despite the dramatic findings, U.S. and worldwide policy, statements, and actions toward CFC production and use continued to be inconsistent and contradictory. On the one hand, CFC production continued—at a rate of 700,000 tons per year in 1986—just as Australia announced that the incidence of malignant melanomas (deadly skin cancer) had doubled in the last ten years. CFC industry spokespeople claimed that ground-level ozone, produced as a pollutant in many forms of combustion, would migrate to the stratosphere and fill the ozone hole[11] (given the reactivity of ozone, the suggestion has no scientific merit). On the other hand, United Nations officials were planning a 1988 meeting in Montreal to deal with what was clearly seen as the problem.

The "Montreal Protocol" called for a reduction of CFC production by 50 percent by the year 2000; 45 nations agreed to the plan. Shortly thereafter, however, DuPont Chairman Richard Heckart told a delegation of U.S. senators that "at the moment, scientific evidence does not point to the need for dramatic CFC emission reductions,"[12] even as other DuPont spokespeople announced that the company would halt all CFC production by the end of the century.

What motivated DuPont's (second) announcement? This might be of no consequence to the fate of the ozone layer, but the discipline of ethics is deeply concerned with issues of human motivation. While forming an opinion of the ethical aspects of an act, we take into account the motives and character of the agent at least as much as the act's consequences. So it was predictable that the DuPont announcement would bring mixed responses, depending on the observer's beliefs about the company's motives. Some people thought that the company must have developed (and was eager to sell) an appropriate substitute for CFCs; others suspected that the company's lawyers feared being sued by skin cancer victims. DuPont said they were acting purely out of concern for the environment. Mustafa Tolba, director-general of the U.N. Environmental Program, disagreed. He said "it had nothing to do with whether the environment was being damaged or not...it was who was going to get an edge over whom; whether DuPont could come out with an advantage over the European companies or not."[13] The best guess, on the basis of our experience with such incidents, is that DuPont's true motives fall somewhere among all the guesses, since human motives are generally mixed. The ethical questions remain, however: If you are going to do the right thing, do you have *ipso facto* the right to claim you are doing it for the right reasons? If you are trying to persuade someone (such as a large company) to do the right thing, should you cite all the wrong reasons (such as fear of lawsuits) to aid in your persuasion?

Meanwhile, a 1987–88 expedition to Antarctica, led by Dr. Susan Solomon of the United States, produced evidence that resulted in the definitive implication of CFCs in ozone destruction. The smoking gun was the discovery of unusually high concentrations of chlorine monoxide, the predicted ozone destroyer—1 part per billion (ppb)—in conjunction with ozone destruction.[14] This evidence, along with 1987 and 1989 ozone holes of 50 percent or greater, probably contributed to the decision by the European Economic Community (EEC) on March 1, 1989, to eliminate CFCs by the year 2000[15] and the convening of a London meeting in June, 1990. At this time the industrialized nations pledged a total ban on CFC production by the year 2000 and a ban on other ozone-depleting chemicals by 2005; Third-World nations pledged a similar ban by 2010, in conjunction with promised aid from industrialized nations to help pay for putting substitutes in place.[16] At the same time, some individual nations pledged earlier bans and industries voluntarily stopped using CFCs. Given the enduring nature of CFCs, these bans, even carried out to the letter, will not solve the problem of ozone depletion in the short term, but they might stop it from getting worse indefinitely.

THE UNCERTAIN CHEMISTRY OF OZONE DEPLETION

Scientists do not like surprises, and "the Antarctic ozone thing came as a surprise,"[17] indeed. No single event in recent scientific history better illustrates our incomplete knowledge of the workings of nature, in general, and of the atmosphere in particular. Dr. Robert Watson, quoted earlier, continued in his testimony: "Scientific uncertainty scares me more than absolute knowledge."[18] In a similar vein, Michael Oppenheimer, atmospheric physicist, warns that earlier miscalculations about the threat of ozone depletion might be followed by a "repeat performance with global warming."[19]

Even those scientists who had predicted that CFCs would catalytically destroy ozone were surprised by the dramatic decline, only in Antarctica and only in the spring. The answer was found in Polar Stratospheric Clouds (PSCs). The general wisdom among the atmospheric chemists studying the phenomenon, as described earlier, was that chlorine (Cl) would become chlorine monoxide (ClO) and, as such, be capable of catalyzing ozone destruction at a rate of one part chlorine to 100,000 parts ozone—predictions that have held true. The chemists went further, however, and predicted that a large amount of the free chlorine would react with other chemicals also, especially methane (CH_4) and nitrates ($-NO_x$), and become trapped as inactive chlorine nitrate ($ClONO_2$) and hydrochloric acid (HCl), resulting in minimal ozone depletion by ClO.

How then can we explain more than 50-percent depletion in only one season and in one place? Enter PSCs. At very low temperatures, as low as -190° C., found only in the Antarctic winter, nitrogen oxides, sulfur oxides, and water form tiny frozen crystals that accumulate as a cloud. The cloud serves two functions: (1) It inactivates the nitrogen that would otherwise trap chlorine, as we have described, and (2) it provides surfaces for the molecules already in the inactive "chlorine reservoir" to become adsorbed, which promotes their breakdown, thus regenerating the chlorine. This process (which was unforeseen in the Antarctic stratosphere) is known as the "ice-crystal-surface catalysis phenomenon."[20] The return of solar radiation in the spring sets the chlorine free from the cloud (it has already broken away from any nitrates it had been attached to) and able to start the ozone-destroying cycle.[21]

Another condition unique to Antarctica is the *polar vortex,* the tight circulation of air over the South Pole. This vortex isolates that area from the rest of the atmosphere; the ozone-poor air does not diffuse, and the hole gets deeper and deeper. As the spring season progresses, the clouds melt and the nitrogen that was once part of them is set free again to react with chlorine. At the same time, the polar vortex breaks down, the ozone-depleted air mixes with its surroundings, and the hole fills in.

OZONE LOSS SINCE THE FIRST HOLE

The difficulties that ozone-layer research presents to scientists might become clearer if we tracked the findings for the last several years. The amount of ozone present in the stratosphere is usually measured in Dobson units (after G. M. B. Dobson, mentioned earlier). Each unit represents a slice of atmosphere 0.01 millimeter (0.00039 inch) thick. (The measuring of such tiny slices of air is done indirectly, by measuring wavelengths of light that penetrate the atmosphere.) The average ozone levels above Antarctica in 1977 were about 300 Dobson units, with peaks as high as 380 units; earlier, "normal" levels were 500 units.[22]

The October, *1985,* measurements showed that ozone had decreased by about 40 percent to 180 Dobson units since 1977; however, in the spring of *1986,* the decrease was not as great. The hole returned with a vengeance the next spring and measured 125 Dobson units, the lowest yet, in October *1987.*[23] The year *1988* followed the every-other-year pattern, showing less depletion, and in *1989* the October hole was as deep as in *1987.*

The year *1989* produced other surprises, too. Scientists investigating ozone over the Arctic Circle found an ozone decrease of 15 to 17 percent from the norm and a concentration of the troublemaking chlorine monoxide one hundred times greater than that over the United States; U.N. Environmental Protection (UNEP) scientists reported a 3- to 5-percent loss over mid-latitudes in the winter; and scientists from Norway's Institute of Geophysics found a 10-percent decrease of ozone over mid-latitudes in Europe and North America since 1967. Later Arctic explorations, using high-altitude aircraft, found North Pole ozone decreases at 25 percent.[24]

On October 4, 1990, the Antarctic hole broke the record again, weighing in at 123 Dobson units; this surprised most people, because it was an off year. (The two-year cycle is generally credited to air currents affecting the polar vortex.)[25] In *1991*, scientists at the National Aeronautics and Space Agency (NASA) and EPA announced that ozone loss over the United States was proceeding at twice the expected rate, falling 4.5 to 5 percent in the fall, winter, and spring and reaching into southern sections of the country.[26] The year 1991 also brought the lowest loss in Antarctica that had yet been measured, 110 Dobson units,[27] as well as the news that ozone depletion of about 3 percent had been found over the United States in the *summer*.[28]

The ozone slide continues. Reports in 1992 revealed very high concentrations of ozone-destroying chlorine monoxide: 1.5 ppb over the northern U.S., Canada, Europe, Russia, and Asia (in contrast to the Solomon expedition's finding of *1* ppb in 1988 in Antarctica). It was estimated that such a concentration could result in a 1- to 2-percent depletion per day, or a loss of between 20 and 40 percent. Other accounts equate a 1 ppb ClO concentration with the Antarctic hole, and report finding a mid-latitude loss of 8 percent in the winter and 3 percent in the summer.[29]

The hole over the Northern Hemisphere did not appear in spring 1992, although there was some ozone depletion, according to NASA. The unusually warm winter is given credit for the lack of the PSCs that cause the release of chlorine, as described earlier. Then, in December, January, and February of 1992–93, the hole returned: Scientists from the U.N.'s World Meteorological Organization reported a 9–20 percent loss of ozone in Northern Hemisphere latitudes. Concentrations of ozone even lower than the previous year prompted Rumen D. Bojkov of that organization to comment, "To have two years in a row that hit [such] values is clearly extraordinary." Concomitant with lowered ozone measurements were increased levels of chlorine monoxide (ClO), the chemical most destructive to ozone.[30] Measurements for the Northern Hemisphere in spring of 1993 (when solar energy would increase the action of ClO) have not been released at this writing. Stay tuned.[31]

THE POLITICAL RESPONSE

As we have reported, the London meeting in 1990 resulted in pledges by industrial nations to halt the production of ozone-destroying chemicals by the year 2000 (allowing a ten-year grace period) and to assemble a $240-million replacement fund for poorer nations. The fund, to be administered by representatives of 14 nations, was not agreed to without argument. It is generally agreed that, although Third-World nations contribute a small percentage of ozone-destroying emissions, their CFC productive potential is huge, given the population represented. Given that potential, several developing nations proposed that the nations that are primarily responsible for the present problem—the United States, European countries, Japan—should provide financial and technological aid to the nations whose development is being shaped, and made much more expensive, by these bans. Ominous divisions developed between "the North" (Europe, the United States, Canada, Japan) and "the South" (South America, Black Africa, South and Southeast Asia), mimicking the 50-year adversarial alignments of East and West. The North–South arguments were acrimonious and heated: India accused U.S. businesses of promoting and selling CFC technology in Third-World nations with full knowledge that it would become obsolete; the United States objected to making any contribution to the fund, on the grounds that such a contribution would set a precedent for industrialized nation's largess to the Third World that might be very expensive to continue in the future.[32] To the credit of the world's politicians, diplomacy prevailed and an agreement was reached.

The revelations that followed the meeting must have made the disagreements seem petty. The reports of the 3-percent decline in ozone in the latitudes populated by the world's wealthy, at the time of highest exposure, accompanied by cancer predictions 12 times greater than expected,[33] caught the attention of the powerful and put much more energy into the work of emissions enforcement. "Now that there's the prospect of a[n ozone] hole over Kennebunkport," remarked (then) Senator Al Gore, "perhaps [President] Bush will comply with the law."[34] At any rate, the U.S. Senate resolved to speed up CFC phaseout, and the Bush administration announced on February 11, 1992, that the United States would stop CFC production by 1996.[35] Meanwhile, industry had been ahead of the politicians: DuPont had pledged to stop CFC production by 1997, and many companies were finding it easier than they had originally expected to substitute for CFCs.[36]

THE KNOWN, THE UNKNOWN, AND THE MEANING OF IT ALL

We know that the stratospheric ozone layer is becoming depleted at an accelerated rate. We also know that this depletion is not limited to the relatively unpopulated polar latitudes, in the winter, but exists also to a lesser degree in the mid-latitudes, where most of the world's population lives, and in the summer, when this population is most at risk for exposure to ultraviolet radiation. We know that a 1-percent decrease in stratospheric ozone is equivalent to a 2-percent increase in u.v. radiation penetrating the atmosphere. We know, too, that u.v.B—the most damaging u.v. wavelength—causes damage to DNA and can thus cause mutations and is immediately responsible for skin cancer, cataracts, and damage to the immune system in humans; it probably also disrupts the ecosystems of the world. Lastly, we know that the ozone destruction is caused by stable, man-made compounds containing chlorine (and bromine to a degree), primarily CFCs, that catalyze the breakdown.

The disparity of ozone loss at various latitudes and seasons can be attributed to temperature and circulation, as we have described. Less well-understood are the conditions that might promote the liberation of destructive chlorine atoms in mid-latitudes. One hypothesis is that the sulfate particles from sulfur dioxide pollution might act as PSCs do at the poles, inactivating compounds that might otherwise trap the chlorine; there is also some evidence that those same particles might filter out some of the u.v. radiation that has gotten through the atmosphere at ground level. One report states that u.v.B has been reduced by sulfur dioxide haze (SO_2) by 5 to 18 percent since preindustrial times.[37] Meanwhile, the Clean Air Act Amendments, passed by the U.S. Congress and signed by President Bush in 1990, call for a 50-percent decrease in SO_2 emissions, primarily to control acid rain. If these emissions, unpleasant as they might be, are helping us to limit u.v. injury, though, should we take such great pains to reduce sulfur dioxide pollution? Ironically, we might find that some of our pollution is canceling the effects of other pollution: How then shall we decide between them?

One further projection is that, as there becomes less ozone to absorb u.v. radiation in the Arctic latitudes, winter temperatures will decrease, because whenever u.v. radiation is absorbed by anything, its energy is converted to heat. This positive feedback would favor the formation and prolongation of the polar vortex that, in turn, contributes to the hole.[38]

Because it can take up to a decade for a CFC molecule to reach the stratosphere, the ozone that is being destroyed today is very probably, in part, being destroyed by CFCs put into the atmosphere before the first ozone hole was discovered. As a result, CFC concentrations in the stratosphere are expected (by one source) to double from 1989 to 2000, and decades will pass before we feel the full effects of the resultant 5- to 20-percent increase in u.v. radiation.[39] Another source claims that half of the total amount of CFCs produced since 1930 will be produced from now until the phaseout is complete,[40] and yet another source predicts increasing ozone destruction for some 20 years and a return to pre–ozone-layer hole concentrations around 2050.[41]

THE UNKNOWNS

The unknowns in this situation include the Third-World phaseout and suitable refrigerant replacements. Today, China and India jointly produce only 3 percent of the world's CFCs, but the potential for the use of these chemicals by one-fourth of the world's population is immense. Today only 10 percent of the houses in China contain a refrigerator, but China's leaders have promised a refrigerator for every kitchen by the year 2000.[42] Substitutes for other uses of CFCs have been found more easily than originally expected, but an equally effective and inexpensive refrigerant remains elusive. One of the better ones, HCFC, must itself be phased out by 2040, and others (such as propane) have explosive characteristics. One further concern is that the CFCs now in use as refrigerants will eventually be added to those in the atmosphere.[43]

Reports of actual measurements of increased u.v. radiation are hard to come by, as are accounts of effects directly attributable to increased u.v. radiation. Questionable anecdotal material exists, such as cataracts in cattle in the Southern hemisphere and sunburns from minor exposure, but there is little confirmed, hard evidence. It is certainly possible that haze reduces the incident radiation, as we have suggested, or that other unknown factors contribute to the equation. Measurements at two sites substantiate the suspicion that pollutants are trapping some of the increased u.v. radiation. U.v. measurements in New Zealand's air were twice as high as in Germany's more polluted air. The two measurements were made at almost identical northern and southern latitudes, using the same instruments, thus increasing our confidence in their reliability. The result reinforces previous findings that Alpine air receives more u.v. radiation than does the United States.[44] Whatever the combination, an increase in human skin cancer is a virtual certainty. It is well-documented that U.S. skin cancers have been on the rise since long before the discovery of the ozone hole; an Australian report cites a 300-percent increase in skin cancers.[45] Furthermore, the link between u.v.B and skin cancer has been firmly established.[46] Other possible effects on humans have been noted, yet many questions remain, such as the effect on children ten years old and younger who have presumably been exposed to excess u.v. radiation all their lives and whether other speculated effects (for example, increases in herpes infections, leprosy, tuberculosis, and lupus), will materialize. We have just begun the research.

Of immediate concern are the effects of increased u.v. radiation on other species. Threats to crops have been predicted, based on laboratory experiments in which plants have been exposed to excessive u.v. radiation. Marine algae seem to be the greatest at risk; their photosynthetic rate is known to be reduced by u.v. radiation.[47] In Antarctica, although the algae populations are not (yet?) shrinking, they are producing u.v.-absorbing pigments (a natural adaptation), and a reduction in productivity, as well as genetic damage, has been documented.[48]

Our concern for marine phytoplankton goes beyond their survival for their own sake: They form the base of all marine food chains, indirectly providing much of the world's food and, because oceans cover three-quarters of the planet's surface, marine plants, through photosynthesis, produce most of the atmosphere's oxygen. A threat to these microscopic plants, truly essential to all other life, is serious indeed.

As noted, many plant species have evolved adaptive mechanisms to protect themselves from u.v. radiation, just as humans tan (produce more melanin) as a protective response to exposure to the sun. The unanswered question is: At what point does the incidence of u.v. radiation exceed the power of nature's protective mechanisms? We can find the answer in our own species, by noting when, and to what degree, we observe an increase in skin cancer. Of course, if we stay indoors or wear hats, we will prevent the u.v. radiation from reaching, and damaging, our skin—but is that the solution of choice?

One of the most worrisome aspects of the ozone-hole problem is that the worst is yet to come. The first public prediction of ozone depletion, after all, was as recent as 1974. But the phaseout of CFC production will not be completed worldwide until 2010—that is, if everything goes according to schedule. The maximum CFC concentration in the stratosphere will not occur until 2020, however, and the ozone layer will not return to normal until 2050. We simply do not know how much damage we have done (or will do) to ourselves, to other species, and to the natural balance among the forces that control the biosphere. We know that some destruction will happen, indeed *is* happening, but the effects are presently impossible to calculate.

CONSIDERATIONS OF JUSTICE

The CFC problem—the depletion of the ozone layer—is about sunlight and refrigeration, u.v.-loaded sunlight that poses far more danger to humans in agrarian regions where people must live and work out of doors and threatens the agricultural product of the world more than the industrial. Even though the polar regions are now suffering more than the tropics, we can predict that, as ozone depletion increases, its effects will spread to the mid- and equatorial latitudes too, with devastating effects on the health and prosperity of those regions. In a pattern that must begin to seem familiar to the leaders of developing nations, the North caused the problem and the South will predictably suffer most from it.

Consider the matter from the perspective of a member of Parliament in a developing nation of the South: Refrigeration (which is, for at least part of the year, merely a convenience in the North) is essential for health in the South. The North—the developed countries in the temperate zones of Eastern and Western hemispheres—invented refrigeration to keep their food fresh and air-conditioning to keep themselves comfortable without sharing that technology with the South—Africa, Asia, and Latin America. Now, just as technological advance, including mass access to home refrigeration and air-conditioned workplaces, becomes a real possibility for the Third World, the North announces that it would prefer that no more refrigeration be introduced anywhere. The reason advanced for this concern must ring false to the same Third-World leaders: that the North has discovered that refrigeration is damaging the ozone layer and that harmful radiation is being rained down on all who must live or work under the sun (especially those too poor to afford effective sunshade), compelling a halt to the spread of all technology that relies on refrigerants.

Not only must the South patiently await some new (probably more expensive) technology to preserve its food and its comfort, but the South must apparently suffer disproportionately the effects of the damage done so far to the ozone layer. Meanwhile, while the North phases out CFC technology (at a pace that will not inconvenience its consumer economies), the damage to the ozone layer will double and again cause more suffering in the South than the North. It hardly seems fair.

That, of course, was the point of the acrimonious debate at the London meeting in June, 1990. The South argued, plausibly enough, that if, as Northern data suggested, the South has been badly damaged by the destruction of the ozone, then the North, who is responsible for that damage, ought to pay them compensation. Further, if those refrigerants are so damaging that the South cannot now introduce them, it seems that the North ought at least to fund the introduction of a less-harmful technology. Otherwise, as politicians everywhere can easily appreciate, the governments of the South will have the very devil of a time convincing their own people that it is somehow their duty to forego economically advantageous technology for the sake of the ozone layer. Indeed, if we have trouble convincing the well-educated businesspeople and politicians of the First World that the ozone depletion is a real threat and that changing our technology is an obligation, how will we *ever* convince the less-educated (and sweltering) populations of the Third World that they ought to remain in the nineteenth century while their big brothers in the North find some environmentally safe way for them to advance to the twenty-first century?

On the other hand, the U.S. delegates argued just as convincingly that *they* were not to blame for the technological backwardness of the Third World; the disparity was determined by chance, history, and a myriad of factors over which the United States had no control. If we accept responsibility for catching them up in this area, where will it all end? Shall we "compensate" them for the disparity in medical technology? transportation? education? cable television? Where does it stop, once it starts?

The conclusion reached at the London meeting was simplicity itself: CFCs damage the ozone layer; the ozone layer protects crops, animals, and health; therefore, the world must cease production of CFCs. Stratospheric ozone is no respecter of persons nor pursuer of justice. The ozone layer does not distinguish between CFCs produced in the United States and CFCs produced in India or China and, if those nations undertake mass CFC production, we will *all* die under the sun. Further, the Third World, the agrarian South, will die under that sun a good deal faster than we will in the North, which suggests that it is even more in *their* interest to see world CFC production slowed and stopped. There is no just compensation to pay a nation for doing what is only in its own best interests.

Then, what *do* we owe the Third World? The question is huge, and we are just beginning to think about it. If we owe them nothing, then what do we owe to the biosphere and to the ozone layer that protects it? Suppose that China, for instance, should claim that its people's need for refrigeration well outweighs the world's need for a cessation of CFC production—at least since the North is not interested in financing that cessation in China. Suppose that China proceeded full speed ahead, manufacturing CFCs to be introduced all over China in leaky, inexpensive refrigerators. Suppose, further, that we could show that this manufacturing project, if it went through to completion, would reduce the ozone layer by another 85 percent and injure terrestrial life beyond recovery. Would we then be ethically justified in invading China (supposing that we could do it successfully) to halt the production? Would we be obligated to do that? Why? Or rather, by our duty to what? other species? the biosphere itself? When justice to the planet is concerned, what *are* our obligations?

QUESTIONS FOR DISCUSSION AND REFLECTION

✦ The ozone layer is somewhat like a *commons*, a communal good shared by all humans and, indeed, all terrestrial life. What obligations do we have to our fellow species not to destroy the commons? What obligations, if any, do we have to future generations of humans (yet unborn) to preserve the ozone layer as a necessary condition for their life?

✦ Our decision to halt beneficial economic activity in order to save the ozone layer is bound to hurt some human beings. How certain do we have to be that the activity we are ceasing is really harmful to the ozone, to justify eliminating a hundred jobs? 10,000 jobs? 20,000 jobs, besides stunting the development of two of the less-developed nations? After all, people can wear hats out in the sun, but animals and plants, including the crops we are growing to try to feed the developing nations, cannot of course wear hats, nor hide in any other way from the searing, unfiltered rays of the sun.

✦ No human group has ever taken responsibility for the protection of something whose function bears more on other species than on our own. Is it possible for us to unite as a species to protect the ozone layer? Can we draw up a scenario of cooperation that would make that possible?

Notes

1. David E. Fisher, *Fire and Ice* (New York: Harper & Row, 1990): p. 41 ff. See also Steven Schneider, *Global Warming* (San Francisco: Sierra Club Books, 1987).

2. Interestingly, these primitive organisms that had existed in an oxygen-free atmosphere poisoned themselves with the oxygen they were producing; now they are found only in anaerobic environments such as intestines, swamps, and soils (Schneider, *Global Warming*).

3. Beth Hansen, insert accompanying Francesca Lyman, "As the Ozone Thins, the Plot Thickens," *Amicus* (Summer 1991).

4. Fisher, *Fire and Ice*, p. 45 ff., and Malcolm W. Browne, "Costlier and More Dangerous Chemicals Foreseen in Saving Ozone," *The New York Times* (1 July 1990): p. 12. (Both Fisher and *The Times* credit Midgley, but Fisher has him working for DuPont, *The Times*, Frigidaire. Both companies were evidently involved.)

5. Schneider, *Global Warming*, p. 218 ff.

6. Fisher, *Fire and Ice*, p. 45 ff.

7. *Ibid.*

8. A recital of the events leading to the banning of CFCs in spray cans can be found in Fisher, *Fire and Ice*; Schneider, *Global Warming*; and Lyman, "Plot Thickens."

9. Lyman, *The Plot Thickens*.

10. Fisher, *Fire and Ice,* pp. 110 ff.

11. *Ibid.*, p. 116.

12. *Ibid.*

13. *Ibid.*, p. 117.

14. Michael Lemonick, "The Ozone Vanishes," *TIME*, vol. 139, no. 7 (17 February 1992): p. 60.

15. Schneider, *Global Warming*, p. 117

16. Malcolm W. Browne, "93 Nations Agree to Ban Chemicals that Harm Ozone," *The New York Times* (30 June 1990): p. 1; also reported in R. Monastersky, "Nations to Ban Ozone Harming Compounds," *Science News*, vol. 38 (7 July 1990): p. 6.

17. Dr. Robert Watson of the National Aerospace Agency, in testimony before the Senate Committee on Energy and Natural Resources, August, 1988, quoted in Schneider, *Global Warming,* p. 27.

18. Schneider, *Global Warming.*

19. Michael Oppenheimer, "Climate Catastrophe, the Rerun," *The New York Times* (27 April 1991): Op-Ed section.

20. Fisher, *Fire and Ice,* p. 113.

21. Owen B. Toon and Richard P. Turco, "Polar Stratospheric Clouds and Ozone Depletion," *Scientific American* (June, 1991).

22. Richard Stolarski, "The Antarctic Ozone Hole," *Scientific American,* vol. 258, no. 1 (January, 1988): p. 30.

23. R. Monastersky, "Antarctic Ozone Bottoms at Record Low," *Science News,* vol. 138 (11 August 1990): p. 228.

24. These figures were reported in several sources, including: R. Monastersky, *Science News* (24 March 1990): p. 183; Phillip Shabecoff, "Scientists Report Faster Ozone Loss," *The New York Times* (24 June 1990); and William K. Stevens, "Ozone Losses in Arctic Are Larger than Expected," *The New York Times* (19 September 1990).

25. Malcolm W. Browne, "Ozone Hole Reopens over Antarctica," *The New York Times* (19 October 1990).

26. Malcolm W. Browne, "Ozone Loss Over U.S. Found to Be Twice as Bad as Predicted," *The New York Times* (5 April 1991).

27. Malcolm W. Browne, "The Worst Ozone Hole Stirs Health Fears," *The New York Times* (10 October 1991).

28. William K. Stevens, "Summer-Time Harm to Shield of Ozone Detected over U.S.," *The New York Times* (23 October 1991).

29. The latest findings were reported by several sources: Philip J. Hilts, "Senate Backs Faster Protection of Ozone Layer as Bush Relents," *The New York Times* (7 February 1992); Lemonick, "The Ozone Vanishes," p. 60; Warren E. Leary, "Ozone Harming Agents Reach a Record," *The New York Times* (4 February 1992): p. C4.

30. R. Monastersky, "Northern Hemisphere Ozone Hits Record Low," *Science News,* vol. 143 (20 March 1993): p. 180.

31. Warren E. Leary, "Scientists Say Warm Winter Prevented Arctic Ozone Hole," *The New York Times* (1 April 1992).

32. Browne, "93 Nations Agree," p. 1; and Monastersky, "Ozone Harming Compounds."

33. "Researchers Report Depletion of Ozone in Temperate Zones," *The New York Times* (22 October 1991); and Stevens, "Ozone Losses."

34. Lemonick, "The Ozone Vanishes," p. 60.

35. Hilts, "Bush Relents"; and Rose Gutfield, "U.S. to Step up Bid to Protect Ozone Layer," *The Wall Street Journal* (12 February 1992).

36. Philip Shabecoff, "Industry Acts to Save Ozone," *The New York Times* (21 March 1988).

37. J. Raloff, "Haze May Confound the Effects of Ozone Loss," *Science News* (4 January 1992).

38. Lemonick, "The Ozone Vanishes."

39. Gary E. McCuen, *Ending War Against the Earth,* Ideas in Conflict Series (Hudson, Wisc.: GEM Publications, 1991), p. 51; and James Gleick, "Even with Action Today Ozone Loss Will Increase," *The New York Times* (20 March 1988): p. A1.

40. Lyman, "The Plot Thickens."

41. Toon and Turco, "Ozone Depletion."

42. George J. Mitchell, *World on Fire* (New York: Charles Scribner's, 1991): p. 164.

43. Browne, "Costlier and More Dangerous Chemicals."

44. *Science News*, vol. 142 (29 September 1992): p. 180.

45. Lemonick, *The Ozone Vanishes.*

46. Natalie Angier, "Ultraviolet Radiation Tied to Gene Defect Producing Skin Cancer," *The New York Times* (19 November 1991).

47. Sayed El-Sayed, "Fragile Life Under the Ozone Hole," *Natural History* (October 1988): p. 73.

48. The effects of u.v. radiation on marine algae are discussed in Lemonick, "The Ozone Vanishes"; Gleick, "Ozone Loss Will Increase"; and Schneider, *Global Warming.*

Suggestions for Further Reading

Fisher, David E. *Fire and Ice.* New York: Harper & Row, 1990.
Mitchell, George J. *World on Fire.* New York: Charles Scribner's, 1991.
Schneider, Steve. *Global Warming.* San Francisco: Sierra Club Books, 1987.

CHAPTER 8

Life in the Greenhouse

Scientists Confront a Changing Climate

PREFACE: QUESTIONS TO KEEP IN MIND

What do we mean by "Science has proved..."? Why is that always a persuasive line in advertisements for new products? Why does the endorsement of science carry more weight than other disciplines (say, philosophy)?

Why is there so much uncertainty about global warming (the greenhouse effect)?

How do policymakers usually proceed when they are really not sure of the facts? How do you think they should proceed? Does inaction have as many consequences as action? How would you balance the relative advantages and disadvantages of a decision to do nothing and a decision to do something?

ON NOT REALLY KNOWING

Summing up the worst dilemma of our discipline, one of our colleagues posted a cartoon on his office door: Two worried men pace the executive suite; one concedes to the other, "It's really still too early to know if it's too late to do anything about it."

Global warming presents a similar dilemma—as does acid rain, pollution of the oceans, and, until recently, the deterioration of the ozone layer: We are still not really sure what we are seeing, and by the time we are sure that the effect is there, that there really *is* damage from pollution and unsound use of resources, it will be much too late to reverse the effect and save ourselves and that sector of our planet.

On the other hand, we must be very wary of acting *without* being sure of the effect. When we have only suspicions, an untested logic, and "Space Odyssey" computer projections to base it on, we might be able to justify advancing hypotheses and scheduling symposia in the annual conventions of learned societies—but can we justify suspending economically beneficial activities, throwing people out of work, and damaging the economic infrastructure of whole regions, solely on computer-projected scenarios of horror? After all, the lost jobs are real and the poverty endured for lack of them is also real, but the computer fantasies are not—certainly not yet. May we sacrifice the real present welfare of real people for the future possible welfare of future people? What ethical obligations exist between our generation and those to follow?

JIM HANSEN BLOWS THE WHISTLE

On June 23, 1988, Dr. James Hansen, Director of the National Aeronautics and Space Administration's (NASA) Goddard Institute for Space Studies, testified before the U.S. Senate Committee on Energy and Natural Resources: "It's time to stop waffling so much and say that this evidence is pretty strong that the greenhouse effect is here."[1] This event occurred in Washington, D.C., which is always steamy in summer, at the beginning of a summer that was to be the hottest on record (with warmer ones yet to come) and was to usher in one of the worst droughts in U.S. history.

There were banner headlines the morning after Dr. Hansen's comment, and many less forthright scientists were shocked that such an unequivocal statement had come from a scientist with such impeccable credentials. This was the first time that a member of "the club" had exhibited such candor before a public and highly visible forum; the club tends to address such problems either in dry, obscure journals or at boring, low-profile, scientific meetings.

Many felt Dr. Hansen had been absolute to the point of being unscientific; others agreed with him but wished that he had used modifiers, had hedged his bets a bit, or had given more attention to the imperfections of computer climate models. Nevertheless, four years later, his testimony is still credited as the single most effective witness, the first voice that cried out in the wilderness near enough to be heard. Jim Hansen's testimony might well be the event that first raised, in the public eye, the distinct possibility that humankind is changing the climate of the planet.[2]

Hansen made more headlines in May, 1989; again, during Senate testimony, he publicly announced that the Bush administration's Office of Management and Budget had, despite his objections, altered the record of his testimony. Specifically, his assertion that global warming would lead to "drought intensification at most middle-and-low-latitude land areas" had been modified to include that "these changes should be viewed as estimates from evolving computer models and not as reliable predictions."

Once again, the public was caught in the middle, with cries of "politics!" and "censorship!" coming from one large sector of the scientific community and conservative dismay from another: "To say that we've seen the greenhouse signal is ridiculous," asserted Timothy P. Barnett of the Scripps Institution of Oceanography; Danny Harvey of the University of Toronto concluded simply that "Jim Hansen has crawled out on a limb." Steven Schneider of the National Center for Atmospheric Research, a friend of Hansen's, shared his commitment to computer climate models and believed, with Hansen, that the issues of climate change should be addressed but did not share his confidence that the documented global temperature increase was clearly due to "greenhouse gases."

Nor was Schneider at all sure about the computer model's ability to pinpoint future effects, such as droughts; as Schneider put it, Hansen "has more confidence in his tools than I do." Hansen himself cited no etiology of climate change—no proven causal chain from carbon emissions to temperature rise—but simply said (of the increase in carbon dioxide in the atmosphere since 1880), "It's just inconceivable that that is not affecting our climate."[3]

THE GREENHOUSE EFFECT

The *greenhouse effect* is the imperfect analogy used to explain the atmospheric phenomena that keep our planet warm enough to sustain life. Our atmosphere allows about half of the incoming solar radiation to reach the Earth's surface; the balance is either directly reflected back into space or absorbed and retained for a while. The energy that does get through is either bounced back as heat or is used to do work (for example, photosynthesis, evaporation, creation of winds), then degraded to heat energy, and returned to the atmosphere. Here is where the greenhouse effect kicks in: Some gases in the atmosphere, notably water vapor and carbon dioxide, have the capacity to hold onto the heat for a while, just as the glass panes in a greenhouse do. Without this heat-retaining quality, the Earth's surface would cool to about -18° C. (-4° F.), instead of maintaining an average temperature of 14° C. (57° F.), and there could be no life on the planet.

Our current concern is not whether the greenhouse effect exists—we would not be here if it didn't—but that the effect might be exacerbated by anthropogenic increases in the effective gases, thus threatening a disruption to the equilibrium between incoming and outgoing energy, and warming of the globe: Each year's average temperature would be higher than the previous year's. Since the start of the industrial revolution, humankind has been adding to the natural amounts of carbon dioxide entering the atmosphere, primarily through the burning of fossil fuels. We humans have also caused increases in other *greenhouse gases,* among them methane from rice paddies and cattle flatulence and nitrogen oxides from fertilizers, combustion, and other activities.

A BRIEF HISTORY
OF OUR CLIMATE

The history of our climate is no simpler than its science. Gases trapped in ice cores and paleontological and anthropological discoveries reveal much about the climate of the past; still, a great deal of supposition exists about the history of the Earth and its creatures. What follows is a brief look at some of the current interpretations of our past.

If we go back just a hundred million years ago, during the age of the dinosaurs, the average temperature was about 10–14° F. warmer than it is today, close to the maximum global-warming predictions. About 65 million years ago, the dinosaurs became extinct. We once assumed that this extinction was caused by a gradual cooling brought on by the incoming ice age, a cooling that cold-blooded reptiles could not survive. With the recent discovery of huge craters in Mexico and the Caribbean, another theory has gained ground: that the temperature drop came suddenly as a huge meteor kicked up a cloud of dust that blocked the sun. Whether the change was sudden or gradual, the climate got colder and the dinosaurs did not survive. Mammals survived, and primates (including, finally, *Homo sapiens*) evolved.

Depending on the source and its definitions, primates appeared about two to five million years ago; the first humans, around 2.5 million to 500,000 years ago; *Homo sapiens* became established about 30,000 years ago; and the beginnings of agriculture occurred about 15,000 years ago. Ice ages came and went, lasting some 50,000 years each time,[4] with warmer and cooler periods within them. (It has been suggested that the evolution of the human brain resulted from the natural selection of those most able to survive the coldest periods.) The respite between ice ages seems to have been about 10,000 years.

Agriculture and civilization both began in the warming interglacial period some 15,000 years ago. If the same intervals still apply, we should now be on the verge of another ice age—not preempted by the "Little Ice Age" that occurred from 1550 to 1850 A.D., when the average temperature was about 2° C. colder; the Thames and the New York Harbor froze, and English grapevines died.[5] Shouldn't we then expect the Earth to be getting colder? The Earth has not been warmer, though, even by one degree, than it is today for the last 8,000 years,[6] and the last time it was 2° C. warmer than preindustrial times was around 125,000 years ago, when any *Homo sapiens* extant were strictly hunter-gatherers and a long way from being dependent on agriculture.[7]

THE PAST AS A CRACKED MIRROR

What does all this tell us about global warming today? Certainly it tells us that there is a lot of uncertainty. We know that the concentration of carbon dioxide and other gaseous emissions from human activity have increased in the atmosphere and that these gases have the capacity to hold heat. We do not know where these gases are going, if not into the atmosphere. We know that temperature fluctuation over geological time is the rule rather than the exception, but we also know that seemingly small temperature changes have in the past had significant effects on the history of life on the planet. Scott L. Wing, a Smithsonian paleontologist, points out that "none of us feel the past is a crystal ball. It's a cracked and warped mirror, but it's the only mirror we've got."[8] Dr. Wallace Broecker of the Lamont-Doherty Laboratory commented on the possibility that the increase in carbon dioxide could put us into a "super inter-glacial" phase: "We're living in a system that can do strange things. Small forcings have produced large things and to say a priori that this gas [carbon dioxide] can't produce large changes is just bloody insanity."[9]

By many measurements, the global average temperature has increased by 0.5° C. from 1880 to today. Predictions for the twenty-first century, without a change in the current emissions, range from an increase of 2–5° C. (approximately 4–9° F.). To put that into perspective, at the height of the last ice age, 18,000 years ago—when the ice had reached as far south as Long Island, New York, and had covered the Great Lakes—the average temperature was only 3–5° C. cooler than it is now.[10]

THE BACKGROUND
OF A WHISTLE-BLOWER

Dr. James Hansen, the mild-mannered scientist at the center of the controversy, was born in Iowa, the son of a tenant farmer and a waitress. In good American style, he earned money for college with a paper route and, by his own account, did no studying until he reached college and met his mentor, Dr. James Van Allen (of Van Allen Radiation Belts fame). Van Allen encouraged him to follow a career at the Goddard Institute, which he did; he eventually went on to direct the institute. This obscure organ of NASA flourished under his direction, expanding its staff to a high of 140, using NASA funds, and EPA funds when NASA's dried up. In 1981, Hansen published the first evidence of global warming and continued to sound the alarm through congressional testimony in 1982, 1986, and 1987, although attracting little notice. (As we have noted, he received more attention than he was looking for in 1988 and 1989.)

After Hansen's 1988 testimony, NASA received calls of displeasure from the White House, and he himself received veiled job threats; he suspects that the present shortage of funds can be traced to his unpopularity in political quarters. But his revelation that OMB had altered his testimony in 1989 attracted the attention of (then) Senator Albert Gore, who seized the initiative, put the White House on the defensive, and eventually orchestrated a White House conference on global warming.

Hansen continued to annoy his superiors. As the satellites that had produced the raw data on the climate went out of commission, Hansen proposed small, inexpensive ones to produce data until the year 2000. NASA had already proposed a huge and very expensive system, however, with all the instruments that Hansen wanted and more, not to be deployed until a politically convenient 1998. Hansen somehow neglected to inform his superiors about his suggestion until after he had published it.

Meanwhile, there is a significant division of opinion in the scientific community about the facts and the appropriate action to be taken. First, no one is sure just what is happening with the global climate; second, there is significant disagreement about what can, or should, be done politically in the face of serious uncertainty. Hansen's interpretation of the data accumulated from the computer runs of climate change models led him to 99-percent certainty that the Earth is warming; it convinced him that the warming is due to the accumulation of greenhouse gases and that signal events, like droughts, will be on the increase. Hansen's critics, the "greenhouse agnostics," claim that the temperature record is not reliable; that there are too many climate variables to lay the blame on greenhouse gases; and that, in short, we do not understand the climate. These people conclude that we should therefore go no further with our attempts to deal with purported climatic crises.

Hansen is fully aware of the problems entailed in extrapolating from the very slight changes in the climate that have occurred over the last few decades, in the light of the climate's much larger natural variability. "I think you have to do what you think is right," he says. "We're not environmentalists; we're not trying to defend some position that we've taken in the past. We're trying to advance our understanding. We're changing the atmosphere. What's that going to do? Now, when the time comes, if we have a result that's important, we're not going to be bashful about presenting it."[11]

Programming computer models to predict the climate of the future is clearly an imperfect science at the very best. As Oppenheimer and Boyle said in *Dead Heat,* "In short, we face uncertainty, indefinitely."[12] David Fisher, on the other hand, states in *Fire and Ice* that Hansen's models are among the best.[13]

CASSANDRA'S TRAIL

As long ago as 1827, Jean-Baptiste-Joseph Fourier compared the atmosphere to a "greenhouse" and, in 1896, Svante Arrhenius predicted a rise in temperature by 4–6° C., with a doubling of carbon dioxide in the atmosphere. With the end of the "Little Ice Age," industrialization proceeded apace in England, fueled by coal. By 1910, atmospheric carbon dioxide had increased by 7 percent. From 1900 to 1920, the consumption of gasoline for automobiles in the United States went from four thousand to four million gallons. By 1938, a British meteorologist, G. D. Callendar, was able to inform the Royal Society of London that global warming had occurred, due to increases in carbon dioxide in the atmosphere and, in 1954, G. Evelyn Hutchinson of Yale University warned that deforestation would contribute to global warming; no on paid him much attention.

In conjunction with the International Geophysical Year in 1957, two scientists from Scripps Institute of Oceanography published their finding that the oceans were not absorbing as much carbon dioxide as had been postulated. In the same year, one of their students, C. David Keeling, started making CO_2 measurements from the observatory in Mauna Loa, Hawaii, which is 11,000 feet high; to this day, these observations are probably the most quoted and graphed as indicators of the CO_2 rise. The 1957 measurement was 315 parts per million (ppm); in 1988, 350 ppm, a 25-percent increase since the estimated 280 ppm of 1800. At that rate, it is estimated that atmospheric CO_2 will double from its 1800 level by the year 2075.

Keeling's work sparked academic interest, if not a public outcry; computer simulations of the future climate followed rapidly in the wake of their publication of these findings. By 1975, several respected scientists, including Hansen, had sounded the first alarms about CO_2; they added that other gases, especially methane, nitrous oxide, and CFCs (of ozone-depletion fame), were together equalling the CO_2 effect, and they indicted deforestation as a major cause of the increase. In 1983, both the National Academy of Sciences and the Environmental Protection Agency released studies: The former predicted the now famous 3–8° F. increase in temperature with a doubling of CO_2 and proclaimed that there was cause "for concern, but not panic";[14] the latter predicted that CO_2 doubling would occur by the year 2030, accompanied by major agricultural, economic, political, and climatic disruptions. Now the public was aroused. By 1985, global warming had received global attention.[15]

In 1988, Jim Hansen's models, using the average temperature from 1950 to 1980 as the baseline for comparisons, found an increase of 0.5° F. from 1880 to the baseline and the same increase from 1980 to 1988. By then it was clear that 1981, 1983, and 1987 had been the warmest years on record, and 1988 was on its way toward breaking another record. Even though many models had by then predicted a 2° rather than a 1° increase, even that seemed significant, given the cooling effect of volcanos—and the presumption, mentioned earlier, that we would be entering a new ice age.[16]

A study done by the University of Chicago's Veerabhadran Ramanthan, based on satellite observations and ocean temperature readings, confirmed that the increased water vapor resulting from increased temperature would amplify the warming picture. (Water vapor is itself a greenhouse gas, a classic case of positive feedback.) This finding was essential to the integrity of the computer models being used, because water-vapor amplification was programmed into all of them.[17] (This is why Hansen wanted new satellites, to replace them as they broke down.)

THE SCIENTISTS CALL FOR ACTION

In April 1990 (just before the convening of the previously mentioned White House conference), a team of U.N. scientists confirmed a 3–8° temperature rise over the next 60 years;[18] in November of the same year, at the second World Climate Conference, 700 scientists called for cuts in emissions of CO_2 and other greenhouse gases, saying it could be done without economic disruption. The United States was the only industrialized nation other than the oil producers (the Middle East, USSR, Venezuela) that did not concur. The chairman of the International Council of Scientific Unions, Maurice la Riviere, a biologist, said that "given what we know, there is absolutely no excuse for governments not to save on energy."[19] Two studies released simultaneously by the United States and the United Kingdom ranked 1990 the warmest year yet and documented that the seven warmest years since 1880 were all after 1980.

Those findings prompted a variety of comments: Hansen predictably said that "the case for a cause-and-effect relationship is becoming harder to deny," and that "seasonal temperature is still a crap shoot, but the global warming is loading the dice." However, Tim Barnett, a climatologist at the Scripps Institute, said the warmest year cannot be attributed to any single cause.

"Is it green house gases or is it natural variability?" James K. Angell of the National Oceanic and Atmospheric Administration's Air Resources Laboratory admitted, "I've been a skeptic, but as these warmish years come one upon the other, you begin to waver a little bit." The British statement was: "Although it is still too early to confirm whether...it [the warming trend] is related to the greenhouse effect...it is likely it has played some role in contributing to the recent warmth."[20] (If you thought science was the domain of "hard facts," of the irrefutable evidence of carefully calibrated instruments, think again.)

In 1992, the year 1991 was found to be the second warmest on record, (1990 was still ahead), but glaciers were also found to be shrinking at "record rates." One glacier revisited after a 1983 study showed no record of the intervening years; it had melted too fast to leave yearly traces, an event that had not happened before in its 500-year history. This event certainly indicates global warming, but not its cause. (Interestingly, in the second half of 1991, the glacier cooled to 0.5° C. below the prior year.) The question was raised whether this was due to the Mount Pinatubo eruption in the Philippines; the dust from that had been predicted to cool the atmosphere for a couple of years. On the other hand, atmospheric scientists were expecting another El Niño current, which usually warms the atmosphere.[21] At this writing in the fall of 1992, it is easy to believe that Mount Pinatubo is masking the warming, given the cool year that we have experienced in this part of the world. We will all just have to stay tuned.

COMPLICATING THE CLIMATE

Events such as the Mount Pinatubo eruption and the El Niño current that confound the computer modelers provide considerable grist for the mills of the "global warming agnostics," to use Jim Hansen's term. A huge number of variables are involved in producing our climate, and probably not all of them are known. Let us consider a few of these.

The effect of the clouds is the most difficult factor to quantify in the overall climate picture. They reflect shortwave radiation from the sun but absorb the longwave (heat) radiation from the Earth's surface; the first cools, the second warms. A distinction is also made between the kinds of clouds and their net effect on temperature (high cirrus clouds are more reflective), but the variables go beyond that. Most existing studies were done over land, and yet the effect of ocean clouds is still unknown. There are 15 percent more clouds over the oceans than over land, and ocean clouds are higher. They become thicker when they cool over water; the reverse is true over land. In the tropics, the clouds are very high and absorb a great deal of energy but cause a great deal of cooling. If these clouds were driven even higher, they would release less heat than they absorb.

One study shows that the net effect of clouds is a cooling effect; however, that can change when more clouds are present. Most climate models assume an increase in clouds due to evaporation that will exert a positive feedback—that is, produce more warming. Interestingly, 11 different computer models project the same outcome when the clouds are removed from the equations, and 19 of the best models treat clouds differently. Because the heating and cooling effects of clouds exist in such a delicate balance that can be altered by small temperature changes and because their effects vary with their location (latitude, whether over land or water), it could be ten years before these models can be considered accurate with respect to clouds.[22]

There are other variables: These include the paths that carbon takes as it cycles through the biosphere, the capacity of the oceans to absorb CO_2, the role played by coral reefs; but the factors receiving the most current attention are volcanic activity, atmospheric pollutants, and—yes—sunspots.

There is considerable opinion that the effects from the eruption of Mount Pinatubo and the expected El Niño current will cancel each other out, but the influence of Mount Pinatubo is expected to *peak* at about the time that any effects of El Niño will end—in late 1992 or early 1993. Other reports postulate that the effects from Mount Pinatubo will last three or four years and decrease average temperatures by 0.5° F. and remind us that the last volcano of this intensity brought on the "year without a summer" in 1815.[23]

You can see the problem. It gets worse: The pollutant sulfur dioxide further clouds the issue. The combination of SO_2 from the volcano plus that poured into the atmosphere from power plants and other sources add to the global reflection of sunlight back into space and, therefore, more global cooling. In January, 1992, the Intergovernmental Panel on Climate Change reported that "the cooling effect of sulfur emissions may have off-set a significant part of the greenhouse warming in the northern hemisphere during the past several decades." If this is true, it would explain the less-than-expected cooling in this hemisphere and also the disproportionate increase in temperature at night (because sunlight cannot be reflected at night) over the United States, the former USSR, and China.[24]

Sunspots have also entered the fray, because their activity has been seen to parallel rises in the Earth's temperature. Analyses also reveal correlations between the "Little Ice Age" and minimum sunspot activity. Whether this is coincidental or not, sunspots now have to take their place among all the other complicating and possibly random influences (besides greenhouse gases) on global temperatures: pollutants, volcanos, El Niño, and random changes beyond our fathoming.[25]

Finally, a study published in *Nature* demonstrated a correlation between atmospheric CO_2 and average temperatures from 1958 to 1988, suggesting positive feedback. That is to say, increases in temperature might increase the natural movement of carbon into the atmosphere as carbon dioxide; for example, increases in temperature speed decomposition, respiration, and diffusion from soils, wetlands, and oceans—all resulting in increases in CO_2 in the air.[26]

TRYING TO DO SOMETHING ABOUT GLOBAL WARMING

The world is getting warmer. So what? Why is global warming undesirable? For starters, there is a strong possibility that the lowlands of the world could become flooded, due to the expansion of the oceans and the melting of the polar ice caps. The Alliance of Small Island States has been publicizing their possible plight wherever possible, including, of course, at the Rio Conference (see Chapter 9). Some predictions say that a one-foot rise in sea level would eliminate some ecosystems and, at worst, immerse whole islands. Beyond the concerns of the islanders, Stephen P. Leatherman, director of the Laboratory for Coastal Research of the University of Maryland, predicts that a three-foot rise in sea level would displace 72 million people in China, 11 million in Bangladesh, and 8 million in Egypt (25 percent of the world's population lives less than 1.1 meters above sea level). In the United States, it is predicted that 45,000 people would have to be evacuated from the Marshall Islands if the predicted flooding should materialize.[27]

Coastlands everywhere would be wiped out. Poorer nations in general would be expected to suffer because of their greater dependence on natural resources for their livelihood,[28] but richer nations would not be exempt: In 1988, 53 percent of the U.S. population lived within 50 miles of a coast.[29] Among the accepted predictions are flooding, increased storm intensity, damaged ecosystems, droughts (in places unused to them), and changes in agriculture.

On the other hand, amid the myriad predictions of disaster, some suggest that there might even be potential advantages to the warmer climate of the future. There is a general reluctance to point out possible advantages accompanying global warming because of a fear that that would defuse the efforts to cut the emissions of the causative gases. But northern Europe, the northern United States, Canada, and countries of the former USSR might all benefit from warmer and wetter conditions for producing crops.

In the same vein, it is hoped that an increase in CO_2 will act as a fertilizer to plants (especially crops) in general—given that this gas is the source of carbon from which plants build all their organic nutrients through photosynthesis—but experiments indicate that CO_2 alone does not provide the hoped-for increase in crop productivity and that other nutrients (such as water and trace minerals), the availability of light, and competition from other species are just as important.[30] Other studies, however, indicate that U.S. agriculture should not suffer more than the northward shift we have mentioned, depending on the intensity of the warming.[31]

Surely, the projected miseries outweigh these putative benefits: One of the purposes of the White House conference was to find out what might be done to reverse the warming trend. There are also reasons against jumping in with expensive solutions to unproven problems, however. Jesse H. Ausubel points out that "a stitch in time saves nine *if* you know the right stitch."[32]

THE SEARCH FOR SOLUTIONS

What might that stitch be? Among the most attractive of the proposed cures for global warming—at least attractive to the politicians—is reforestation. Just as carbon dioxide is put into the atmosphere by many natural carbon sources (the respiration and decomposition of plants and animals, for instance) as well as roundly condemned human activities (primarily burning fossil fuels), so can CO_2 be removed from the air by many *carbon sinks*. These sinks include the oceans, into which CO_2 dissolves, and the forests and other vegetation that remove CO_2 from the air through photosynthesis. The destruction of trees through logging and burning indirectly contributes to the increase of CO_2 in the atmosphere. Therefore, one obvious solution would be to stop deforestation and plant more trees.

In an extensive analysis of these possibilities, Roger A. Sedjo estimated that, to achieve the goal of removing excess CO_2 from the atmosphere by planting trees, about $500 billion would be required in the United States, about half of that in the tropics. He computed the costs and effects of reducing lumbering and the possibility that forests might increase naturally with CO_2 acting as a fertilizer. He also points out that, although the price seems high for any of the reforestation proposals, the costs still fall well within U.S. means, and such a move would give us time to devise a more permanent solution to the problem.[33]

With fossil fuels seen as the global-warming villain, nuclear energy (predictably enough) is back in the news. The nuclear industry claims that the disadvantages of cost, wastes, and safety concerns are less negative than the problems that would be caused by global warming. According to one analysis, that argument does not consider the problems of the less-developed countries: Whereas they contributed only 7 percent of the world's carbon dioxide in 1950, this figure was 28 percent in 1987 and, it is estimated that, by 2020, they could be responsible for more than 40 percent of the world's energy use and 50 percent of the world's CO_2 emissions. To be effective, therefore, nuclear power plants should be in place in the Third World by the year 2010, which is unlikely because of the cost, the politically undesirable increase in debt that would be required, the necessity for transfer of technology from industrialized countries, and—perhaps most important—because coal is more abundant and cheaper in these countries. (China, for example, has the largest coal reserves in the world.)[34]

THE POLITICS AND PROGRESS OF GLOBAL WARMING

The politics of global warming is treated at length in the chapter on the Rio Conference. To summarize, on the global level, the North wants the South to develop in a sustainable fashion that minimizes emissions of greenhouse gases; the South wants the North to send money to subsidize such sustainability and also to demonstrate the will to change its own destructive ways. Most of the industrialized world is more sympathetic to the southern view than is the United States, which stands firm in its conviction that any commitments to reduction of greenhouse gases will hurt its already ailing economy. In the United States, the Democrats have generally pushed for more cooperation on the global-warming scene, with (then) Senator Albert Gore in the lead; the Republicans, led by former President Bush's chief of staff, opposed any action.

This opposition deserves further comment. The role played by former chief of staff John H. Sununu is noteworthy; in a world dominated by collectivities and mass communication, it demonstrates the power that can still be exerted by a single person on an issue that affects the planet's entire population. Sununu developed his own computer projections, and he trusted them more than he trusted NASA's. At one point, he evidently prevailed over the arguments of the Secretary of State, the Administrator of the Environmental Protection Agency, the Secretary of the Department of Energy, and the White House Science Advisor—all of whom were advising action on global warming. Mr. Sununu's explanation of the scientists' climate concerns was simply that some people in this country were trying to "create a policy...that cuts off our use of coal, oil, and natural gas." While Sununu held office, no action was taken on the problems of global warming, either in domestic policy or by participation on the international scene. His qualification for making this policy decision was a degree in mechanical engineering.[35]

Yet, such political effects can be no more than temporary. As the dispute came to the Rio Conference, the only available estimates of global warming came from the computer models simulating the world's climate—either the EPA's or John Sununu's. But at this writing, progress in the science of predicting climate change has come in the form of "a substantial independent check on the models: an analysis of how the Earth's climate responded to changes in atmospheric heat-trapping carbon dioxide and other influences in the distant past, based on geological and geophysical evidence."[36]

The new calculations are contained in a study by Dr. Martin Hoffert of New York University and Dr. Curt Covey of the University of California and predict that, if no means are undertaken to restrain carbon dioxide emissions, the average temperature will soar during the next century "to perhaps the highest levels in a million years ..." The study predicts that the results, for us and the rest of the biosphere, would be "disruptive and possibly catastrophic."[37] The article also grimly points out that these calculations are "no mere academic exercise" but essential guides to the new Clinton administration in setting policy, especially with regard to the guidelines adopted at Rio.

To bring our account full circle, the report cites Dr. James E. Hansen of NASA's Goddard Institute for Space Studies as affirming that the Hoffert-Covey analysis is "extremely valid; the best method we have for estimating climate sensitivity." Not all uncertainties have been banished from the question; for instance, we must continue to factor in the cooling effect from volcanos.[38]

CONTINUING THE STORY

A study of pine trees in the Sierra Nevada has yielded evidence that the sun has influenced climate over time. A 2,000-year record of tree rings has associated fluctuations of growth with Carbon-14 (isotope) concentrations, which indicate higher temperatures. Louis A. Scuderi of Boston University said of these findings, "I think this is some of the best proof we have to date that the sun is actually forcing climate." Other studies show that the effects of greenhouse gases are greater than any solar influence in determining climate changes. The jury is still out.[39]

Meanwhile, Jim Hansen struck again, predicting (again, through his computer models) an average of 0.5° C. cooling due to the effects of Mount Pinatubo's eruption. Actual measurements show that the post-Pinatubo years averaged 0.6° C. cooler than the previous year. According to Hansen's predictions, we can make the final observations at the end of 1993, when Mount Pinatubo's influence is expected to diminish.[40]

Here, again, there is scientific disagreement. Another 1993 study predicts that the cooling effect of Mount Pinatubo's airborne debris will last two to four years.[41] There is no assurance, though, that the tests we carry out in the next two years will tell us which estimate is correct, but at least for the first time we will be able to make direct and unambiguous measurements after a major climatic disruption.

We must not let these continuing disagreements among scientists discourage research or provide an excuse for inaction. There is now, and there will continue to be, real progress. Science will ultimately find ways to escape ideology and not stay hostage to politics.

QUESTIONS FOR DISCUSSION AND REFLECTION

+ What does the future hold? As we have abundantly demonstrated, no one really knows. The data that supports an increase in the planet's average temperature over the next 50 years or so is increasingly accepted, not only by scientists but by policymakers. The question is: How much will the temperature rise? When will it happen? and What, finally, will be the effects? These questions are still arguable.

+ How shall we best serve our long-run interests in the face of global warming? The interest of the European community and Japan in cooperation with the Third World on this issue is likely to influence U.S. policy eventually—especially since this interest springs from what the Third World sees as economic advantages in energy conservation and pollution control technologies. Does U.S. economic advantage also lie in the direction of climate-sensitive technology and cooperation with the South?

+ Shall we try again to get global cooperation to address this issue? The climate treaty signed in Rio, as watered-down as it was, nevertheless had a provision for revisiting the issue as circumstances warranted, a provision that will probably serve us well.

+ In conclusion, we can observe that, whatever else the climate treaty accomplished, it demonstrated that climate change and other environmental issues have moved to one of the global front burners. With the end of the Cold War, increasing attention is being paid to the *new* international conflict—that between the rich, industrialized North and the poorer, arguably exploited, South. Thanks primarily to the threat of global warming, these parties are at least talking to each other. If international cooperation on addressing global concerns, or at least an accepted set of procedures for addressing these concerns as they arise, should be a by-product of the threat of drastic climatic change, it will be worth all the fuss it has caused.

Notes

1. Michael Oppenheimer and Robert Boyle, *Dead Heat* (New York: Basic Books, 1990): p. 51; and George J. Mitchell, *World on Fire* (New York: Charles Scribner's, 1991): p. 26.

2. Oppenheimer & Boyle, *Dead Heat*; and Richard A. Kerr, "Hansen vs. the World on the Greenhouse Threat," *Science,* vol. 244 (2 June 1989): p. 1041.

3. Kerr, "Hansen vs. the World."

4. Ice ages come about because of changes in the orbit of the Earth and the angling of surfaces that the Earth presents to the sun, a topic that is beyond the scope of this chapter.

5. Oppenheimer & Boyle, *Dead Heat,* p. 18 ff.

6. World Resources Institute Report, 1987.

7. J. Raloff, "Tough Carbon Budget Could Slow Warming," *Science News* (2 December 1989): p. 359.

8. Richard Monastersky, "Swamped by Climate Change?" *Science News,* vol. 138 (22 September 1990): p. 184.

9. William K. Stevens, "In the Ebb and Flow of Ancient Glaciers, Clues to a New Ice Age," *The New York Times* (16 January 1990): p. C1. For more information on the history of the Earth's climate, see the books noted above and articles from the Bibliography (Chapter 8) by William F. Allman and Betsy Wagner; Richard Monastersky; James Kasting et al.; William K. Stevens; and J. Raloff.

10. For more detailed descriptions of global warming and the history of the Earth's climate, see Steven H. Schneider, *Global Warming* (San Francisco: Sierra Club Books, 1989); Oppenheimer & Boyle, *Dead Heat*; and Mitchell, *World on Fire.*

11. Virtually all of the previous information about Jim Hansen is from Karen Wright, "Heating the Global Warming Debate," *The New York Times* magazine (3 February 1991): p. 24.

12. *Ibid.,* p. 57.

13. *Ibid.,* p. 92.

14. Oppenheimer & Boyle, *Dead Heat,* p. 39.

15. Virtually all of the foregoing is taken from Oppenheimer & Boyle, *Dead Heat,* pp. 18–39.

16. Philip Shabecoff, "Temperature for the World Rises Sharply in the 1980s," *The New York Times* (29 March 1988): p. C1.

17. William K. Stevens, "Study Supports Global Warming Prediction," *The New York Times* (14 December 1989): p. A36.

18. Philip Shabecoff, "Team of Scientists Sees Substantial Warming of Earth," *The New York Times* (16 April 1990): p. B7.

19. Marlise Simons, "Scientists Urging Gas Emission Cuts," *The New York Times* (5 November 1990): p. A5.

20. William K. Stevens, "Separate Studies Rank '90 as World's Warmest Year," *The New York Times* (10 January 1991): p. A1; and R. Monastersky, "Hot Year Prompts Greenhouse Concern," *Science News,* vol. 139 (19 January 1991): p. 36.

21. R. Monastersky, "Pinatubo and El Niño Fight Tug of War," *Science News* (18 January 1992); and "Signs of Global Warming Found in Ice," *Science News,* vol. 141 (7 March 1992): p. 148.

22. Richard A. Kerr, "How to Fix the Clouds in Greenhouse Models," *Science,* vol. 243 (6 January 1989): p. 28; "Clouds Keep Ocean Temperatures Down," *Science News* (11 May 1991): p. 303; R. Monastersky, "A Moisture Problem Muddles Climate Work," *Science News,* vol. 141 (4 April 1992): p. 212; and William K. Stevens, "Clouds Are Yielding Clues to Changes in Climate," *The New York Times* (24 April 1990): p. C1.

23. *Science News* (18 January 1992); see also William K. Stevens, "Volcano's Eruption in Philippines May Counteract Global Warming," *The New York Times* (19 June 1991): p. 1.

24. Richard Monastersky, "Haze Clouds the Greenhouse," *Science News,* vol. 141 (11 April 1992): p. 232.

25. Internal lecture at Environmental Defense Fund by Michael Oppenheimer and Stuart Gaffin (Spring 1992); see also Wallace S. Broecker, "Global Warming on Trial," *Natural History* (April 1992): pp. 6–14.

26. William K. Stevens, "Warming of the Globe Could Build on Itself, Some Scientists Say," *The New York Times* (19 February 1991): p. C4.

27. Paul Lewis, "Island Nations Fear a Rise in the Sea," *The New York Times* (17 February 1992); and Paul Lewis, "Danger of Floods Worries Islanders," *The New York Times* (13 May 1992).

28. William K. Stevens, "In a Warming World, Who Comes Out Ahead," *The New York Times* (5 February 1991): p. C1.

29. Larry Long, "Population by the Sea," *Population Today* (April 1990): p. 6.

30. Fakhri A. Bazzaz and Eric D. Fajer, "Plant Life in a CO_2-Rich World," *Scientific American* (January 1992): p. 68.

31. R. Monastersky, "Warming Shouldn't Wither U.S. Farming," *Science News,* vol. 137, p. 308.

32. Jesse H. Ausubel, "A Second Look at the Impacts of Climate Change," *American Scientist,* vol. 79 (May/June 1991): p. 210.

33. Roger A. Sedjo, "Forests: A Tool to Moderate Global Warming?" *Environment,* vol. 31, no. 1 (Jan./Feb. 1989): p. 14.

34. Alan Miller and Irving Mintzer, "Global Warming: No Nuclear Quick Fix," *The Bulletin of the Atomic Scientists* (June 1990): p. 31.

35. James H. Scheuer, "Bush's 'Whitewash Effect' on Warming," *The New York Times* (3 March 1990): Op-ed. section.

36. William K. Stevens, "Estimates of Warming Gain More Precision and Warn of Disaster," *The New York Times* (15 December 1992): pp. C1 & C9.

37. *Ibid.*

38. Special to the *Los Angeles Times,* "Scientists Document Cooling Effect from Volcanoes," *The Hartford Courant* (13 December 1992): p. A19.

39. R. Monastersky, "Here Comes the Sun-Climate Connection," *Science News* (6 March 1993): p. 148.

40. Richard A. Kerr, "Pinatubo Global Cooling on Target," *Science,* vol. 259 (29 January 1993): p. 594.

41. P. Minnis et al. "Relative Climate Forcing by the Mount Pinatubo Eruption," *Science,* vol. 259 (5 March 1993): p. 1411.

Suggestions for Further Reading

Flavin, Christopher. *Slowing Global Warming: A Worldwide Strategy.* Worldwatch Paper 91. Washington, D.C.: Worldwatch Institute, 1989.

Mitchell, George J. *World on Fire.* New York: Charles Scribner's, 1991.

Oppenheimer, Michael, and Robert Boyle. *Dead Heat.* New York: Basic Books, 1990.

CHAPTER 9

North Against South

The UNCED Summit
at Rio de Janeiro

PREFACE: QUESTIONS TO
KEEP IN MIND

> Humans are the most curious creatures. A few are billionaires, ready to drop $4,000 on a New York hotel suite, and a billion are impoverished, unlikely to see that much money in years. Twelve men have walked on the moon, riding an industrial revolution few can fully comprehend, and 500 million women can't find an invention as simple as an IUD. One third of American homes have Nintendo, and two thirds of the developing world still burns wood for all of its energy.

Therefore,

> This June 30,000 people will descend on Rio de Janeiro for the "Earth Summit" to bargain for a better deal for people and the planet.[1]

What is the relationship of that list of the massive disparities in the human condition to the conference we now call "Rio"? What assumptions link those facts and that gathering?

For that matter, what assumptions lie behind calling a conference to get a job done—let alone a conference of world leaders to take action on the global environment?

It might help us to understand the development and the sequelae of Rio to put these in some logical order.

JUSTICE

First, that list of massive disparities carries a moral message that is only obliquely alluded to, in the last sentence, in the reference to a "better deal." Behind the list lies the assumption that these disparities constitute a wrong, crying for remedy, and that a better deal is therefore called for. Why? Why is the present deal, as described, a bad one? What sorts of disparities need to be fixed? Some trees are taller than others, and some horses faster than others, but these differences do not constitute injustice. For that matter, not all differences among humans are unjust—differences in height, for instance, intelligence, genetic endowments, family background, country of origin, or color of eyes or hair. Blondes might have more fun, but that does not give me a right to reparations, if I am born brunette.

This list of disparities surely intends to suggest that, at least concerning access to material goods and favored lifestyles, significant inequality constitutes inequity, without further specification as to merit. According to the author of that passage, I do not have to know how the fortunate few got rich, nor why the multitude of starving have no food, to know that the few should do something to help the multitude.

That assumption is significant. We have vast disparities in wealth in the United States, and we do not ordinarily assume that the disparity by itself creates injustice. Indeed, the whole premise of the free market is that what Adam Smith called the "invisible hand" will produce all the economic justice we need. So this assumption is not universally accepted—but is it valid? Ought we go beyond market forces and economic power to seek justice for future generations of people and other species? Do the people and the planet really deserve a better deal, without having done anything to earn it?

CONFERENCES

The calling of a world conference brings with it another group of assumptions. Some of these are straightforward and factual: We have discovered, through the best application of available science, that problems foreseeably arising from actions that affect the natural environment cannot be addressed by one person, region, or even nation, for they affect resources that are truly global—air, climate, oceans, and the diversity of species. Some of the assumptions are problematic and political: for instance, that humans from all over the world should, and can, all work together to accomplish a common good. This claim sounds reasonable enough, but all the evidence of human experience argues against it. We can, and do, fight and die for our own groups and nations, but we have tremendous difficulty seeing our own interests as linked with humanity's. We compete easily and cooperate with difficulty. The convening of the conference at Rio bespeaks infinite hope. This chapter will evaluate that hope, consider the problems that arise in realizing it, and look for ways to render it operational in the future.

There was some basis for that hope: Twenty years before Rio was the first such meeting in history, the United Nations Conference on the Human Environment, the Stockholm Conference, was held in that city in 1972. That conference recognized environmental issues as global concerns for the first time and was marked by a number of prescient statements, including Indira Gandhi's question, "How can we speak to those who live in villages and in slums about keeping the oceans, the rivers, and the air clean when their own lives are contaminated at the source?" That conference produced 109 recommendations, international treaties on ocean dumping, protection of endangered species, and whale hunting, and ended in the creation of the United Nations Environment Program (UNEP), which has been monitoring the global environment ever since.[2] The Stockholm delegates proclaimed that "the capability of man [sic] to improve the environment increases with each passing day." Russell Train, one of the delegates, called the conference "a catalytic event that raised consciousness about the issue and energized politicians."[3]

Since the Stockholm Conference, three factors have governed the consideration of environmental problems by industrialized nations: economic feasibility, scientific consensus, and public safety. The United States has concentrated primarily on the first factor; other industrialized nations have been more willing to consider the other two. The world community has also informally adopted what is called the "precautionary principle," the belief that action should be taken even without firm scientific evidence that an environmental threat is real. (This belief was first evidenced by the Montreal Protocol, which called for cuts in ozone-depleting gases, despite the lack of proof of cause and effect at that time.)[4]

Ten years later, the second Environmental Conference in Nairobi reinforced the statements from Stockholm, started to plan the Rio Conference, and also appointed the World Commission on Environment and Development, to be headed by Gro Brundtland, the Prime Minister of Norway and a highly respected global environmentalist. It was probably the Brundtland Commission Report, *Our Common Future*, released in 1987, more than any single document or event, that brought the extreme complexity of contemporary environmental issues to the forefront. The report laid the groundwork for understanding that economics and the environment are irrevocably intertwined, and introduced policymakers to the concept of sustainable development. Later, the Montreal Protocol mandated reduction in CFCs. Then, the Second World Climate Conference was held in Geneva in 1990; by 1991, the Global Environmental Facility had evolved as an international institution to facilitate the flow of money for environmental cleanup from the rich to the poor.

With this history of modest success as motivator, the United Nations General Assembly passed Resolution #44/228 in December, 1989, calling for a United Nations Conference on the Environment and Development (UNCED) to be held June 1–12, 1992. The conference soon acquired the nickname of "Earth Summit" and—after Rio de Janeiro was chosen as the site and the commencement of the conference was imminent—merely "Rio."[5] Rio de Janeiro, Brazil, was an interesting choice of location: Brazil is a Third World country with one-third of the world's forest and one-fifth of the world's fresh water, the fifth-largest nation in the world in area and the sixth-largest in population.[6]

GOALS

The goals of the Rio Conference included an "Earth Charter," to set down principles of environmental behavior, and "Agenda 21," a list suggesting the implementation of such principles, as well as substantive treaties on global warming, deforestation, and biodiversity, to be signed by heads of states and ratified by world legislative bodies. James Gustave Speth, President of the World Resources Institute, felt that the word "conference" was a misnomer, that the event was really a mega-negotiating session to explore the connection between environmental degradation and underdevelopment and to promote environmental protection and economic development.[7] More simply, the goal at Rio was to "devise a way that countries may pursue economic growth that does not result in environmental destruction."[8]

Maurice Strong, a Canadian diplomat who had headed the Stockholm Conference, was asked by U.N. Secretary General Javier Perez de Cuellar to be the Secretary General of this conference also. Strong, the son of a poor railway worker, ran away from home at 14 and made his fortune in oil. (He has confessed to having been an "environmental sinner" at one time.) He is known for his diverse interests; he also ran Canada's foreign-aid program. Michael Oppenheimer of the Environmental Defense Fund described Strong as "a unique character whose background has enabled him to convince business and political leaders to take the environment seriously."[9]

Once Strong had been assigned the task, he began immediately to set the scene for fruitful negotiations. The first problem he confronted was the polarization of the world along political and economic lines. Now that the Cold War is over, a conflict hitherto overshadowed has come into focus: the conflict between the rich, high-consumption, high-emission, resource-exploiting North and the poor, over-populated, deforesting, materially ambitious South. The conflict arises with the realization that, if the South, with about four-fifths of the world's 5.5 billion people, were to attain the living standards of the North, via the routes that the North used (burning fossil fuels, using the land without limit, polluting the air and water, and creating more and more ecosystem-threatening products), there would simply be no hope for the survival of the planet— at least as we now know it.

So, Strong set out to convince the Third World that pollution is no better than poverty; to convince the North to spend their former military budgets on the environment; and to convince Japan to get more interested in environmental issues as foreign-policy matters. One ambassador said, "Strong crosses the North–South line and the public–private line better than anyone else in the world," and Strong himself said, "This [conference] will not lay an egg."[10]

WARMING UP: THE "PREP COMS"

Four preparatory committee meetings ("Prep Coms") were scheduled for August, 1990, in Nairobi; March and August, 1991, in Geneva; and April, 1992, in New York. Individual nations were asked to prepare an accounting of their national experience in environmental affairs since 1972. Regional reports were prepared, and three working groups were organized to deal with climate change, biodiversity, management of biotechnology, protection of the oceans and fresh water resources, and legal and institutional issues involved in the Earth Charter.

The International Council of Scientific Unions (ICSU), a well-respected nongovernmental organization (NGO) that represented 75 national Academies of Science, was asked by Strong to be the official science adviser to the entire conference. A *nongovernmental organization* is a nonprofit international organization, such as the International Red Cross, with a cultural or humanitarian agenda of its own but that is beholden to no government. NGOs from all over the world brought to Rio agendas ranging from the protection of indigenous peoples in rainforests to the prevention of flooding island nations. NGOs tend to be impartial, reliable, and carry clout in situations where nations can become locked in conflict, because of their international scope and independence, and also (on occasion) because of the world-respected leaders that govern them.

The Alliance of Small Island States met to discuss their concerns that global warming might well cause enough ocean rise to inundate their nations. There were also conferences on individual issues, such as the status of women, agriculture, finance, technology, and health; the findings were reported to the Prep Coms. Generally, the conference was organized so that research and negotiations would precede each Prep Com, which in turn would prepare positions to be signed at Rio, but it didn't quite work out that way.[11]

The very complexity of the enterprise created a circus atmosphere, especially in conference logistics. Preparations had to be made for the arrival of the representatives of the NGOs. The "Global Forum," a few miles from the actual meeting place, was set aside to accommodate 400 workshops and 650 exhibition stands for the 10,250 registrants representing 2,202 NGOs from 116 nations—at a cost of $1 billion to Rio.[12] To this mass migration was added the excitement engendered by Brazil's own problems at the time: President Fernando Collor de Mello was accused of corruption (on September 29, 1992, he was impeached on those charges); there were fears of a possible cholera epidemic; there was conflict with an Islamic festival; and, just before the conference, Collor fired his own environmental chief, an official who was highly regarded internationally for his efforts to save the Amazon.

Brazil was always sensitive on the topic of deforestation and had planned to claim that it was down from burning 11,580 square miles to 4,299 square miles over a one-year period (that is, that an area only twice the size of Delaware had been burned in the past year).[13] In the middle of all this, President Collor was calling President Bush, urging him to attend the conference, while preparing for 30,000 attendees. Of these attendees, there were 60 heads of state, including those from most industrialized nations.[14]

SUSTAINABILITY: THE BATTLE IS JOINED

The North came to the table with ideas about how the South should live *sustainably*—that is, without polluting and without diminishing the resource base and, incidentally, accepting a lifestyle of modest consumption. The South arrived very angry at the North for causing the major part of the global ecological crisis and then having the gall to ask them not to behave in the same way. The South was also prepared to ask the North what price it would be willing to pay to have the South develop in an environmentally acceptable way. In a long indictment, the South blamed the North for exploitation of resources, for the nuclear arms race, for CFC production, and for carbon dioxide emissions and asked the North to change its overconsumptive ways; also, the South argued, the North should compensate the South for avoiding the Northern sins, for not following in its footsteps.

One American diplomat described the Southern attitude as, "You've had your turn; you're fat, happy, and breathing dirty air and you have no trees. We want our turn and when we're rich, we can start worrying about the environment."[15] The North had arrived expecting the South to understand that it must not develop the way the North had done; the North wanted the South to reduce its population and stop cutting down its forests (while tactfully avoiding any discussion of the cutting of the great forests in the North).[16] "The more I watch this," commented Michael McCloskey, of the Sierra Club, "the more I come to understand that it really does turn on the idea of a global bargain."[17]

A bargain entails bargaining power. The *Third World*, the less developed or developing nations—collectively, the South—had lost bargaining power at the end of the Cold War and the East–West confrontation, because they could no longer sell themselves as military clients to the highest bidder. From the data available on the environmental sins of the First World, the South attempted to draw new leverage for the negotiations. Paul and Anne Erhlich frequently define North–South differences, for instance, in population terms: "Measured by commercial energy use, each American, on average, causes 70 times the environmental damage as a Ugandan or Laotian, 20 times an Indian, 10 times a Chinese, and roughly twice that of the U.K., France, Sweden or Australia. Viewed in this light, the U.S. is the world's most overpopulated nation."[18]

As another example of the confrontation, in negotiations about deforestation, Brazil wanted the word *tropical* removed and cautioned that the United States especially was contributing as much to the problem in its own Northwest as they were in Brazil. The sins of the Second World were not forgotten, and there were complaints that Eastern Europe was taking too much attention (and foreign aid) from poorer nations.

Bargaining positions were adopted in the Prep Coms on sensitive issues of national sovereignty: It was decided, for instance, that the country that owned the rainforest should benefit from any pharmaceutical discoveries made within its boundaries and that any intrusion into a nation's population policy was a threat to national sovereignty.[19]

So *sustainability* became the catchword of the conference. Sustainability "posits that economic growth cannot take place at the expense of the Earth's natural capital—its stock of renewable and non-renewable resources… Humanity has the ability to make development sustainable—to ensure that it meets the needs of the present without compromising the ability of future generations to meet their own needs."[20] A twin to sustainable development is the notion that, if it is to occur, it must go hand in hand with improved lifestyles for the least fortunate: "Unless the multiple facets of poverty are dealt with, we have little hope of reducing the environmental damage of people eking out a living on fragile ecosystems."[21] Sustainability was the club that both sides could wield as the positions became clear and the battle continued.

THE GREENHOUSE ISSUE

The climate change (global warming) treaty commanded the most publicity about preconference jockeying, primarily because the United States ended up standing alone. The generally accepted scientific consensus is that increased emissions of "greenhouse gases," especially carbon dioxide, will cause an increase in the average global temperature that, in turn, could cause tremendous global ecological disruptions, resulting in changes in agricultural systems, increased flooding in low-lying areas, increased storm intensity, and other unknown global perturbations. The problem is that the burning of fossil fuels (coal, oil, and natural gas) produce the most carbon dioxide, and fossil fuels keep the U.S. economy going. Indeed, the United States is the single largest emitter of carbon dioxide. While the European industrialized nations and Japan were all committed to a cap on carbon dioxide emissions at the 1990 level by the year 2000, the U.S. position was that such an agreement would cause further economic disruption to an economy already in recession and was, therefore, unacceptable.

Was that a legitimate objection? As the conference proceeds, we find the United States often isolated in positions centered on national interest—insisting that, because U.S. interests would be damaged by a certain provision, the United States simply could not consider the provision. It is reasonable to protect national interests, but the point of such a bargaining session is that each side must give up some of its interest to promote the common good and, ultimately, the good of each. Can the leader of a country agree to damage even a little of the interests of his nation, however, absent a specific authorization from his own people? What was that leader elected to do?

At Rio, the official rationale for the U.S. rejection of the climate change treaty was that the science itself might well be flawed, and that any agreement should be flexible and tailored individually to each country; further, that European or Japanese arguments in favor of the treaty could be discounted as political (they were just playing to their own "green" constituencies) and self-interested (they were just exploiting their advantage in the efficient-energy technologies). At any rate, the United States said, we are already contributing to reducing greenhouse gases, equal to the proposed cap, because of our cuts in CFC production and our plans to plant many trees, which would absorb plenty of carbon dioxide.

Virtually the entire rest of the world lined up against the U.S. position. The United States is known as the largest consumer of fossil fuels and energy, the worst offender when it comes to carbon dioxide emissions (the United States is responsible for one-fourth of the world's emissions), and it happens also to be the world's richest nation and best able to absorb the economic costs of reducing the pollution. The delegates tended, grimly, to see the U.S. commitment to a decrease in carbon dioxide as an indication of how much the industrialized nations were truly committed to shouldering their share of the global burden.

The U.S. position was by no means supported by U.S. scientists nor those of the usual allies. After the departure of John Sununu, President Bush's former Chief of Staff (notorious for his opposition to giving any credence to the possibility of global warming), the Environmental Protection Agency released a paper that had "been shelved in the days of Mr. Sununu,"[22] demonstrating that a cap on carbon dioxide would not cost the economy anywhere near the price suggested by other White House departments. Also, a report of the Union of Concerned Scientists contradicted Sununu's assertions that decreasing carbon dioxide emissions would cause economic disruption; in fact, the report showed that the energy saved would ultimately result in corporate savings.[23]

A further development questioned the validity of Bush administration claims about another greenhouse gas: Research by the U.N. Intergovernmental Panel on Climate Change revealed that CFCs, although uncontestedly greenhouse gases, also result in atmospheric cooling because of their destruction of ozone, which warms the atmosphere.[24] This finding undercut the White House contention that U.S. reduction in CFC production would contribute to a reduction in global warming. None of this scientific work found its way into the official U.S. position at the Rio Conference.

Not all U.S. policymakers were aligned with the official Bush administration position. Then-Senator Albert Gore (a U.S. delegate at the convention) said that President Bush had shown "an abdication of leadership" and served "the forces of short-term greed." Bush retorted that his "environmental strategy...seeks to merge economic and environmental goals..."[25] Bush found himself without allies. Gore and the other delegates found Bush's strategy painfully transparent: Bush was running for reelection; Americans were out of work; jobs and the economy were the big election issues; it is easy (if false) to blame loss of jobs on environmental regulation; therefore, Americans will be happy with their president, and will reelect him, if he opposes environmental regulation.

Tommy Koh, a respected diplomat from Singapore, probably summed up many delegates' feelings when he said, "The U.N. must never hold a conference during an American election year."[26] *Must* an upcoming American election have the effect of rendering the United States totally worthless in world affairs for the duration of that year? Where do the legitimate claims of the political process leave off and the legitimate claims of the world begin, and vice versa?

As the negotiations were nearing the final Prep Com, speculation began about the political implications (for the conference) of President Bush's stands on the issues before Rio. He still had not announced whether or not he would attend, his advisers were worried that he might be walking into a political nightmare if he did attend, and it was assumed that he would not sign a carbon dioxide treaty unless the language were changed to avoid the set limits. In an attempt to overcome some of the image-damaging isolation, Bush reversed his position and announced that the United States would contribute $75 million to help developing countries deal with emission controls. The Bush administration was probably none too pleased by the conference's response: "a very encouraging first step" said a British delegate; "it is clear that the President has abandoned the Flat Earth Society approach to global warming..." said a Sierra Club spokesperson.[27]

While economists played with figures to find acceptable language for President Bush,[28] U.S. representatives at a Prep Com meeting were vetoing the following language: "...one of the most serious problems now facing the planet is that associated with historical patterns of unsustainable consumption and production, leading to environmental degradation, aggravation of poverty, and imbalances in the developments of countries."[29] By May 13, when the Bush administration announced that Bush would attend the meeting, the climate treaty had been watered down enough (no mention of caps) for him to sign it.[30]

THE BIODIVERSITY ISSUE

The other controversial proposal concerned biodiversity. The U.S. position on that, although less publicized, was as negative as its position on global warming. A treaty agreed to by 98 nations in Nairobi on May 22 called for integrating species and ecosystem protection into economic planning, while emphasizing that abolishing poverty is the first concern of the Third World nations in which most endangered species exist. The proposed reconciliation of these disparate objectives required the infusion of money from rich nations to help poorer ones develop in a sustainable fashion. The U.S. position was that its biotechnology industry would be threatened by the treaty and thus the treaty should not be signed as written. Although President Bush had committed himself to going to the Rio meeting and signing a compromise global warming treaty, as he left for the meeting, there was no consensus on whether any other progress that required U.S. cooperation would occur.[31]

When the conference finally began, Brazil welcomed representatives from 178 nations, including 118 heads of state, 8,000 journalists, and 10,000 environmentalists.[32] The atmosphere took on the adversarial tones of the preparation period soon enough, in the inevitable conflicts and confrontations between the richer Northern nations and the poorer Southern nations; Southern anger focused inevitably, on the United States.[33]

It was easy, too easy, to cast the United States as a villain. The news that this nation would not sign a climate treaty that had specific targets and timetables preceded the delegation to the conference, and this was exacerbated by the news that the United States would probably not sign the Biodiversity Treaty either. President Bush's last-minute pledge of $150 million for forest protection was greeted with skepticism as a cynical attempt to divert attention from other U.S. failures to support this massive international effort. According to James Brooke in *The New York Times*, there was "anti-American sentiment not seen since the days of the Vietnam war." A Brazilian congressman is quoted as saying "United States intransigence is recreating the polarized atmosphere of the 1960s: all civil society and the press are against the United States."[34]

That statement is surely extreme, but such assertions were entirely acceptable in the ugly mood of the conference as the day of President Bush's arrival approached. The feeling was tense enough to cause U.N. officials, who feared demonstrations, to limit press access—and the access of some of their own officials—to the proceedings when President Bush was due to arrive. About 150 nongovernmental U.S. environmentalists marched, displaying banners that stated, "George Bush, you are embarrassing us," and "Bush: Lead Or Get Out Of The Way."[35] One English-language newspaper headlined: "U.S. Singled Out as ECO Bad Guy,"[36] and another local paper published a cartoon picturing President Bush as a devil with horns and a forked tail.[37]

Why the intensity of the resentment against Bush? Partly because, given the commitment to cooperation presupposed by the convening of the conference, the U.S. position could be seen as morally unacceptable but, in large part, also because the United States is the quintessential Northerner. North and South were squared off against each other and, this time—for the first time—the South finally had an environmental bargaining chip in its negotiations with the richer, more powerful North. You don't have to be a rocket scientist to figure out that, if four-fifths of the world's population pollutes the world to the same degree that one-fifth already has (only over the last hundred years or so), the biosphere, at least as we know it and would like to have it, is doomed.

So the South could say to the North: "You want us *not* to behave as you did? Then pay, and *stop* acting that way yourselves." India's State Environment Minister, Kamal Nath, exclaimed, "At meeting after meeting, we have told the developed world, especially the United States, that the North has far greater responsibility to clean up its act. They have polluted the most, per capita and in gross national terms, and they should carry the burden of cleaning up."[38]

One very attractive formula for reform had emerged from one of the Prep Coms: "We all have the right to the same standard of living. You (the North) may decide what it shall be." The implications of the formula included massive North-to-South subsidies to bring the South up to the North's standard of living; or massive sacrifices in energy use and other consumption on the part of the North, to bring it down to the South's standard; or both.

Let us pause to examine this suggestion. The justice of it is evident: The most attractive feature of the bargain is that it is absolutely fair. Among the first alternative (bring all up to the Northern standard) and the second (bring all down to the Southern standard) and the third (bring all to a standard in between), there is no difference, as far as the human condition is concerned. The vast disparities listed in the paragraph that opens this chapter would be eradicated, the solution achieved.

These alternatives are not at all equivalent, however, as far as the natural environment is concerned: If the ideal of equality at the Northern level is ever achieved, the Earth is doomed. Earth dictates one and only one of these alternate positions: Reduce the standard of living; stop polluting the air; have many fewer children; slow down manufacturing and service; go back to primitive agriculture, if possible (better yet, rediscover the nomadic hunter-gatherer life); in short, *back off*. We will not find that perspective well-articulated here at Rio; Rio was, essentially, about human beings, not about the Earth.

THE CONFRONTATION CONTINUES

Even human truths were hard to get across at Rio, though. The negotiators from the Third World had difficulty persuading their richer neighbors that, as far as they were concerned, environmental protection is linked to economic growth, to raising living standards out of poverty. "You cannot freeze people into permanent poverty while the West continues to sustain unsustainable life-styles," said Indian diplomat Chandrashekar Dasqupta.[39] Northern delegates complained meanwhile that they were already financing Southern development, with funds that were sometimes misused and diverted to corrupt politicians.[40] The crux of the matter, as one U.S. delegate stated flatly, is that "the United States standard of living is not up for negotiation." The U.S. delegation fought virtually every mention of changes in Northern habits of high consumption in any document.[41]

The conflicts built into the situation at the conference made cooperation very difficult. The South wanted assurances that the North would pay, not only for cleaning up its own mess but also for instituting sustainable technologies in the South. The North wanted to monitor the South's economic development in general and, specifically, to be sure that foreign-aid funds were being properly used. The North wanted the South to control population growth, although pressure from the Pope had succeeded in removing all language on population control and family planning from the documents under consideration. (Under similar pressure, of different origin, the Reagan administration had previously agreed not to allow foreign-aid funds to be used for any program that includes abortion as a population control alternative.)

The poorer Southern nations' suspicion that the North's commitment to global environmentalism was less than sincere was intensified when word got around that President Bush would not sign the Biodiversity Treaty. The consensus was that the treaty favored Third World nations (there were financial advantages built into the treaty), whereas the Climate Treaty was more favorable to the industrialized nations (it provided for less carbon dioxide production worldwide, a blow to the less-developed nations, especially those like China, with large coal reserves). That discrepancy itself became a bargaining point; some Southern delegates asserted that, "If the North won't do Biodiversity, the South won't do Climate." That simple formula fell apart as the Southern coalition found itself badly divided on other issues: The poor island nations were enthusiastic about a treaty that would address the flooding predicted to accompany global warming, whereas some countries with tropical forests felt that the Biodiversity Treaty threatened their sovereignty.[42]

There yet remained the Southern suspicion that the convention's dedication to "sustainable development" was merely a recycled attitude that would maintain the Southern existence "of poverty and dependence while Northern economies continue their profligate ways."[43] The resentment over the global distribution of wealth was based in fact: In the host country itself, the wealthiest 20 percent are 26 times richer than the poorest 20 percent (as compared to a 9:1 gap in the United States); in the world as a whole, the ratio is 150:1![44]

SUMMARY: THE FOCAL TREATIES

The Climate Treaty

As we have mentioned, the U.S. opposition to a strong, specific climate treaty resulted in its virtual isolation from the rest of the world. The convention saw the attitudes of the industrialized world toward reducing carbon dioxide emissions—and, by implication, reducing fossil fuel use, thus reducing industrial output GNP, national income, and standard of living—as a test of its sincerity regarding the threat of global climate change. Of the delegations, India and China were especially suspicious of both the North's attitude and the effect of the treaty itself on their countries. Both countries were still reeling from the London Conference on the use of ozone-depleting CFCs that resulted in a decision to phase out the chemicals entirely. Together, these two countries, with 33 percent of the world's population, used only 2 percent of the world's CFCs, but because these chemicals are the cheapest refrigerants known, they were prominent in the development plans of both nations.[45]

The climate treaty itself was watered down to suit the current U.S. administration, and it was clear by now that President Bush would come to Rio to sign it. Ultimately, this version of the treaty received more than the requisite 50 signatures—including that of India, who had not yet signed the CFC treaty. Other industrialized nations started drives to prepare supplementary documents. Germany pushed for an additional treaty *with* targets and timetables for those who wished to sign it; Austria, Switzerland, and the Netherlands urged commitments to immediately stabilizing carbon dioxide emissions at current levels. William K. Reilly, Administrator of the U.S. Environmental Protection Agency and head of the U.S. delegation, tried to defuse the German effort with quiet lobbying. He was not at all helped by Senator Gore, who announced that he found it "incomprehensible that we would object to other countries declaring that they want to meet targets and timetables."[46]

The Biodiversity Treaty

The U.S. opposition to the Biodiversity Treaty withstood numerous attempts to break it. Although the treaty needed only 30 nations to ratify it to go into effect, it required Northern approbation, because U.S. dollars were written into it. The treaty also provided for technical assistance from the North and pledged to protect threatened areas, restore damaged ecosystems, integrate protection into economic planning, and promote sustainable development of ecologically valuable sites, through nondamaging industry such as ecotourism and the harvesting of food and medicine. The isolated U.S. position was based on a perceived threat to its biotechnology industry (the possibility of shared patents) and on the ambiguity of the funding provisions. Although the treaty contained stipulations for future meetings to make amendments, the United States came to Rio determined to oppose it.[47]

Originally, both Japan and the United Kingdom were inclined to go along with the U.S. position, acknowledging the failings of some portions of the treaty, but "green" groups at home caused them to change their stand. When they announced that they would sign the treaty, along with Germany and Canada, the United States was again alone. That left Reilly, as head of the U.S. delegation, with the task of calming the waters. He might very well have wished he had stayed home.

The delegation was consistently on the defensive. As the United States became more and more isolated, Reilly tried mightily to find a way that

President Bush could sign the Biodiversity Treaty—by meeting with delegates of other nations and exploring compromises that might satisfy the President. On June 1, he met with Brazilian officials and came away with suggestions for changes in the treaty; on June 2, he called Clayton Yeutter, the White House Director of Domestic Policy, and alerted him to some possible compromises; on June 3, he faxed a memo with a draft of the proposed changes to Yeutter, urging acceptance, and said that the U.S. position was "the major subject of the press and delegate concern here." On June 4, this memo was leaked to *The New York Times* by an administration official, apparently to embarrass Reilly and to block his efforts. The U.S. position did not change. Reilly, normally a mild-mannered man, was reportedly furious and extremely embarrassed that his attempt to convince the White House had been made public.

President Bush deplored the leak and publicly supported Reilly, saying "For someone...opposed...to the treaty, or any changes, to leak it, it's insidious."[48] Yet the damage was done, and Reilly had been discredited. Members of other delegations were appalled. One Brazilian diplomat said, "What is the White House trying to do to their man here?" Reilly himself said it was "most unfortunate that some chose to leak information...about efforts that demanded diplomatic discretion." Another (anonymous) delegate said, "Reilly's embarrassment contributes to a growing climate of cynicism about the U.S. in Rio," and suggested that the leak was "a little hand grenade from a middle-level White House staffer to whom 'biodiversity' is a disease." Senator Gore commented that "once again the principle official in charge of the U.S. environmental policy has been overruled—and this time the whole world is watching."[49] To no avail was an eleventh-hour attempt by Japan, France, and the United Kingdom, to get the United States to sign, by proposing a separate paper describing the U.S. administration's interpretation and allowing a U.S. veto over financing.[50]

The Forest Treaty

At this point, friends of the United States proclaimed that the U.S. isolation at the conference had reached a crisis stage. Their representatives met with U.S. delegates in an attempt to figure out a way to diffuse the anti-American sentiment at the conference. They decided that they would all enthusiastically support the U.S. forest initiatives. From the beginning, President Bush had evinced an interest in preserving the world's forests (to the amusement—at best—of some, given that the U.S. Forest Service had been allowing clear-cutting in the magnificent U.S. Northwest). Forest preservation seemed an attractive way to reduce atmospheric carbon dioxide. But U.S. efforts to generate a comprehensive treaty on forest preservation were thwarted by Third World nations, where deforestation for fuel is common and where lumber export is sometimes a major source of income; they objected to what they saw as an invasion of their sovereignty.[51]

When the United States started to push the forest initiative, it was greeted with a certain amount of skepticism. Many developing nations pointed to U.S. destruction of its old growth in the Pacific Northwest and its status, with Malaysia, as one of the top two lumber exporters, and dismissed the initiative as a political ploy for consumption at home, while indicating that they would do whatever they pleased with their own forests. Other industrialized nations and many nongovernmental organizations supported the agreement just for the sake of reaching an agreement, although it was considered weaker than some conventions already in existence. To support the initiative, William Reilly announced that the United States would stop clear-cutting; he also noted that, overall, the United States had a good forest record and that its forests were more extensive now than a hundred years ago.[52] (Some critics noted that this is because the United States abandoned many small farms that have since reverted to forests.) Even as Reilly was announcing the Bush plan to save the world's forests, the administration in Washington was introducing legislation to open four million more acres in the Northwest to lumbering.

As it became increasingly apparent that the forest treaty might not be ratified, President Bush announced that the United States would spend $150 million to save forests in the Third World and encouraged others to jump on the bandwagon.[53] When even that move failed to garner support, the U.S. delegation promoted a post-Rio conference on forests, to produce a nonbinding treaty; that suggestion acquired few backers. As a last-ditch effort, as the conference neared the end, parliamentary processes were streamlined in the hope that some consensus could be reached on the forests. According to some delegates, the adversary atmosphere was still too strong, and the determination to embarrass the United States persisted.

THE BOTTOM LINE: THE LESSONS OF RIO

What was accomplished at Rio? What was not accomplished? and What did it all mean? Two major documents, signed by all, expressed ideals and principles but were nonbinding:

The **Rio Declaration** established the link between environmental cleanup and economic development in the Third World, asserting that the first cannot occur without the second and that industrialized nations will have to help the Third World to clean up.

Agenda 21, signed by all delegates (President Bush had reservations but went along), was an 800-page laundry list of environmental and social priorities for the twenty-first century; it addressed ocean dumping, hazardous waste, human health, women's status, poverty, and so forth—a blueprint for cleaning up the planet that also reiterated the United Nations' long-standing goal of getting the richer nations to donate 0.7 percent of their Gross Domestic Product to poorer ones. (The United States has never come close to that figure, but the standard is achievable; Norway reached it long ago.)

The **Climate Treaty** was watered down to placate President Bush, with no targets or timetables, and signed by all 153 nations. It did contain *pledges* by signatories to reduce greenhouse gases and, most important, it provided for future consideration of global warming if events should warrant it. (Just such a provision in the Montreal Protocol allowed the nations to reconvene, when ozone depletion became greater than expected, and reach agreement to stop all CFC production.)

The **Biodiversity Treaty,** described earlier, was signed by all nations except the United States. The treaty is, however, open for signing for a year following the conference, which leaves some hope on the horizon.

No treaty or formal agreement was reached on **Forest Preservation,** but a statement on principles did emerge, and further negotiation is expected.

No decision was reached on the mechanics of transferring **Money** from the industrialized nations to Third World nations, to help them develop in a sustainable manner. Nevertheless, funds were pledged. Generally, the North wanted funds managed by existing international financial institutions, such as the World Bank, whereas the presumed recipients wanted more control. In the end, the South deferred on the U.N.'s 0.7-percent GDP goal (which, if universally enacted, would double aid to the Third World); in turn, the developed nations promised to try to meet the goals of Agenda 21, which is meaningless without Northern dollars.

There was practically no movement on **Population Control,** although the subject is mentioned in Agenda 21. Diverse groups joined with those in the Third World that resented being lectured on population control, especially by the very rich nations that cause most of the environmental degradation. The Pope, some women's rights groups, and Islamic groups joined in stonewalling the issue.

The delegates did form a **Sustainable Development Committee,** designed to oversee individual nations' compliance with the treaties and the non-binding agreements but with no enforcement power. Governments will be asked to report to the committee, however, and individual nongovernmental organizations (NGOs) are expected to be the whistle-blowers on non-compliance, just as private human rights groups, such as Amnesty International, keep the U.N. Human Rights Commission informed. (Bad publicity has a power all its own.) The British were in the forefront of advocating the commission; India and China—two who joined the United States as the foot-draggers of the conference—went along unenthusiastically. The

Bush administration went along too, kicking and screaming but unwilling to risk further adverse publicity after the biodiversity scuffle.

One perhaps unexpected development of the conference was the integration of NGOs dedicated to environmental advocacy from around the world. Presumably, many networks evolved that will serve the formal governments well in the future, especially as watchdogs for the Sustainable Development Committee. It is entirely possible that this union of like-minded volunteers will produce the most powerful force for the environment that the Earth has yet seen; the next century will determine this.

It is too early to propose a final evaluation of the conference. It might have been, overall, a "...fractious 12 days of diplomatic free-for-all among 178 nations," as William K. Stevens described it in *The New York Times*.[54] The U.S. performance was disappointing by virtually all accounts. President Bush's final news conference was defensive, denouncing critics in Rio and at home; other administration officials attempted to blunt the effects of the U.S. isolation at the conference by downsizing its importance, suggesting that some Northern nations had no intention of conforming to the provisions in treaties they had signed. White House aides were pleased at what they saw as excellent politics at home for an election year—the U.S. hard line against environmental regulation, sure to appeal to the political right and the unemployed.

The performances of many other nations was hardly inspiring, however. India and China evinced similar tendencies toward obstruction. Said one frustrated U.S. delegate, "Every time the U.S. says something [about the forest proposal], India pops up and says the opposite." India's perspective on the proposal, of course, was that "it was neither new, nor was it an initiative."[55] By the midpoint of the conference, Eugene Linden reported that "trivialities and private agendas derailed serious debate over the plan of action called Agenda 21. Arab delegates pushed for oblique references to emotional and irrelevant issues like the plight of Israel's occupied territories, while oil states worked to strip out any language implying that petroleum might be bad for the environment..."[56] Bringing the nations to work together in harmony will never be easy; indeed, the ideal of unity in pursuit of common purpose might possibly be beyond human capability.

POLITICS AND
NATIONAL INTEREST

There was general agreement among the delegates that the Bush entourage was playing to the conservative right at home; that the conference would have been more successful with a more positive U.S. leadership; and that the United States, once considered the world leader in environmental issues, had abdicated that leadership, ironically, at a time when those issues had reached top international priority.

Yet, there is some doubt about the ultimate political value of the Bush administration's tactics, even in the Bush camp's own terms. The effect on the 1992 presidential election is, of course, well known. Beyond the election, though, is the crumbling state of U.S. industry and the chronic failure to market U.S. products abroad—both strong causal elements in the recession. The assumption behind the "Competitiveness Council," run by (then) Vice President Dan Quayle, was that environmental regulation (requirements that products and the processes that make them be harmless or beneficial to the natural environment) work against the present and future prosperity of business and, by raising production costs, make it harder for our products to compete in world markets. We might have this backward: Both Germany and Japan, makers of many of the automobiles gracing U.S. roadways, seem to see economic benefits in environmental technology and believe that energy efficiency will eventually benefit business. If these nations turn out more environmentally safe products than the best of ours and pass the tougher environmental rules to match, they will inevitably compete favorably in our markets, laws or no laws. What is worse, they will be able to squeeze us out of their markets by demanding that our products conform to *their* laws (a reasonable request).

Japan's interest in the conference was illustrated by the size of their delegation: 100 delegates as opposed to 45 from the U.S. Their enthusiasm was also matched by our customary allies in Northern Europe. As Paul Lewis phrased it in *The New York Times,* Japan and the Northern allies "unlike the Administration...see safeguarding the environment as an unavoidable challenge that will strengthen their industry in the long run, not as a new and sinister threat to their way of life."[57]

Despite all the haggling and politicking at Rio, it appeared that a consensus had been produced: that the environment has top international priority and that progress will not occur unless the nations' economies are factored into the equation. (The factoring can be done, as the delegates observed, in more or less enlightened ways.) The conference closed with the remarks of U.N. Secretary-General Boutros Boutros-Ghali: "Today we have agreed to hold to present levels the pollution we are guilty of. One day we will have to do better—clean up the planet."[58]

Since the Rio summit, some helpful changes have taken place. The Clinton administration is reversing "the Bush administration's diplomatic floundering at the Earth Summit..."[59] U.S. officials are predicting that, at the talks in Geneva to renegotiate the International Tropical Timber Agreement of 1987, an agreement could be reached between tropical and temperate countries that both shall log their forests in a sustainable fashion, with regard to long-term preservation. (Tropical timber exporters in Rio insisted that Northern exporters be included in any agreement, a position that was opposed by the United States at the time.)[60]

Additionally, President Clinton made an Earth Day announcement that the United States would comply with the cap of reducing greenhouse gases to 1990 levels by the year 2000 and that he would sign the Biodiversity Treaty.[61] Earth Day, April 22, has apparently acquired a permanent home in the U.S. calendar, and there is reason to believe that the protection of the environment lies close to the heart of people highly placed in this administration. Stay tuned.

QUESTIONS FOR DISCUSSION AND REFLECTION

+ There can be no doubt that Rio left frustration in its wake, but the process itself seems to have been valuable for the participants. Consider the following comments:

> Enrique Penalosa, who led the Colombian delegation:

> The two-year preparation period had brought the issues of sustainable development—progress without destruction of the environment—before hundreds of officials from developing countries [who would take them home].

and again,

> Even if the conference has been a failure on specific treaties, it would be a success...because for the first time we are alerting the planet that development is not necessarily good if it sacrifices future generations.[62]

+ Also underlined at Rio was what we do *not* know. As Vaclav Havel, then President of Czechoslovakia, said,

> The world we live in is made up of an immensely complex and mysterious tissue about which we know very little and which we must treat with utmost humility.[63]

+ What, finally, can we say with certainty? What is the primary lesson to emerge from Rio? That the global environmental situation is too complicated to do anything about at all? That some individuals can still be effective—but only in negative ways?

+ Is collective action on global problems possible at all? If the answer to that question is negative, should such high-profile conferences as

UNCED in Rio be discontinued? Or do we believe that collective process has value even though collective results are unlikely?

+ Some have suggested that there is hope that the agreements reached, even compromised, will serve as the foundation for building the tougher and more effective conventions of the future. Where should we start? What sorts of conventions would do the most good?

Notes

1. Will Nixon, "Can Talking Heads Save an Ailing Planet?" *E Magazine,* vol. III, no. 3 (May/June 1992): p. 37.

2. *Ibid.,* p. 38.

3. William K. Stevens, "Earth Summit Finds the Years of Optimism Are a Fading Memory," *The New York Times* (9 June 1992): p. C4.

4. Peter M. Haas, "Climate Change Negotiations," *Environment* (Jan./Feb. 1992): p. 2.

5. *Ibid.*

6. Elizabeth Heilman Brooke, "As Forests Fall, Environmental Movement Rises in Brazil," *The New York Times* (2 June 1992): p. C4.

7. James Gustave Speth, "On the Road to Sustainability," *Environment, Science and Technology,* vol. 26, no. 6 (June 1992): p. 1075.

8. Scott Bronstein, "Is Bush Trashing Earth Summit? Critics Say Yes," *Atlanta Journal* (3 April 1992).

9. Paul Lewis, "Rio Planner: A Magnate Who Meditates," *The New York Times* (4 June 1992): p. A10.

10. John Newhouse, "The Diplomatic Round Earth Summit," *The New Yorker* (1 June 1992): p. 64.

11. The details of the preparations that went into the conference are too intricate for our purposes; suffice it to say they were extensive. Sources used as background include: Stephen Collett, "PrepCom 3: Preparing for UNCED," *Environment,* vol. 34, no. 1 (January 1992): p. 3; Judith T. Kildow, "The Earth Summit, We Need More Than a Message," *Environment, Science and Technology,* vol. 26, no. 6 (June 1992): p. 1077; Paul Lewis, "Island Nations Fear a Rise in the Sea," *The New York Times* (17 February 1992).

12. James Brooke, "Cleaning the Environment for Environmentalists," *The New York Times* (14 May 1992): p. A4.

13. James Brooke, "Homesteaders Gnaw at Brazil Rain Forest," *The New York Times* (22 May 1992): p. A1.

14. James Brooke, "For the Environmentalists, Hurdles on the Road to Rio," *The New York Times* (27 March 1992): p. A6.

15. William K. Stevens, "Rio: A Start on Managing What's Left of This Place," *The New York Times* (31 May 1992).

16. John Carey, "Will Saving People Save Our Planet?" *International Wildlife* (May/June 1992): p. 14.

17. Nixon, "Talking Heads," p. 39.

18. Cited in Nixon, "Talking Heads," p. 42.

19. Marlise Simons, "North–South Divide is Marring Environmental Talks," *The New York Times* (17 March 1992): p. A8.

20. Gro Harlem Brundtland, quoted in Nixon, "Talking Heads," p. 39.

21. Joseph C. Wheeler, UNCED's Director of Program Integration, quoted in Carey, "Saving People."

22. William K. Stevens, "Washington Odd Man Out, May Shift on Climate," *The New York Times* (18 February 1992): p. C1.

23. "Viewpoint: USC Tackles Global Problems," *Nucleus*, vol. 14, no. 2 (Summer 1992).

24. Stevens, "Odd Man Out."

25. "U.S. Rejects Limits on Pollution," *Philadelphia Inquirer* (25 March 1992).

26. Newhouse, "Earth Summit."

27. William K. Stevens, "White House Vows Action to Cut U.S. Global Warming Gases," *The New York Times* (28 February 1992): p. A6.

28. Bob Davis, "The Outlook—In Rio They're Eyeing Greenhouse Two-Step," *The Wall Street Journal* (20 April 1992).

29. "The Talk of the Town," *The New Yorker* (4 May 1992): p. 28.

30. Keith Schneider, "Bush Plans to Join Other Leaders at Earth Summit in Brazil in June," *The New York Times* (13 May 1992).

31. William K. Stevens, "Striving for Balance," *The New York Times* (24 May 1992).

32. Tom Bethell, "Rio: What Happened," *Friends of the Earth* (August 1992): p. 8.

33. Stevens, "Earth Summit Finds the Years of Optimism Are a Fading Memory."

34. James Brooke, "U.S. Has a Starring Role at Rio Summit as Villain," *The New York Times* (2 June 1992): p. 10.

35. Eugene Linden, "Rio's Legacy: Despite the squabbles, the Earth Summit could go down in history as a landmark beginning of a serious drive to preserve the planet," *TIME* (22 June 1992): pp. 44–45.

36. James Brooke, "To Protect Bush, UN Will Limit Access to Talks," *The New York Times* (8 June 1992).

37. James Brooke, "Earth Summit Races Clock to Resolve Differences on Forest Treaty," *The New York Times* (10 June 1992): p. A8.

38. Sonjoy Hazarika, "India Dam Plan: Environmental Symbol," *The New York Times* (2 June 1992): p. A10.

39. *Ibid.*

40. Vaclav Havel, "Rio and the New Millennium," *The New York Times* (3 June 1992): Op-ed. section.

41. "The Talk of the Town," *The New Yorker* (29 June 1992): p. 25.

42. Paul Lewis, "Storm in Rio: Morning After," *The New York Times* (15 June 1992): p. A1.

43. Mark Hertsgaard, "A View from El Centro del Mundo," *Amicus Journal* (Fall 1992): p. 12.

44. *Ibid.*

45. Hazarika, "India Dam Plan."

46. Brooke, "U.N. Will Limit Access."

47. William K. Stevens, "U.N. Chief Charts Defense of Nature" and "To U.S., Treaty's Flaws Outweigh Its Benefits," *The New York Times* (4 & 6 June 1992): p. A10.

48. Rosenthal, June 8, 1992.

49. James Brooke, "Britain and Japan Split with U.S. on Species Pact," *New York Times* (6 June 1992).

50. Brooke, "Britain and Japan Split"; and William K. Stevens, "Bush Plan to Save Forests Is Blocked by Poor Countries," *The New York Times* (9 June 1992): p. A1.

51. Stevens, "Defense of Nature."

52. William K. Stevens, "U.S., Trying to Buff Its Image, Defends the Forests," *The New York Times* (7 June 1992).

53. Stevens, "Bush Plan to Save Forests."

54. William K. Stevens, "Lessons of Rio: New Prominence and an Effective Blandness," *The New York Times* (14 June 1992).

55. James Brooke, "Earth Summit Races Clock to Resolve Difference," *The New York Times* (10 June 1992): p. A8.

56. Linden, "Rio's Legacy."

57. Paul Lewis, "U.S. at the Earth Summit: Isolated and Challenged," *The New York Times* (10 June 1992).

58. James Brooke, "U.N. Chief Closes Summit with an Appeal for Action," *The New York Times* (15 June 1992): p. A8.

59. William K. Stevens, "U.S. Cracks Door to World Forest Agreement," *The New York Times* (13 April 1993): p. C4.

60. *Ibid.*

61. Richard L. Berke, "Clinton Supports Two Major Steps for Environment," *The New York Times* (22 April 1993): p. A1.

62. Linden, "Rio's Legacy."

63. Havel, "The New Millennium."

Suggestions for Further Reading

The UNCED at Rio de Janeiro is too recent for any book-length or other good evaluations to be readily available at this time. Check your library for more recent work than these preliminary pieces; contemporary articles from *The New York Times* are listed in the bibliography.

Bethell, Tom. "Rio: What Happened." *Friends of the Earth* (August 1992): p. 8.

Kildow, Judith T. "The Earth Summit: We Need More Than a Message," *Environment, Science and Technology,* vol. 26, no. 6 (June 1992): p. 1077.

Speth, James Gustave. "On the Road to Sustainability." *Environment, Science and Technology,* vol. 26, no. 6 (June 1992): p. 1075.

Summation
and Portents

We stand at a Janus point of the environmental movement, if *movement* is the proper word for the fearful realization, now nationwide, that something is drastically wrong with the way we are treating our natural environment. We are becoming aware that we are dangerous to the environment, that consequently much about that environment that used to be safe for us is now dangerous, and that something has to be done about all this—and soon. Looking to history with the backward-looking face of the two-faced Janus, we can draw some very tentative generalizations about the genesis of the defining moments of environmental consciousness. With Janus' forward-looking face, we can discern some traces of the future, the patterns that the consciousness will assume as a consequence of the past. The past is, if only in retrospect, sadly understandable; the future is characterized more by conflict than hope, more by prophecies of war than visions of peace. Let us consider both past and future very briefly.

The past is so ordinary as to be boring. The "environmental disasters" of our experience, those covered in this volume and many more, did not result from malice, evil schemes, or magical demonic influences. These disasters can all be attributed to either inattention or ignorance. Inattention, or complacency, is a very ordinary and distinctly human attribute: In the presence of inherently dangerous activities, substances, and technology, there is a tendency to become careless, if sufficient time goes by without incident. We humans have a very short attention span. When danger looms real and near, we devise excellent policies to protect the safety of everyone concerned, we formulate prudent rules to ensure that all activities are carried out safely, and we promise to keep safeguards always in place. Then, after a while, when nothing disastrous happens and everything we do, it seems, is really perfectly safe, we begin to feel a little silly about enforcing inconvenient rules and paying someone to go around checking to make sure the policies are in effect, and those safeguards begin to seem unnecessarily expensive.

The enabling conditions for the wreck of the Exxon Valdez are much the same as the enabling conditions for the escape of methyl isocyanate gas in Bhopal, India, or the blowup at Chernobyl: Safety equipment that was promised to the community and that was supposed to be in place was broken, unavailable, or simply inadequate to the task; company safety policies were violated, and safety rules were simply ignored.

In our community, the fire department gets calls almost every day about something—a brush fire by the highway, a midnight blaze from a faulty electrical system in the back of a store, a flare-up of grease in a busy restaurant kitchen. Usually, the problems are small and easily handled, but no one could doubt the potential for disaster. So although the official policymakers of the community might quibble about the details of the fire fighters' contract, there is no real dissension on the need for a well-equipped and well-trained fire department. But suppose there never were any little fires. Suppose that there were only roaring infernos, three-alarm fires, that only came along every 77 years—not predictably, of course, but every 77 years on the average. Whole generations would go by without a fire. Under those conditions, with money as tight as it is, imagine the difficulty of maintaining the fire department in a state of readiness to fight a three-alarm fire. Well, an oil spill of the magnitude of the Exxon Valdez debacle comes along only every 241 years. So who could blame the managers (the "bottom-line types") for deciding that it was not cost-effective to maintain special teams for the containment of oil spills?

The other governor of the past, along with inattention, is ignorance. We generally learn only on a need-to-know basis and are unlikely to tax our brains without compelling reason. We simply did not know about the possibility of damage to the ozone layer when we started using CFCs in refrigeration and spray cans; we only recently figured out the relationship between CO_2 and climate change (the greenhouse effect); and the loggers of the Northwest Coast can say, quite honestly, that until very recently it never occurred to them that the trees might be gone someday, or at least that the oldest and most beautiful trees might someday be considered valuable enough to preserve from cutting. Nor have we appreciated, until very recently, the advantages of biodiversity and the reasons, outside of childish sentiment, for attempting to protect endangered species of all kinds. There were historical warnings, of course, but these were not understood and certainly not heeded.

We can apologize for inattention and ignorance; we can promise to remedy these things by developing enlightened policy (now that we know what such policy should be) and by complying with that policy to the letter, forever—and then, by actually following through—but the future cannot be resolved as easily as all that. The unintentional blunders of the past are being replaced by *intentionality* in the new environmental consciousness, and that intentionality can take several forms; all of them portend war.

The war spawned by the new environmental consciousness could take several forms: (1) radical violent environmentalism, best represented by the organization Earth First!; (2) an anti-environmental reactionism, represented by the Wise Use Movement; or (3) environmental kidnapping—holding the environment hostage, primarily in military operations but, occasionally, for ransom money. The oil fires in Kuwait, following the 1991 Gulf War, represent the wartime use of kidnapping; the tactics of the "inholders" in National Parks are the peacetime equivalent. Let us discuss these one at a time.

ENVIRONMENTALISM TURNS RADICAL

It is a fundamental tenet of democracy that extralegal violence accomplishes nothing, threatens the basis of the democratic system, and should never be resorted to by any party to a political debate. Still, however well-accepted we hold that tenet to be, it is equally clear (to participants in a dispute) that violence can alter a situation, sometimes dramatically. In the Northwest Forest, for instance, if spotted owls (and other inconvenient birds) are wiped out, no further limitations on logging can be imposed under the Endangered Species Act, and logging may then proceed unhindered by those laws. On the other hand, if loggers' lives are in danger in the woods, no one will dare go into the woods to cut down the trees, and thus the trees will be saved for the moment. If extralegal violence is the only way to save something valuable, is it then justified?

Since the publication of the Federalist Papers, we have agreed that legal political means should be sufficient for the resolution of all policy disputes in the United States. That agreement has met, and absorbed, only one serious challenge, when Martin Luther King, Jr., and his followers nonviolently violated laws against trespassing—and cheerfully went to jail for their offenses—during the efforts to crack open the legal barriers unjustly restricting African Americans' access to public facilities and career advancement. The important feature of King's revolution was that it was committed to nonviolence; it would not have been acceptable otherwise. We Americans have been very firm in our decision that violence is never justified in the pursuit of a political cause.

On the other hand, we do concede that there have been times and places (the Third Reich under the dictatorship of Adolf Hitler comes to mind) when *lawless*—even lethal—violence was welcome and praised, to protect the rights of those threatened by government policy, if found effective in saving lives. We are agreed that the unconscionable genocidal actions taken by the Reich, for example, however legal under German law at the time, were not only totally wrong, but wrong enough to justify (proportionate) violent resistance.

True pacifists might have foreseen that the Reich would not last forever and counseled us to wait and work patiently for reform until sanity and enlightenment returned—but every day that Hitler's policies stayed in force, innocent people died. Compensation would never have been possible; people who are killed today can never be brought back. As a simple extension of basic *just war* theory: If an aggressor threatens human life under color of law, and there is no other way to stop the aggressor, we have a right to resort to proportionate violence if there is good reason to think it will be effective. Similarly, it would have been morally permissible to kill Adolf Hitler, if it would have stopped the slaughter, and those who tried to do so, and failed, are heroes.

The ecosystems of the world, like individual human beings, are unique and completely irreplaceable. They are being destroyed, though, in very large numbers, even at this writing, despite evidence that the American people would very much prefer to have them preserved and are willing, if necessary (if the question is put to them), to tax themselves to make sure that this happens. If it were possible to put all the cutting of trees on hold and in some suitably open public forum debate whether we want the forests saved or cut, giving weight to the opinions of all Americans, we would clearly have an obligation to abstain from violence and participate in the debate, but trees continue to be cut as the debate seems to continue. Each day that goes by means that sanity and enlightenment will arrive too late for yet more groves of the tropical rainforest, for example, or the old-growth forest of the Northwest.

If we have for these groves the sort of respect that we should have for any irreplaceable living system, then it would seem that we have a right to resort to (effective) violence against property to protect them when they cannot be protected any other way—at least to hold off the cutting until the debate has taken place. The remaining provisions of just war theory must also be observed: that violence be avoided whenever nonviolent means will protect the trees from destruction, that violence at all times be kept to an absolute minimum and proportionate to the object of the violence. Those who have advocated such extralegal means have interpreted the rule of proportionality to mean that only property is an appropriate object for such violence; killing, or even hurting, human beings is forbidden.

EARTH FIRST!

That argument has been presented by one of the newest and most interesting environmental groups around, Earth First! (The punctuation is part of the name.) Earth First! realized early on that trees would not be saved by peaceful means alone, so they advocated stopping the logging the only way they could, by "monkeywrenching." The term was taken from a popular novel (*The Monkey Wrench Gang*, by Edward Abbey), and it includes all manner of property sabotage in the name of the Earth (pouring maple syrup and other nasty substances in bulldozers' motors, for instance, or clogging padlocks with epoxy, or spiking trees with threepenny nails).

The Earth First! logic is simplicity itself: A day spent fixing machines is a day spent not cutting trees, a day of reprieve for the trees. A threepenny nail in a tree will damage the saws at the mill and maybe stop work for a while. So, if the logging companies know that the trees are spiked, they will leave the trees alone to save their saws. (Spikes do not hurt the trees.) If the logging companies know that trees all over the North Coast are probably spiked, they will leave all the trees alone. Trees left alone, not cut, are trees preserved, there for the rest of us, and our grandchildren, to enjoy.

Earth First! never really carried out its published plans to monkeywrench the timber industry in northern California, although they did stage some peaceful sit-ins and guitar-sings. It has never been more than a tiny group of people more lost and explorative than committed and active. The organization does not seem to pose much danger to the body politic by advocating pouring maple syrup in bulldozer engines or spiking trees, especially when these practices exist exclusively as paper threats.

Yet the FBI, threatened with obsolescence as the Cold War ground to a halt, found this insignificant group enough of a threat for it to deploy all of its communist-hunting skills to bring the group to its knees. The FBI's tactics toward this end will be familiar to veterans of the antiwar movement of the Vietnam era. FBI agent Ron Frazier infiltrated a four-member Arizona outpost of Earth First! and encouraged the group's plans to engage in some unsophisticated local sabotage: to cut the bracing cables for ski lift pylons and power poles in a ski resort outside Flagstaff. The group had no idea how to go about this, so the FBI researched the cables and then rented the acetylene torch and taught the group how to use it. When it turned out that the group did not have either a car or money for gas to reach the site of the planned sabotage, the FBI procured both and drove the conspirators to the spot, where they were arrested.[1]

By this time, another FBI agent, Michael Fain, had been sent in with specific instructions to entrap David Foreman, the spokesperson for Earth First!, who lived in Tucson and had nothing to do with this enterprise, into encouraging not just pylon sabotage but nuclear sabotage: the destruction of nuclear plants in California, Colorado, and Arizona. The tape recorders that the FBI agents wore to every encounter with Foreman provide no evidence of conspiracy on his part: On the contrary, all that Foreman does on those tapes is try to talk Fain out of such actions, especially with regard to the nuclear plants. The agents did inadvertently record themselves agreeing in the parking lot that it was important to involve Foreman somehow, to "send the message" to all those undesirables out there. The tape raises the strong possibility that the FBI should have been convicted of conspiracy to deprive Foreman of his rights, but that did not happen.

When the other Earth First! members were arrested, Foreman was arrested too, roused from his bed at gunpoint and led away in handcuffs as a conspirator. It is not clear that there was ever a case against the five but, given the severity of the charges leveled at the hapless bunch, the amount of prison time that would have to be served, the risk of a guilty verdict from a small-town jury, and the certainty of wasted years trapped in the legal system, David Foreman counseled the group to accept a plea bargain—and he himself pleaded guilty, in September 1991, to one count of conspiracy, with sentencing to be delayed for five years, during which time he must keep silent on political matters. This transparent plan to silence Earth First!'s leader and keep his voice out of the political process cost taxpayers $2 million and served no useful purpose: "In its obsession to tie the issue of monkeywrenching to nuclear sabotage, the FBI had to invent a conspiracy where none existed; whatever 'message' it intended to send was lost along the way."[2]

Environmentalists with a political background found the parallels too obvious to ignore: "The real lesson of this case is as old and American as the abolitionists before the Civil War, as the labor movement of the late 19th and early 20th century, as the civil rights movement of the 50s... Government likes to crush social movements with trials because it has in its employ cops, lawyers and courthouses, and the movements don't. What determines the success of government in these instances of repression are the reactions of citizens. And that verdict was not decided in Prescott, Arizona, in September. That jury is still out, way out there."[3]

So the major effect of this small band of paper radicals has been to trigger an entirely disproportionate legal/political reaction. Earth First! might be a poor example of the potential for violence in defense of the Earth; on the other hand, it might just be that those who defend the Earth are unsuited, by background, temperament, and further ideological commitments, to be violent. Whatever the fate of these little organizations, their logic remains intact and their potential is worth watching.

THE WISE USE MOVEMENT

More prone to violence are the new antienvironmentalists. The interests behind this new movement are themselves old and well known: property owners who object to environmental restrictions that limit the use of their property and reduce its value in sale; timber and extraction industries that have depended on virtually unrestricted taking of natural resources for profit; recreational and other users of natural areas (for instance, the operators of off-the-road recreational vehicles) who are prohibited from certain activities deemed to be destructive of the environment. These groups have never before made common cause, however, and they have never been activist and collectively interventionist. All that has changed.

Antienvironmentalist activism seems to have arisen from a series of articles written in 1979 for *Logging Management* by Ron Arnold; he called for an activist alliance to oppose the environmental movement in all its forms.[4] The alliance was organized by Alan Gottlieb of Washington state, who had made his fortune as a direct-mail fundraiser for conservative politicians and causes. (One of Gottlieb's creations was the Citizens Committee for the Right to Keep and Bear Arms.) After Gottlieb spent a year in prison for tax evasion in 1984, he was ready for a new right-wing cause to keep his mailing list together, so he came up with the Center for the Defense of Free Enterprise. Ron Arnold, joining him as executive vice president, promoted his antienvironmentalist crusade as the *Wise Use Movement*; the term "wise use" was borrowed, without permission, from Gifford Pinchot, Teddy Roosevelt's chief of the U.S. Forest Service.

Gottlieb and Arnold were, in turn, joined by Charles Cushman, executive director of the National Inholders Association. (An *inholder* owns a plot of private land in the middle of a federal park or other reservation.) Together with other like-minded associations, the CDFE battles environmental regulation, seeks concessions for private industry on public land, and—above all—carries on ideological campaigns against any efforts to preserve the environment for its own sake.

The constellation of allies in the Wise Use Movement is instructive: These range from the Wilderness Impact Research Foundation, founded in 1986 by Grant Gerber, a Nevada attorney, as a Christian organization dedicated to the defeat of pagan environmental movements to the Blue Ribbon Coalition of Idaho, an alliance of 200 dirt-bike and snowmobile clubs that want access to public lands for their sport. (The coalition's approach to the woods is summed up by past president Henry Yake: "Wilderness has no economic value.")[5]

Legal action is being explored by the Mountain States Legal Foundation, led by William Perry Pendley—a holdover from the 1970s Sagebrush Rebellion, which tried to get all federal lands transferred to states or private parties. Charles Cushman also heads the Multiple Use Land Alliance, dedicated to opening up federal lands for mining and lumbering. The People for the West (PFW) is one of the largest organizations, recruiting most of its membership from rural sections of the Western states and capitalizing on unemployment (actual or feared) and resentment of central government "interference" in individual lives. All in all, there are between 400 and 500 organizations in the Wise Use Movement, and they tend to be very angry (and apocalyptic, seeing their war, whether or not cast in traditional Christian terms, as a cosmic struggle of Good against Evil).[6]

The sponsors of the Wise Use Movement and the suppliers of the money for literature, mailings, and the many conferences, are also worthy of note. One of the more interesting participants is the Reverend Sun Myung Moon's Unification Church, connected to Wise Use through the American Freedom Coalition (AFC), which sponsors the conferences. The AFC was organized in 1987 by Colonel Bo Hi Pak, a ranking associate of the Reverend Moon for U.S. activities, and fundamentalist Gary Jarmin, as the basis for a third political party through which Moon's political agenda might be funneled. Ron Arnold was president of the Washington State AFC in 1989 and 1990 and a registered agent for Moon in 1989. Alan Gottlieb was a Washington State AFC director in 1989 and owns the office building where that organization has its headquarters.[7]

The Unification Church is not the only source of money for Wise Use. The Western States Public Lands Coalition, an association of mining companies set up in 1988, was incorporated to establish "a permanent coalition between industry and local government officials in the western United States to protect their mutual interests, ensuring that timber, grazing, ranching, oil and gas, and mining activities continue on public lands."[8] That would mean continuation of the 1872 Mining Law, which gives mining companies right over all other uses on public lands and demands no royalties—an enormously profitable deal.

The WSPLC spun off the PFW in the next year, realizing that political allies were essential to keep the law so solidly in their interests. The grassroots following of the PFW was then collected by an extensive, and expensive, mailing campaign, funded by $1.7 million from the mining industry—"peanuts," according to Jim Jensen of the Montana Environmental Information Center, "by comparison to what they should be paying and will be paying when the law changes."[9] A list of the directors of the WSPLC shows corporate executives of ten different mining companies, with yearly corporate contributions of well over $350,000. That is a tidy war chest for spreading a message.

And spread it they do, by all the traditional means at their disposal:

> An op-ed article about PFW in a Santa Fe newspaper, *The New Mexican,* appeared to be a heartfelt piece by local Pecos PFW orga-

nizer Hugh Ley. But on investigation it turned out to be a press release from Pueblo headquarters.[10]

What is traditional is the cloaking of right-wing causes in grassroots garb, funded by the major corporations of affected industries pushing an agenda favorable to those industries. What is new in all of this is the anti-environmental message.

Other examples of this technique are listed in a recent issue of *National Wildlife:* A group called the "Information Council on the Environment (ICE)" argued that the average temperature in Minnesota was falling and that global warming was therefore not to be feared; when it turned out that ICE had been created and funded by coal and utility companies, and that the average temperature in Minnesota was actually rising, ICE "melted away." Then we have the Marine Preservation Association, 15 oil companies dedicated to "promote the welfare and interests of the petroleum and energy industries"; the National Wetlands Coalition, sponsored by oil and gas companies and developers, whose purpose is to remove restrictions on wetlands use; the Environmental Conservation Association, with the same agenda; the Endangered Species Reform Coalition, sponsored by utility companies and others in an effort to weaken the Endangered Species Act—and the list goes on.[11] (If you received a mailing from one of these organizations, featuring only the organization's name and a typical logo [ducks flying over marshes, for example], would you assume that its agenda was to *oppose* environmental protections?)

Wise Use got its start in Reno, Nevada, when about 200 organizations came together in conference in August, 1988, to establish a plan of action. The papers from that conference were published by the Free Enterprise Press in 1989 as *The Wise Use Agenda.* Items from that agenda include positions on issues we have discussed in this volume: for instance, immediate petroleum development in the Arctic National Wildlife Refuge; cutting all old growth on national forestland; rewriting the Endangered Species Act to remove protection for "nonadaptive" species—and, something new, "civil penalties against anyone who legally challenges 'economic action or development on federal lands.'"[12] All parts of this agenda are being taken to the Congress for enactment: The WSPLC is a nonprofit 501(c) (6) tax-exempt corporation, which entitles it to lobby for favorable legislation.

The major campaign, though, is directed toward the Constitution and the Supreme Court. Above all, Wise Use wants a ruling that any government regulation that reduces the value of property constitutes "taking" and requires compensation. Because the value of any property is arguably reduced if its potential uses are reduced and because every environmental regulation does that, such a ruling would require every property owner affected by a federal environmental law to be paid by the taxpayers to obey it.

One small federal court whose membership was composed entirely of Reagan appointees actually made such findings in the course of the late 1980s; those decisions are on appeal.[13] The major court precedents are against the ruling (see, for example, *Hudson Water Company v. McCarter* 1907), and municipal zoning regulations are entirely legal, but environmentalists should not be overconfident: With the present composition of the Supreme Court, nothing is safe.

THE ENVIRONMENT AS MILITARY HOSTAGE

Before the opening salvoes of Operation Desert Storm (the 1991 military action in the Persian Gulf in which General Norman Schwarzkopf and an international task force rescued Kuwait's autocratic ruling family from Iraq's war machine), Iraqi leader Saddam Hussein took hostages from among the many Americans and Europeans living in Kuwait at the time he took over. When he became convinced that human hostages were counterproductive, he released them and altered his tactics: Should the Allied forces be so unwise as to attempt to drive him out of Kuwait, he announced, he would sabotage all the oil-refining facilities on Kuwait's Gulf Coast, allowing all stored oil to flow into the Persian Gulf; destroy all the oil wells in Kuwait, so that they could never again pump oil; and set as much oil as possible afire in a massive conflagration that could never be extinguished.

This threat amounted to blackmail, extortion, whatever you like to call it, and exactly duplicated the hostage situation that had existed before the war began. If we wanted the environment back alive, Hussein warned, we would have to meet his terms. This was the first time in the history of world conflict that the ecosystem had been held as a hostage of war. The vanquished army warned that the hostage would be killed unless the victors met the vanquished's demands.

As we know, no negotiations took place. The Iraqi army was routed from Kuwait, and, true to form, the Iraqis blew up refineries and set afire as many Kuwaiti oil wells as they could as they left the country—the most complete and deliberate "scorched earth" policy in the annals of combat. The first order of business was, clearly, to put out the fires.

The world has some experience in this task; the legendary Texan oil-fire fighter Red Adair has been doing this for years, and there are now a handful of companies in that line of work. Initial projections for completion of the work were very gloomy. Red Adair himself, viewing the scene, estimated that it would take four or five years to put the fires out.

The *National Geographic* had a terrifying photographic essay in its August, 1991, issue, bringing home with sickening clarity the effect of a huge mass of leaking and burning petroleum on the fragile ecosystem of the desert at our feet and the air above us. The scene can only be described as hellish—everything you imagined hell to be, including the limitless, mindless malice that brought it about. "Strategically it was senseless," said Abdullah Toukan, Science Adviser to King Hussein of Jordan. "The only casualty was the environment."[14]

The damage was inflicted on water, land, and air. An estimated six to eight million barrels of oil (or roughly 300 million gallons) spilled into the Gulf after January 18, 1991. That was about 25 times the spill from the Exxon Valdez, and it was made much worse by the airborne pollution from the damaged wells on land. The wind carried soot and oil-bearing mist, eventually about twice as much oil as was originally spilled, into the sea. Crucial breeding grounds for fish and waterfowl were damaged; research on the extent of that damage was carried on by all the Gulf nations, including Iran, 40,000 of whose citizens fished those waters.[15]

At the outset, no one knew how much damage would eventually be caused by the plumes of smoke towering into the sky over the Arabian desert—predictions ranged from nuclear winter (from the shade of the smoke) to global warming (from the CO_2 and other greenhouse gases)—or how much the land would be damaged, where lakes of burning oil flowed ever further from the wellheads.

Inevitably, the prospect of terrible environmental devastation brought into question the actions taken by the United States in prosecuting the war. Tom Wicker, a writer whose syndicated column "In the Nation" appears in *The New York Times* and many other newspapers, argued in April, 1991, that Hussein's threat might have been taken more seriously. First, he gives a description of the inferno:

> About six million barrels of oil, weighing roughly a million tons, around 10 percent of the world's daily oil ration, are going up in smoke *every day* from the 550 Kuwaiti wells set afire by Iraqi occupiers. None of the fires have yet been put out, and at the projected extinction rate of five days per well, the job could take as long as two years … Joel S. Levine of NASA, an authority on biomass burning, told Mr. Horgan the Kuwaiti well fires were "the most intense burning source, probably, in the history of the world."[16]

The estimate of the number of wells set afire was later revised up to 650–700. Next, a crisp assessment of responsibility:

> Saddam Hussein's forces, of course, actually set the fires and caused this immense environmental threat. He had plainly warned that he would do it, however; so the United States, by its decision to launch the war anyway, rather than rely on non-combat pressures, bears some responsibility.[17]

A later column continued the bad news. There was very pessimistic evidence from testimony presented on July 11, 1991, to a Senate subcommittee on the environmental effects of the war, chaired by Senator Joseph Lieberman, a Democrat from Connecticut: 199 wells had been capped, but about 500 were still burning, and some lakes of oil that had leaked from nonburning wells were starting to catch fire. Tom Wicker quotes E. L. Shannon, Jr., chairman of Santa Fe International, an oil-drilling company owned by Kuwait:

> [He] said the Kuwaiti Government had set a goal of 500 wells "secured" by the end of the year, and all by March 1992. But Mr. George [James George, former Canadian ambassador to Kuwait and an environmental scientist who led a Friends of the Earth inspection team to Kuwait in June], in much more pessimistic testimony, said his F.O.E. team had concluded the fires "will not be controlled for years—perhaps four or five years—as Red Adair told the committee a month ago."[18]

Work on the wells went very slowly at first, bearing out the worst predictions. Everything arrived in reverse order: first the volunteer fire fighters, then some of their equipment, then the machine-ship backup to develop the right equipment, then the minesweepers to make the area safe enough to work in. As of late July, 1991, only 240 of (by then) 732 fires had been extinguished. The goal for finishing the job was March, 1992, but a Greenpeace assessment agreed with Red Adair's testimony, cited earlier by Wicker, that "we're talking five years" before all the fires would be out.[19]

Talk of an official conspiracy to repress news of the fires began to surface ("Instead of cleaning up, the government is covering up") probably, Wicker speculated, because government officials knew beforehand of the deadly effects of the burning but were afraid to discuss them, concerned that such gloom would lend support to the antiwar movement.[20]

Then, suddenly, it was over. By October, two months after those gloomy accounts had been written (and before the Greenpeace assessment was published), the end was in sight—and it wasn't such a bad end after all. "Most Oil Fires Are Out in Kuwait, but Its Environment Is Devastated," read *The New York Times* banner headline on October 19, 1991, but the bulk of the article went on to deny the second half of the banner. Mostly, it quoted officials who were amazed at how fast the wells were being extinguished and how little damage had been done compared to previous estimates.[21] All fires were out in early November. (On November 6, one was reignited so that the Emir of Kuwait could put it out amid pomp and ceremony.) Four American and Canadian companies had put out three-quarters of the fires; 27 companies from other countries assisted with the work. The whole enterprise had taken eight months.

When the damage was added up, the value of the lost oil was given as $12 billion, compared to earlier projections of $43 billion. By November, many of the wells were back in production, and Kuwaiti oil production stood at 320,000 barrels a day (compared to 1.5 million barrels per day before the war), but production was projected to go up to two million barrels a day by the end of 1993. The cost of the fire fighting and initial cleanup was between $1.5 and $2.2 billion; estimates had reached more than twice that figure.

There had been seven deaths, all accidents, during the fire fighting—altogether, an amazing accomplishment. Airborne studies of the smoke from the fires, which had been carried out during the height of the blazes in the spring of 1991, showed the smoke nowhere near as damaging as expected, falling short of the stratosphere and short-lived in the troposphere. The damage simply did not measure up to anyone's expectations.[22]

So it came out more or less all right—not completely, for the desert will be stained and poisoned by the oil for a long time to come—but with some very serious questions left unanswered. Saddam Hussein is not the only madman in the world. Who will the next one be, and where? Who will threaten to blow up or burn or otherwise destroy some fragile, beautiful ecosystem for some selfish purpose? Saddam Hussein's purposes were nationalistic, as are those of the Islamic fundamentalists who take human hostages, but nationalism is not the only possible motive. Most people who take human hostages do it for money, and the same process can work with the environment.

A new tactic of *inholders*, for instance, is to threaten to clear-cut or develop a plot of land that they hold within the federal property, generally an environmental reserve, unless they are immediately bought out by the government, for a very high price. The proceeds of the maneuver can be used to purchase another inholding and repeat the threat. Those threats, incidentally, would have been technically impossible to carry out when the inholding was formed, since access to an inholding is generally restricted to one small logging road, but it is now entirely possible, at some cost, since materials can be transported by helicopter. What other forms of legal extortion can be used to feed off our new concern for the environment?

CONCLUDING POSTSCRIPT ON THE UNSCIENTIFIC METHOD

These last reflections on the environment—these unpleasant portents of Environment Future—raise some new and serious questions. We might discount, on the evidence, any danger from the Earth First! variety of zealots. Wise Use and environment hostaging, however, will be with us for a while, and they underline a theme that has recurred in the body of this volume: There are things we don't know, where the science is still uncertain, where we cannot surely say what the outcome will be. Scientific uncertainty hounds all work on causes and cures of global warming and other climate change, acid rain, depletion of the ozone layer, pollution of the oceans, and desertification, to mention just a few areas. Then how shall we proceed?

The division of opinion on courses of action has been seen to form along purely political lines: A faction that identifies itself as "conservative," "politically right," or "probusiness" will decide that all allegedly polluting activities should continue without change until all the evidence is in and we are sure that the activities are harmful; a faction that identifies itself as "proenvironment," "liberal," or "politically left" will (usually) urge a halt to all potentially harmful activities until we know for sure that they are not harmful.

In the absence of scientific witness, each side will marshal *unscientific* witness as far as it can to support its side: projections of dire consequence and damage on one side, projections of insignificant damage and complete environmental recovery on the other. Science itself is not at fault: The science is just complex, and the ideologues count on the public's misunderstanding of extrapolations from generally reliable computer models programmed by knowledgeable scientists. Too, the trend intensifies as the time approaches the present.

The unusual alliance between the remains of the antiwar movement and the environmental activists in opposition to the Gulf War can be seen as a convenient way to further both agendas: The activists used the war and the drama of the Kuwait fires for publicity; the antiwar movement recruited the projections of environmental disaster to strengthen regret for the war. Neither party to this amalgam can advance the cause clearly as long as this highly political process of association by convenience continues.

In conclusion, let us plead for clarity and honesty, above all. In environmental *science*, we are venturing into uncharted waters; let us leave the scientists free to study, and report honestly, and let us keep the scientific process distinct from the political as much as possible. In environmental *politics*, we are blazing new paths, testing whether traditional legislation and adjudication of rights can be bent and adapted to accommodate new environmental interests in an increasingly crowded world. Finally, in environmental *ethics*, we are also exploring strange territory; we do not yet have consensus on whether we can have obligations to nonhuman entities, let alone how those obligations ought to be carried out in individual cases. Let us get used to living and acting in an uncertain world; let us keep the dialogue open, maintain respect for our opponents, seek the help of the journalists, poets, philosophers, churches, and all the thinkers and artists of the world and hope that we can take the sad experiences chronicled in these pages and use them to form a safer and better world.

Notes

1. Taxpayers might be interested to know that we were paying Frazier a salary of $53,000 per year to carry out this detective work.

2. Christine Keyser, "Compromise in Defense of Earth First!: A Monkeywrencher Trial Ends, and No One's Happy," *Sierra* (Nov./Dec. 1991): pp. 45–47.

3. Charles Bowden, "Government First, Earth Last: Lessons of the Earth First! Trial," *E Magazine*, vol. 3, no. 1 (Jan./Feb. 1992): pp. 56–67.

4. Kate O'Callaghan, "Whose Agenda for America?" *Audubon* (Sept./Oct. 1992): pp. 80–91.

5. Thomas A. Lewis, "Cloaked in a Wise Disguise," *National Wildlife* (Oct./Nov. 1992): pp. 4–9.

6. Lewis, "Cloaked in a Wise Disguise," p. 7.

7. O'Callaghan, "Whose Agenda?" p. 87.

8. *Ibid.*

9. *Ibid.*, p. 88.

10. *Ibid.*, p. 89.

11. Thomas A. Lewis, "You Can't Judge a Group by Its Cover," *National Wildlife* (Oct./Nov. 1992): p. 9.

12. O'Callaghan, "Whose Agenda?" p. 90.

13. Lewis, "Cloaked in a Wise Disguise," p. 8.

14. Quoted in Thomas Y. Canby (senior assistant editor of the *National Geographic*), "After the Storm," *National Geographic* (August 1991): p. 21.

15. John H. Cushman, Jr., "U.S. Ship to Investigate Damage from Oil Pollution in Persian Gulf," *The New York Times* (14 January 1992).

16. Tom Wicker, "In the Nation: Smoke over Kuwait," *The New York Times* (3 April 1991): p. A21.

17. Wicker, "Smoke over Kuwait."

18. Wicker, "In the Nation: Kuwait Still Burns," *The New York Times* (28 July 1991): op-ed. page; see reprint of FOE testimony, "Gulf War Legacy: An Unending Assault Against the Earth," *Friends of the Earth* (August 1991): pp. 1, 6–7.

19. Andre Carothers, "After Desert Storm, the Deluge," *Greenpeace* (Oct.–Dec. 1991): pp. 14–17.

20. *Ibid.*

21. Youssef M. Ibrahim, "Most Oil Fires Are Out in Kuwait, but Its Environment Is Devastated," *The New York Times* (19 October 1991): pp. A1 & 4.

22. Peter V. Hobbs and Lawrence F. Radke, "Airborne Studies of the Smoke from the Kuwait Oil Fires," *Science*, vol. 256 (15 May 1992): pp. 987–991.

Bibliography

Chapter 1 Toxin's Halloween:
The Story of Love Canal

Abelson, P. H. "Chemicals from Waste Dumps." *Science,* vol. 229 (26 July 1985): p. 335.
———."Treatment of Hazardous Waste." *Science,* (1 August 1986): p. 509.
Beauchamp, Tom. "Love Canal." *Case Studies in Business, Society, and Ethics.* Englewood Cliffs, N.J.: Prentice-Hall, 1983.
Blumenthal, Ralph. "Fight to Curb 'Love Canals'." *The New York Times,* (30 June 1980): pp. B1 & 11.
Brown, Michael. *Laying Waste: The Poisoning of America by Toxic Chemicals.* New York: Parthenon, 1980.
Brown, Michael H. "A Toxic Ghost Town: Harbinger of America's Toxic Waste Crisis." *The Atlantic,* vol. 264, no. 1 (July 1989): pp. 23–24.
Carson, Rachel. *Silent Spring.* Boston: Houghton-Mifflin, Anniversary Edition, 1962.
Cavanaugh, Gerard F., and Arthur F. McGovern. *Ethical Dilemmas in the Modern Corporation.* Englewood Cliffs, N.J.: Prentice-Hall, 1988.
Cook, J. "Risky Business." *Forbes* (2 December 1985): pp. 106–109.
Cox, Hank. "Love Canal Special Supplement." *The Regulatory Action Network: Washington Watch* (September 1980).
Elmer-Dewitt, Philip. "Love Canals in the Making." *TIME* (20 May 1991): p. 51.
Epstein, Samuel. *Hazardous Waste in America.* San Francisco: Sierra Club Books, 1982.

Gibbs, Lois Marie. *Love Canal: My Story.* Albany: State University of New York Press, 1982.

Griffin, M. "The Legacy of Love Canal." *Sierra,* vol. 73, (Jan–Feb. 1988): pp. 26–27.

Hammer, J. "The Big Haul in Toxic Waste." *Newsweek,* vol. 112 (3 October 1988): pp. 38–39.

Hevesi, Dennis. "Chronology of Events: Love Canal." *The New York Times* (28 September 1988): p. B1.

Hirschhorn, J. S. "Cutting Production of Hazardous Waste." *Technology Review,* vol. 91 (April 1988): pp. 52–61.

Kadlecek, M. "Love Canal—10 Years Later." *The Conservationist,* vol. 43 (Nov.–Dec. 1988): pp. 40–43.

Klinkenborg, Verlyn. "Back to Love Canal." *Harper's* (March 1991): pp. 71–78.

Leonard, B. "Cleaning Up." *Forbes,* vol. 139 (1 June 1987): pp. 52–53.

Levine, Adeline Gordon. *Love Canal: Science, Politics, and People.* Lexington, Mass.: Lexington Books, 1982.

Marbach, W. D. "What to Do with Our Waste." *Newsweek,* vol. 110 (27 July 1987): pp. 51–52.

Nader, Ralph, Ronald Brownstein, and John Richard, eds. *Who's Poisoning America? Corporate Polluters and Their Victims in the Chemical Age.* San Francisco: Sierra Club Books, 1981.

Niagara Falls, New York, Deed of Love Canal Property Transfer, 28 April 1953.

Pomice, E. "Cleaning up After Industry's Slobs." *Forbes,* vol. 139 (20 April 1987): p. 90.

Postel, Sandra. "Defusing the Toxics Threat: Controlling Pesticides and Industrial Waste." *Worldwatch Paper 79,* Washington, D.C.: Worldwatch Institute, September 1987.

Raloff, J. "Unexpected Leakage." *Science News,* vol. 135 (18 March 1989): p. 164.

———. "EPA Limits Industrial Benzene Emissions." *Science News,* vol. 136 (9 September 1989): p. 165.

———. "Biggest Benzene Risks Hide Close to Home." *Science News,* vol. 136 (14 October 1989): p. 245.

Regenstein, Lewis. *America the Poisoned.* Washington, D.C.: Acropolis Books, 1982.

Revkin, A. C. "Trapping Toxics in the Trenches." *Discover,* vol. 9 (November 1988): p. 10.

Salholz, E. "The Next Love Canal?" *Newsweek,* vol. 114 (7 August 1989): p. 28.

Schmitt, Eric. "Axelrod Says 220 Love Canal Families Can Return." *The New York Times* (28 September 1988): p. B1.

Schneider, Keith. "U. S. Said to Lack Data on Threat Posed by Hazardous Waste Sites." *The New York Times* (22 October 1991): p. C4.

Shabecoff, Philip. "Government Says Abandoned Love Canal Homes are Safe Now." *The New York Times* (15 May 1990): p. B1.

Smart, T. "Love Canal: A New Clean-up Plan Stirs Old Fears." *Business Week* (31 August 1987): p. 30.

Underwood, Anne. "The Return to Love Canal." *Newsweek* (30 July 1990).

Verhouek, Sam Howe. "After 10 Years, the Trauma of Love Canal Continues." *The New York Times* (5 August 1988): p. B1.

————. "New Findings Delay Resettling of Love Canal." *The New York Times* (7 March 1989): B5.

————. "At Love Canal, Land Rush on a Burial Ground." *The New York Times* (26 July 1990): p. A1.

Vianna, Nicholas. Report to the New York State Department of Health. Reported in *Science* (19 June 1981): p. 19.

Whalan, Robert. *Love Canal: A Public Health Time Bomb.* Report of the New York Department of Health, 1978.

Whelan, Elizabeth. *Toxic Terror: The Truth About the Cancer Scare.* Ottawa, Ill.: Jameson Books, 1985.

Whitney, Gary. "Hooker Chemical and Plastics." *Case Studies in Business Ethics.* ed. Thomas Donaldson, Englewood Cliffs, N.J.: Prentice-Hall, 1984.

Winerip, Michael. "Home Bargains in Niagara Falls: Forget the Toxics." *The New York Times* (29 May 1990): p. B1.

Zuesse, Eric. "Love Canal: The Truth Seeps Out." *Reason* (February 1981).

Articles from The New York Times *(news service or author unknown)*

"U.S. to Burn All Toxic Soil Removed from Love Canal." (2 November 1987): sec. B, p. 2.

"A Judge Orders Company to Pay Love Canal Cost." (24 February 1988): sec. B, p. 2.

(29 September 1988): sec. B, p. 1.

(29 August 1989): sec. D, p. 2.

"Love Canal Defense Setback." (29 August 1989): sec. D, p. 2.

(22 October 1990): sec. B, p. 1.

(18 July 18 1991): sec. A, p. 14.

Editorials and unsigned columns

Chemical and Engineering News. "Occidental Agrees to Store, Treat, Love Canal Wastes." Vol. 67 (19 June 1989): p. 20.

Environment. "Health Aspects of Hazardous Waste Disposal." Vol. 28 (April 1986): pp. 38–45.

Newsweek. "Love Match." vol. 111 (7 March 1988): p. 8.

Science. "CDC Finds No Excess Illness at Love Canal." Vol. 220 (17 June 1983).

Science News. "Last Stage of Love Canal Cleanup." Vol. 132 (14 November 1987): p. 319.

TIME. "A Problem that Cannot Be Buried." Vol. 126 (14 October 1985): pp. 76–78.

TIME. "Love Canals in the Making." (20 May 1991): p. 51.

Wall Street Journal. "Love Canal Suit Threatens to Make Old Errors Costly." (24 October 1990): p. B1.

Conversations

Lois Gibbs, Citizens' Clearing House for Hazardous Waste, Falls Church, Virginia.

Eugene Martin-Less, Esq., Environmental Bureau of the Attorney General of New York State, Albany, New York. Senior Attorney, *New York State vs. Occidental Chemical Company* (suit pending, asking $250 million punitive damages relative to Love Canal dumpsite).

Spokesperson, Love Canal Area Revitalization Agency, Niagara Falls, New York.
Lee Wasserman, Esq., Environmental Planning Lobby, Albany, New York.

Chapter 2 A Cloud of Poison:
The Disaster at Bhopal

Anderson, Warren M. (former Chairman, Union Carbide Corporation) "Bhopal: What We Learned." Distributed by Union Carbide Corporation (Danbury, Connecticut 06817–0001; UCC Document #158).

De Grazia, Alfred. *A Cloud over Bhopal.* Bombay, India: Kalos Foundation, 1985. (Kalos Foundation for the India-America Committee for the Bhopal Victims, 55 Mamta-A, Appasaheb Marathe Marg, Prabhadevi, Bombay 400 025 India.)

Ehrlich, Paul, et al. *Ecoscience: Population, Resources, Environment.* San Francisco: W. H. Freeman, 1977.

Fazal, Anwar. Foreword to David Weir. *The Bhopal Syndrome: Pesticides, Environment and Health.* San Francisco: Sierra Club Books, 1987.

Kalelkar, Ashok S. (Arthur D. Little, Inc.) "Investigation of Large-Magnitude Incidents: Bhopal as a Case Study." Presented at the Institution of Chemical Engineers' Conference On Preventing Major Chemical Accidents, London, England, May 1988.

Kurzman, Dan. *A Killing Wind: Inside Union Carbide and the Bhopal Catastrophe.* New York: McGraw-Hill, 1987.

Lavoie, Denise, writing for the Associated Press. "Bhopal still haunts former Carbide chief." *Hartford Courant* (5 April 1992): pp. D1 & D7.

Mehta, Pushpa S. et al. "Bhopal Tragedy's Health Effects: A Review of Methyl Isocyanate Toxicity." *Journal of the American Medical Association,* vol. 264, no. 21 (5 December 1990): p. 2781.

Oil, Chemical and Atomic Workers International Union. "Union Carbide: A Study in Corporate Power and the Case for Union Power." June 1974.

Peterson, J. "After Bhopal: Tracing Causes and Effects." *Science News,* vol. 127 (30 March 1985): p. 196.

Raman, Anantha K. S., cited in Neal Carlan and Peter McKillop, "Sabotage in Bhopal?" *Newsweek* (1 April 1985): p. 35.

Rennie, John. "Trojan Horse: Did a Protective Peptide Exacerbate Bhopal Injuries?" *Scientific American* (March 1992): p. 27.

Union Carbide Corporation. *Bhopal Methyl Isocyanate Incident Investigation Team Report.* Danbury, Connecticut, March 1985.

———. "Union Carbide Corporation Bhopal Fact Sheet." Available from UCC, Corporate Communications Department, Section C–2, Danbury, CT 06817-0001.

Webster, Donovan. "Heart of the Delta." A Reporter at Large for *The New Yorker* (8 July 1991): pp. 46–66.

Weir, David. *The Bhopal Syndrome: Pesticides, Environment and Health.* San Francisco: Sierra Club Books, 1987.

Yoon, Carol Kaesuk. "Nibbled Plants Don't Just Sit There: They Launch Active Attacks." *The New York Times* (23 June 1992): p. C1.

"India's Tragedy: A Warning Heard Round the World." *U.S. News and World Report* (17 December 1984): p.25.

Chapter 3 Chernobyl:
The Blast Heard 'Round the World

Albright, David. "Chernobyl and the U. S. Nuclear Industry." *Bulletin of the Atomic Scientists* (November 1986): pp. 38–40.

American Medical Association "Health Evaluation of Energy-Generating Sources." AMA Council of Scientific Affairs (10 November 1978).

Barringer, Felicity. "Chernobyl: Five Years Later, the Danger Persists." *The New York Times* magazine (14 April 1991): pp. 28–39 & 74.

Bloomfield, Lincoln P. "Nuclear Crisis and Human Frailty." *Bulletin of the Atomic Scientists* (October 1985): pp. 26 ff.

D'Anastasio, Mark, et al. "The Soviets End Their Silence—but the Damage Keeps Mounting." *Business Week* (19 May 1986): pp. 44–46.

Dickman, Stephen. "IAEA's Verdict on Chernobyl." *Nature* (26 May 1988): p. 285.

Dold, Catherine. "From the Twentieth Century, with Love." *Discover* (October 1992): pp. 22–23.

Edwards, Mike. "Chernobyl: One Year After." *National Geographic* (April 1987): pp. 632–653.

Ehrlich, Paul, et al. *Ecoscience: Population, Resources, Environment.* San Francisco: W. H. Freeman, 1977.

Fialka, John J., and Roger Cohen. "Chernobyl Fallout: Nuclear-Plant Projects in Nations Like Brazil Falter After Accident." *The Wall Street Journal* (5 June 1986): p. A1.

Flavin, Christopher. "Nuclear Power's Burdened Future." *Bulletin of the Atomic Scientists* (July/Aug. 1987): pp. 26–31.

———. "Reassessing Nuclear Power: The Fallout from Chernobyl." *Worldwatch Paper 75*, Washington, D.C.: Worldwatch Institute, March 1987.

———. "Reassessing Nuclear Power." *State of the World—1987*, Washington, D.C.: Worldwatch Institute, 1987.

Jagger, John. *The Nuclear Lion: What Every Citizen Should Know About Nuclear Power and Nuclear War.* New York: Plenum Press, 1991.

Kidder, Rushworth. "Ethics: A Matter of Survival." *The Futurist* (March–April 1992): pp. 10–12.

Kolata, Gina. "A Cancer Legacy from Chernobyl." *The New York Times* (3 September 1992): p. A9.

Lenssen, Nicholas. "Nuclear Waste: The Problem That Won't Go Away." *Worldwatch Paper 106*, Washington, D.C: Worldwatch Institute, 1991.

Levin, S. K. "Who'll Pay For U. S. Chernobyl?" *The Nation* (14 June 1986): pp. 815–818.

Lilienthal, David E. *Atomic Energy: A New Start.* New York: Harper & Row, 1980.

Lockwood, Robert P. "More Heat at Chernobyl." *TIME* (9 May 1988): p. 59.

Lowrance, William W. *Of Acceptable Risk: Science and the Determination of Safety.* Los Altos, Calif.: William Kaufmann, 1976.

Medvedev, Grigori. *The Truth About Chernobyl* (1989). Evelyn Rossiter, trans., New York: Basic Books, 1991.

Mortimer, Nigel. "Nuclear Power and Carbon Dioxide: The Fallacy of the Nuclear Industry's New Propaganda." *The Ecologist*, vol. 21, no. 3 (May–June 1991): pp. 129–133.

Munson, Richard. *The Power Maker.* Emmaus, Penn.: Rodale Press, 1985.

Myers, Nancy. "Coping with Chernobyl." *The Bulletin of the Atomic Scientists* (September 1992): pp. 8–9.

Nader, Ralph, and John Abbotts. *The Menace of Atomic Energy.* New York: W. W. Norton, 1977.

Patterson, Walter C. "Chernobyl—the Official Story." *Bulletin of the Atomic Scientists* (November 1986): pp. 34–36.

Powers, Thomas. "Chernobyl as a Paradigm of a Faustian Bargain." *Discover* (June 1986): pp. 33–35.

Raloff, Janet. "Source Terms: The New Reactor Safety Debate." *Science News,* vol. 127 (20 April 1985): pp. 250–253.

Rippon, Simon, et al. "The Chernobyl Accident." *Nuclear News* (June 1986): pp. 87–94.

Schemann, Serge. "Soviet, Reporting Atom Plant 'Disaster,' Seeks Help Abroad to Fight Reactor Fire." *The New York Times* (30 April 1986): p. A1. Also see supplemental articles by Harold M. Schmeck Jr., Philip M. Boffey, John Tagliabue, Michael Kaufman, Philip Taubman, Steve Lohr, Matthew Wald, Irvin Molotsky, Lee Daniels, and Theodore Shabad, same issue, pp. A1, A10–A12.

———. "Chernobyl Fallout: An Apocalyptic Tale of Fear and Power." *The New York Times* (26 July 1986): pp. 1 & 4.

———. "Soviet Ratifies Nuclear Accident Conventions." *The New York Times* (16 November 1986): p. A19.

———. "Chernobyl and the Europeans: Radiation and Doubts Linger." *The New York Times* (12 June 1988): p. A1.

Serrill, Michael. "Anatomy of a Catastrophe." *TIME* (1 September 1986): p. 26.

Starr, Barbara, and Richard Hoppe. "Battling the Backlash Against Nuclear Energy." *Business Week* (19 May 1986): p. 46.

Thompson, Gordon. "What Happened at Reactor Four." *Bulletin of the Atomic Scientists* (August–September 1986): pp. 26–31.

Weaver, Kenneth F. "The Promise and Peril of Nuclear Energy." *National Geographic,* vol. 155, no. 4 (April 1979): pp. 459–493.

Weinberg, Alvin M. "A Nuclear Power Advocate Reflects on Chernobyl." *Bulletin of the Atomic Scientists* (Aug.–Sept. 1986): pp. 57–60.

Wynne, Brian. "Sheepfarming After Chernobyl." *Environment,* vol. 31, no. 2 (March 1989): pp. 11–15 & 33.

Chapter 4 Oil in Troubled Waters: The Wreck of the Exxon Valdez

Barrett, Paul M. "Environmentalists Cautiously Praise $1 Billion Exxon Valdez Settlement." *The Wall Street Journal* (14 March 1991): p. A4.

Bavaria, Joan. "Business, Clean up Your Environmental Act!: Withholding Investment Can Influence Corporate Actions." *Newsday* (7 September 1989): op-ed page.

Boyd, Gerald M. "Bush Sends Team to Assess Cleanup." *The New York Times* (29 March 1989): p. B5.

Browne, Malcolm W. "Arsenal of Lasers vs. an Angry, Oily Sea." *The New York Times* (29 March 1989): p. B5.

———. "Spill Could Pose a Threat for Years." *The New York Times* (31 March 1989): p. A12.

———. "In Alaskan Disaster, Science Seeking Lessons for Marine Life." *The New York Times* (2 April 1989): p. A22.

———. "Alaska Bans Herring Fishing in Oil-Fouled Sound." *The New York Times* (4 April 1989): p. A1 & B8.

———. "In Once-Pristine Sound, Wildlife Reels Under Oil's Impact: Biologists Say Spill Could Set Records for Loss of Birds, Fish and Mammals." *The New York Times,* Science Times (4 April 1989): pp. C1 & C5.

———. "Experts See Glass Beads as Low-Cost Tool for Oil-Spill Cleanup." *The New York Times* (11 April 1992): p. 12.

Chasis, Sarah, and Lisa Speer. "How to Avoid Another Valdez." *The New York Times* (20 May 1989): p. 27.

Cushman, John H., Jr. "Alaska Cleanup May Drag into '90, U. S. Says." *The New York Times* (11 May 1989): p. A27.

———. "Sparks Fly at Alaska's Spill Inquiry." *The New York Times* (20 May 1989): p. L9.

———. "Coast Guard Studies Need for Improved Ship Traffic Control." *The New York Times* (26 June 1989): p. A17.

———. "Spill Panel Considers Pilots' Timing." *The New York Times* (30 June 1989): p. A10.

———. "Questions Unanswered in Tanker's Grounding." *The New York Times* (2 July 1989): p. 18.

Davidson, Art. *In the Wake of the Exxon Valdez.* San Francisco: Sierra Club Books, 1990.

Deutsch, Claudia H. "The Giant With a Black Eye: An Oil Spill Puts Exxon on the Defensive When Everything Else Is Going Right." *The New York Times* (2 April 1989): business section.

Dionne, E. J., Jr. "Big Oil Spill Leaves Its Mark On Politics of Environment." *The New York Times* (3 April 1989): pp. A1 & A12.

Egan, Timothy. "High Winds Hamper Oil Spill Cleanup off Alaska." *The New York Times* (28 March 1989): pp. A1 & B7.

———. "Fisherman Fear Spill Will Hurt into the 90's." *The New York Times* (29 March 1989): p. B5.

———. "Fisherman and State Take Charge of Cleaning up Alaska Oil Spill: Defensive Steps Taken After Company Fails to Halt Spread of Slick." *The New York Times* (29 March 1989): pp. A1 & B5.

———. "Exxon Concedes It Can't Contain Most of Oil Spill; Admits Delay in Cleanup; Coast Guard Officer Is Said to Have Smelled Alcohol on Breath of the Captain." *The New York Times* (30 March 1989): pp. A1 & A20.

———. "Elements of Tanker Disaster: Drinking, Fatigue, Complacency." *The New York Times* (22 May 1989): p. B7.

Feder, Barnaby J. "Group Sets Corporate Code on Environmental Conduct." *The New York Times* (8 September 1989): pp. D1 & D5.

Gold, Allan R. "Newport Spill Widens, but Harm May Be Limited." *The New York Times* (26 June 1989): p. A1.

———. "Pilot Says He Tried to Warn Tanker Headed for Reef." *The New York Times* (27 June 1989): p. A12.

————. "Exxon to Pay up to $15 Million for Spill." *The New York Times* (15 March 1991): pp. B1 & B2.

Golden, Tim. "Oil in Arthur Kill: Publicity and Peril for Urban Marsh." *The New York Times* (18 January 1990): pp. B1 & B4.

Graham, Frank, Jr. "Oilspeak, Common Sense, and Soft Science." *Audubon* (September 1989): pp. 102–111.

Gutfeld, Rose, and Allanna Sullivan. "Exxon, Alyeska Sued by Wildlife Group." *The Wall Street Journal* (18 August 1989): p. B12.

Hair, Jay D. (President, National Wildlife Federation), Memorandum to Lawrence G. Rawl, Chairman, Exxon Corporation, "Prince William Sound Oil Spill Disaster: Exxon's Responsibilities." (11 May 1989).

————. (President, National Wildlife Federation), Statement at the Exxon Corporation Annual Shareholders Meeting, (18 May 1989).

Holusha, John. "Chairman Defends Exxon's Effort to Clean Up Oil." *The New York Times* (19 April 1989): p. A21.

Keeble, John. "A Parable of Oil and Water." *Amicus Journal* (Spring 1993): pp. 35–43.

Laycock, George. "The Baptism of Prince William Sound." *Audubon* (September 1989): pp. 74–91.

Lemonick, Michael D. "The Two Alaskas." *TIME* (17 April 1989): pp. 56–66.

Lewis, Thomas A. "Tragedy in Alaska." *National Wildlife* (June–July 1989): pp. 4–9.

Luoma, Jon R. "Terror and Triage at the Laundry." *Audubon* (September 1989): pp. 92–101.

Malcolm, Andrew H., Roberto Suro, and Richard Witkin. "How the Oil Spilled and Spread: Delay and Confusion off Alaska." *The New York Times* (16 April 1989): pp. A1 & A30.

Matsen, Brad. "Fishermen Battle Pain, Anger and Spilled Oil." *National Fisherman* (June 1989): pp. 2–4 & 95.

Mauer, Richard. "Unlicensed Mate Was in Charge of Ship That Hit Reef, Exxon Says; Hull Seriously Damaged by Rocks 2 Miles Apart." *The New York Times* (27 March 1989): pp. A1 & B12.

McCoy, Charles, and Allanna Sullivan. "Exxon's Withdrawal of Valdez Pleas Will Maintain Pressure to Settle Case." *The Wall Street Journal* (28 May 1991): pp. A3 & A6.

McGinley, Laurie. "Valdez Decision Spreads Blame for Alaska Spill: Safety Board Cites Exxon, Skipper, His Third Mate, Coast Guard and Officials." *The Wall Street Journal* (1 August 1990): pp. A1 & A4.

Muscat, Paul, and Michael Gilson. "Oilfields Scar Arctic Wildlife Refuge Even Now." Letter to the Editor, *The New York Times* (4 April 1989): editorial page.

Revzin, Philip. "Years Temper Damage of Worst Oil Spill: Starkest Fears of 1978 Amoco Disaster Weren't Realized." *The Wall Street Journal,* p. A10.

Rothman, Andrea et al. "Who's That Screaming at Exxon? Not the Environmentalists." *Business Week* (1 May 1989): p. 31.

Schneider, Keith. "Transfer of Remaining Oil From Tanker Moves Slowly: Salvage Is Risky, Offer of Help Rejected." *The New York Times* (2 April 1989): p. A22.

———. "Under Oil's Powerful Spell, Alaska Was Off Guard: Enriched and Reassured, Industry and State Cut Disaster Preparations." *The New York Times* (2 April 1989): pp. A1 & 22.

———. "New Equipment Enables Alaska to Intensify Cleanup." *The New York Times* (3 April 1989): p. A12.

Shabecoff, Philip. "Captain of Tanker Had Been Drinking, Blood Tests Show; Illegal Alcohol Level; Coast Guard Opens Effort to Bring Charge of Operating Ship While Intoxicated." *The New York Times* (31 March 1989): pp. A1 & A12.

———. "Oil Industry Gets Warning on Image: Lujan Says Public Reaction to Alaska Spill Could Block Drilling in New Fields." *The New York Times* (4 April 1989): p. B8.

———. "The Rash of Tanker Spills Is Part of a Pattern of Thousands a Year." *The New York Times* (29 June 1989): p. A20.

———. "House Panel Urges One-Year Ban on Oil Drilling off Much of U.S." *The New York Times* (30 June 1989): pp. A1 & A10.

Stevens, William D. (President, Exxon, U.S.A.) Statement before the National Ocean Policy Study of the Senate Committee on Commerce, Science and Transportation of the U.S. Senate, cited in Exxon Annual Report, 1986.

Stevens, William K. "Size of Oil Spill May Be No Guide to Its Impact." *The New York Times* (4 April 1989): p. C6.

———. "The Bay Was Lucky, Marine Scientists Say." *The New York Times* (26 June 1989): p. A16.

———. "Despite Gains, Dealing With Big Oil Spills Is Still a Struggle." *The New York Times* (27 June 1989): environment section.

Stevenson, Richard W. "Why Exxon's Woes Worry ARCO: Thriving ARCO May Be Hard-hit if Congress Curbs Alaskan Exploration." *The New York Times* (14 May 1989): business section.

Sullivan, Allanna. "Exxon Discloses Oil-Spill Expenses Over $1.25 Billion." *The Wall Street Journal* (25 July 1989): p. 3A.

———. "Valdez Talks Didn't Consider Natives' Claims." *The Wall Street Journal* (13 June 1991): p. A6.

Sullivan, Allanna, and Amanda Bennett. "Critics Fault Chief Executive of Exxon on Handling of Recent Alaskan Oil Spill." *The Wall Street Journal* (31 March 1989): p. B2.

Wald, Matthew L. "Exxon May Have Small Liability for Spill Claims." *The New York Times* (28 March 1989): p. B7.

———. "Drilling Plans Point up Questions on Oil and Wilderness in Alaska: Industry Showcase or Environmental Disaster?" *The New York Times* (23 April 1989): pp. A1 & 30.

———. "Cleanup of Oily Beaches Moves Slowly." *The New York Times* (23 April 1989): p. A30.

———. "Angry Shareholders Confront Exxon Chief Over Alaska Spill." (19 May 1989): p. B1.

———. "Cleanup Efforts Fail to Hold Delaware Oil." *The New York Times* (26 June 1989): p. A16.

———. "Oil Spills Leaving Trail of Disturbing Questions." *The New York Times* (27 June 1989): pp. A1 & A12.

———. "Liability Issue Stalls Bill on Oil Spills." *The New York Times* (22 June 1990): p. A12.

Wells, Ken. "For Exxon, Cleanup Costs May Be Just the Beginning." *The Wall Street Journal* (14 April 1989): p. B1.

Wells, Ken, and Marilyn Chase. "Paradise Lost: Heartbreaking Scenes of Beauty Disfigured Follow Alaska Oil Spill." *The Wall Street Journal* (31 March 1989): pp. A1 & A4.

Wells, Ken, and Charles McCoy. "Out of Control: How Unpreparedness Turned the Alaska Spill into Ecological Debacle." *The Wall Street Journal* (3 April 1989): pp. A1 & A4.

———. "Exxon Says Fast Containment of Oil Spill in Alaska Could Have Caused Explosion." *The Wall Street Journal* (5 April 1989): p. A3.

Wells, Ken, and Allanna Sullivan. "Stuck in Alaska: Exxon's Army Scrubs Beaches, but Many Don't Stay Cleaned." *The Wall Street Journal* (27 July 1989): pp. A1 & A8.

Wieland, Anne Pacsu. "Legacy of an Oil Spill: Out of Anguish and Despair, a Challenge to Live More Harmoniously in Our Fragile Environment." *Swarthmore College Bulletin* (November 1991): pp. 10–15 & 63.

Wolff, Craig. "Exxon Admits a Year of Breakdowns in S.I. Oil Spill." *The New York Times* (10 January 1990): pp. A1 & B3.

———. "Leaking Exxon Pipe Ran Through Regulatory Limbo." *The New York Times* (11 January 1990): pp. B1 & B7.

Editorials and unsigned columns

Editorial. "The Consequences of Complacency." *Fairpress* (6 April 1989): p. A10.

"Tanker Spills Oil off Hawaiian Coast." *The New York Times* (4 March 1989): p. 6.

"Oilfield Practices Viewed as Threat to Land in Arctic." *The New York Times* (5 March 1989): p. A1.

Editorial. "Late and Lame on the Big Spill." *The New York Times* (12 April 1989): p. A24.

Editorial. "On Oil Spills: Trust Turns into Anger." *The New York Times* (28 June 1989): editorial page.

"Concern for Environment." *The New York Times* (2 July 1989): p. 18.

Editorial. "Dolphins and Double Hulls." *The New York Times* (14 April 1990): editorial page.

Editorial. "The True Cost of Energy." *The New York Times* (19 August 1990): p. E18.

Editorial. "Another Wake-up Call: Save Energy." *The New York Times* (4 September 1990): p. A16.

"Alaska Oil Spill Continues to Spread as Limited Shipping Resumes at Valdez." *The Wall Street Journal* (29 March 1989): pp. A3 & A8.

Editorial. "Fight on, Exxon." *The Wall Street Journal* (2 May 1991): p. A16.

Chapter 5 Forests of the North Coast: The Owls, the Trees, and the Conflicts

Adams, Brock. "A Comprehensive Forest Management Plan: Wood and Work for Washington: *S. 1536.*" U.S. Senate (July 1991).

Adler, Jerry. "Top Talon." *National Wildlife,* vol. 30, no. 2 (Feb./Mar. 1992): pp. 50–59.

Alm, Andy. "Log Fight Comes to Headwaters." *ECONEWS* (July 1991): p. 1.

———. "Who's Messing with the Forests?" *ECONEWS* (December 1991): p. 1.

Associated Press Report. "Northwest Loggers Challenge Rules on Spotted Owl." *The New York Times* (1 September 1991): p. 29.

———. "Land Bureau Seeks to Sell Protected Timber." *The New York Times* (12 September 1991): p. A26.

———. "Logging Limits Sought over Seven Million Acres." *The New York Times* (10 January 1992): p. A12.

Baden, John. "Spare That Tree!" *Forbes* (9 December 1991): pp. 229–234.

Barrett, William. "Aluminum Cow." *Forbes* (6 January 1992): p. 275.

Boland, John: editorial in *The Wall Street Journal.* (10 February 1988).

Booth, William. "New Thinking on Old Growth." *Science,* vol. 244 (14 April 1989): p. 141.

Botte, Gisela, and Dan Cray. "Is Your Pension Safe?" *TIME* (3 June 1991): p. 43.

Bowden, Charles. "Government First, Earth Last." *E: The Environmental Magazine,* vol. 3, no. 1 (Jan./Feb. 1992): pp. 56–57.

Castro, Janice, et al. "A Sizzler Finally Fizzles." *TIME* (22 April 1991): p. 61.

Caulfield, Catherine. "The Ancient Forest." *The New Yorker* (14 May 1990): p. 46.

Corn, M. Lynne. *CRS Issue Brief.* "Spotted Owls and Old Growth Forests" (updated 19 August 1991). Environment and Natural Resources Policy Division, Congressional Research Service, Library of Congress.

Egan, Timothy. "Economic Forces that Knock Down the Oldest Forests." *The New York Times* (8 October 1989): review section.

———. "Forest Supervisors Say Politicians Are Asking Them to Cut Too Much." *The New York Times* (16 September 1991): p. A1.

———. "Politics Reign at Spotted Owl Hearings." *The New York Times* (9 January 1992): p. A14.

———. "Trees That Yield a Drug for Cancer Are Wasted." *The New York Times* (29 January 1992): pp. A1 & A12.

Farrell, James. *National Wildlife,* vol. 29, no. 1 (December 1990): p. 28.

Findley, Rowe. "Will We Save Our Own?" *National Geographic* (September 1990): pp. 106–134.

Foreman, David, and B. Haywood, eds. *Ecodefense: A Field Guide to Monkeywrenching,* second edition. Tucson: Ned Ludd Books, 1987.

Friedman, Milton. "The Social Responsibility of Business Is to Increase Its Profit." *The New York Times* magazine (13 September 1970): p. 32.

Gup, Ted. "Owl vs. Man." *TIME* (25 June 1990): pp. 56–62.

Hamach, Tim. "The Great Tree Robbery." *The New York Times* (19 September 1991).

J. C., "Service to Whom?" *Greenpeace* (Jan./Feb. 1991): p. 6.

Johnson, K. Norman, et al. (The Scientific Panel on Late-Successional Forest Ecosystems, ISC) "Alternatives for Management of Late-Successional Forests of the Pacific Northwest: A Report to the Agriculture Committee and the Merchant Marine and Fisheries Committee of the U.S. House of Representatives" (8 October 1991).

Kelly, David, and Gary, Braasch. *Secrets of the Old Growth Forests.* Layton, Utah: Gibbs Smith, 1988.

Keyser, Christine. "Compromise in Defense of Earth First!: A Monkeywrencher Trial Ends, and No One's Happy." Sierra (Nov./Dec. 1991): pp. 45–47.

Manes, Christopher. *Green Rage: Radical Environmentalism and the Unmaking of Civilization.* Boston: Little, Brown, 1990.

McGourty, Kelly. "The Spotted Owl in the Media." Internship report for the Huxley College of Environmental Studies, Western Washington University (14 June 1991).

McKay, Tim. "Two Birds in Hand May Keep Trees in the Bush: Marbled Murrelet Joins Spotted Owl." *ECONEWS* (July 1991): p. 1.

———. "Crimes Bedevil National Forests." *ECONEWS* (December 1991): p. 5.

———. (Northcoast Environmental Center), and Felice Pace (Klamath Forest Alliance). "New Perspectives on Conservation and Preservation in the Klamath Siskiyou Region." 1991.

McNeil, Donald G., Jr., et al. "The Withering Woods." Special section on the North Coast forests, *The New York Times* (3 November 1991): review section.

Miller, G. Tyler, Jr. *Living in the Environment.* Belmont, Calif.: Wadsworth, 1990.

Mitchell, John G. "Sour Times in Sweet Home." *Audubon,* vol. 93, no. 2 (May 1991): pp. 86–97.

North Coast Redwood Interpretive Association. "Old Growth Redwood: Parks in Jeopardy." 1991.

Pacific Lumber Company, Annual Reports in general, especially the years 1981 through 1984.

Pollack, Andrew. "Lumbering in the Age of the Baby Tree." *The New York Times* (24 February 1991): business section, p. 1.

Porterfield, Andrew. "Railroaded: The LBO Trend on Wall Street Is Playing Havoc with the Nation's Forests." *Common Cause* (Sep./Oct. 1989): pp. 21–23.

Rauber, Paul. "The August Cove." *Sierra* (Jan./Feb. 1992): p. 26.

Reinhold, Robert. "Failure of S&L in California Could Save a Redwood Forest." *The New York Times* (27 March 1991): pp. A1 ff.

Schneider, Keith. "When the Bad Guy Is Seen as the One in the Green Hat." *The New York Times* (16 February 1992): review section.

Schneider, Paul. "When a Whistle Blows in the Forest..." *Audubon* (Jan./Feb. 1992): pp. 42–49.

Seed, J., et al., eds. *Thinking Like a Mountain: Towards a Council of All Beings.* Philadelphia: New Society, 1988.

Shepard, Jack. *The Forest Killers.* New York: Weybright and Talley, 1975.

Taylor, Bron. "The Religion and Politics of Earth First!" *The Ecologist,* vol. 21, no. 6 (Nov./Dec. 1991): pp. 258–266.

Tisdale, Sallie. "Annals of Place: The Pacific Northwest." *The New Yorker* (26 August 1991): pp. 37–62.

———. "Save a Life, Kill a Tree." *The New York Times* (26 October 1991): op-ed page.

U.S. Fish and Wildlife Service, Department of the Interior, Washington, D.C. "Economic Analysis of Designation of Critical Habitat for the Northern Spotted Owl" (August 1991).

U.S. Forest Service, Department of Agriculture; U.S. Bureau of Land Management, Department of the Interior, "Actions the Administration May Wish to Consider in Implementing a Conservation Strategy for the Northern Spotted Owl" (1 May 1990).

Velasquez, Manuel. "Ethics and the Spotted Owl Controversy." *Issues in Ethics* (Santa Clara Ethics Center), vol. 4, no. 6 (Winter/Spring 1991): pp. 1 &6.

Wilcove, David S. "Of Owls and Ancient Forests." *Ancient Forests of the Pacific Northwest* Washington, D.C.: Island Press, 1990

Wilkerson, Hugh, and John van der Zee. *Life in the Peace Zone: an American Company Town.* New York: Macmillan, 1971.

Williamson, Lonnie. "The Forest for the Trees." *Outdoor Life,* vol. 186, no. 5 (November 1990): pp. 54–58.

Wuerther, George. "Tree-Spiking and Moral Maturity." *Earth First!* (1 August 1985): p. 5 & 7.

Editorials

"Scientist on a Hot Seat." *National Wildlife,* vol. 29, no. 1 (December 1990): p. 28.

"Owlmageddon." *The Economist* (4 May 1991): p. 27.

Chapter 6 The Diversity of Life:
Chico Mendes and the Amazonian Rainforest

Ackerman, Diane. "A Reporter at Large: Golden Monkeys." *The New Yorker* (24 June 1991) p. 36.

Brooke, James. "Plan to Develop Amazon a Failure." *The New York Times* (25 August 1991).

Christian, Shirley. "There's a Bonanza in Nature for Costa Rica, but Its Forests Too Are Besieged." *The New York Times* (29 May 1992): p. A6.

Dold, Catherine. "Tropical Forests Found More Valuable for Medicine than Other Uses." *The New York Times* (28 April 1992).

Eckholm, Erik. "Secrets of the Rain Forest." *The New York Times* (17 November 1988): p. 20.

Environmental Defense Fund. "Brazil Creates Rainforest Reserve for Yanomamis." *EDF Letter* (April 1992).

Linden, Eugene. "Playing with Fire." *TIME* (18 September 1989).

———. "Lost Tribes, Lost Knowledge." *TIME,* vol. 138, no. 12 (23 September 1991): p. 46.

Myers, Norman. *The Sinking Ark.* Oxford, England: Pergamon Press, 1979.

———. *The Primary Source.* New York: Norton, 1984.

Perlez, Jane. "Whose Forest Is It, the Peasants' or the Lemurs'?" *The New York Times* (7 September 1991): p. 2.

Preston, Richard. "A Reporter at Large: Crisis in the Hot Zone." *The New Yorker* (26 October 1992): p. 58.

Revkin, Andrew. *The Burning Season.* Boston: Houghton Mifflin, 1990.

Sesser, Stan. "A Reporter at Large: Logging the Rain Forest." *The New Yorker* (27 May 1991).

Shoumatoff, Alex. *The World is Burning.* Boston: Little, Brown, 1990.

Tolan, Sandy, and Postero, Nancy. "Accidents of History." *The New York Times* magazine (23 February 1992).

Wilson, Edward O. *The Diversity of Life.* Cambridge: Harvard University Press, 1992.

Chapter 7 The Hole in the Middle of the Air: The Depletion of the Ozone Layer

Angier, Natalie. "Ultraviolet Radiation Tied to Gene Defect Producing Skin Cancer." *The New York Times* (19 November 1991): p. 53.

Browne, Malcolm W. "93 Nations Agree to Ban Chemicals that Harm Ozone." *The New York Times* (30 June 1990): p. A1.

———. "Costlier and More Dangerous Chemicals Foreseen in Saving Ozone." *The New York Times* (1 July 1990): p. 12.

———. "Ozone Hole Reopens over Antarctica." *The New York Times* (12 October 1990): p. A8.

———. "Worst Ozone Hole Stirs Health Fears." *The New York Times* (10 October 1991).

———. "As Halon Ban Nears, Researchers Seek a New Miracle Firefighter." *The New York Times* (15 December 1992): p. 23.

Fisher, David E. *Fire and Ice.* New York: Harper & Row, 1990.

Gleick, James. "Even with Action Today Ozone Loss Will Increase." *The New York Times* (20 March 1988): p. A1.

Gutfield, Rose. "U.S. to Step up Bid to Protect Ozone Layer." *The Wall Street Journal* (12 February 1992): p. A3.

Hansen, Beth. Insert accompanying Francesca Lyman. "As the Ozone Thins, the Plot Thickens." *Amicus Journal* (Summer 1991): p. 21.

Hilts, Philip J. "Senate Backs Faster Protection of Ozone Layer as Bush Relents." *The New York Times* (7 February 1992): p. A1.

Leary, Warren E. "Ozone Harming Agents Reach a Record." *The New York Times* (4 February 1992): p. C4.

Lemonick, Michael. "The Ozone Vanishes." *TIME,* vol. 139, no. 7 (17 February 1992): p. 60.

Mitchell, George, J. *World on Fire.* New York: Charles Scribner's, 1991.

Monastersky, R. "Nations to Ban Ozone-Harming Compounds." *Science News,* vol. 138 (7 July 1990): p. 6.

———. "Antarctic Ozone Bottoms at Record Low." *Science News,* vol. 138 (11 August 1990): p. 228.

———. "Pinatubo Deepens the Antarctic Ozone Hole." *Science News,* vol. 142 (24 October 1992): p. 278.

Oppenheimer, Michael. "Climate Catastrophe, the Rerun." *The New York Times* (27 April 1991): op-ed section.

Raloff, J. "Haze May Confound the Effects of Ozone Loss." *Science News* (4 January 1992): p. 5.

Schneider, Steven. *Global Warming.* San Francisco: Sierra Club Books, 1987.

Shabecoff, Philip. "Industry Acts to Save Ozone." *The New York Times* (21 March 1988): p. A1.

————. "Scientists Report Faster Ozone Loss." *The New York Times* (24 June 1990): p. 13.

Stevens, William K. "Ozone Loss Over U.S. Found to Be Twice as Bad as Predicted." *The New York Times* (5 April 1991): p. A1.

————. "Ozone Losses in Arctic Are Larger than Expected." *The New York Times* (19 September 1990): p. A 25.

————. "Summer-Time Harm to Shield of Ozone Detected over U.S." *The New York Times* (23 October 1991): p. A1.

————. "Peril to Ozone Hastens a Ban on Chemicals." *The New York Times* (26 November 1992): pp. A1 & A9.

Stolarski, Richard. "The Antarctic Ozone Hole." *Scientific American,* vol. 258, no. 1 (January 1988): p. 30.

Toon, Owen B., and Richard P. Turco. "Polar Stratospheric Clouds and Ozone Depletion." *Scientific American* (June 1991): p. 68.

Wald, Matthew. "Cold Season Loses its Chill." *The New York Times* (30 June 1991): p. 16.

Watson, Robert (National Aerospace Agency). Testimony before the Senate Committee on Energy and Natural Resources (August 1988) quoted in Schneider, Steven H. *Global Warming.* San Francisco: Sierra Club Books, 1989; p. 27.

"Researchers Report Depletion of Ozone in Temperate Zones." *The New York Times* (22 October 1991).

Chapter 8 Life in the Greenhouse:
Scientist Confront a Changing Climate

Allman, William F., and Betsy Wagner. "Climate and the Rise of Man." *U.S. News and World Report* (8 June 1992): p. 60.

Ausubel, Jesse H. "A Second Look at the Impacts of Climate Change." *American Scientist,* vol. 79 (May/June 1991): p. 210.

Bazzaz, Fakhri A., and Eric D. Fajer. "Plant Life in a CO_2-Rich World." *Scientific American* (January 1992): p. 68.

Broecker, Wallace S. "Global Warming on Trial." *Natural History* (April 1992): pp. 6–14.

Flavin, Christopher. "Slowing Global Warming: A Worldwide Strategy." *Worldwatch Paper 91*, Washington, D.C.: Worldwatch Institute, 1989.

Kasting, James F., Owen B. Toon, and James B. Pollack. "How Climate Evolved on the Terrestrial Planets." *Scientific American,* vol. 258, no. 2 (February 1988): p. 90.

Kerr, Richard A. "How to Fix the Clouds in Greenhouse Models." *Science,* vol. 243 (6 January 1989): p. 28.

————. "Hansen vs. the World on the Greenhouse Threat." *Science,* vol. 244 (2 June 1989): p. 1041.

————. "Clouds Keep Ocean Temperatures Down." *Science News* (11 May 1991): p. 303.

Lewis, Paul. "Island Nations Fear a Rise in the Sea." *The New York Times* (17 February 1992): p. A3.

———. "Danger of Floods Worries Islanders." *The New York Times* (13 May 1992).

Long, Larry. "Population by the Sea." *Population Today* (April 1990): p. 6.

Los Angeles *Times* Special Report. "Scientists Document Cooling Effect from Volcanoes." *The Hartford Courant* (13 December 1992).

Miller, Alan, and Irving Mintzer. "Global Warming: No Nuclear Quick Fix." *Bulletin of the Atomic Scientists* (June 1990): p. 31.

Mitchell, George J. *World on Fire*. New York: Charles Scribner's, 1991.

Monastersky, R. "Warming Shouldn't Wither U.S. Farming." *Science News*, vol. 137 (19 May 1990): p. 308..

———. "Swamped by Climate Change?" *Science News*, vol. 138 (22 September 1990): p. 184.

———. "Hot Year Prompts Greenhouse Concern." *Science News*, vol. 139 (19 January 1991): p. 36.

———. "Pinatubo and El Niño Fight Tug of War." *Science News*, (18 January 1992).

———. "Signs of Global Warming Found in Ice." *Science News*, vol. 141 (7 March 1992): p. 148.

———. "A Moisture Problem Muddles Climate Work." *Science News*, vol. 141 (4 April 1992): p. 212.

———. "Haze Clouds the Greenhouse." *Science News*, vol. 141 (11 April 1992): p. 232.

———. "Greenland Ice Shows Climate Flip-Flops." *Science News*, vol. 142 (26 September 1992): p. 199.

Oppenheimer, Michael, and Robert Boyle. *Dead Heat*. New York: Basic Books, 1990.

Oppenheimer, Michael, and Stuart Gaffin, Internal lecture for the Environmental Defense Fund (Spring 1992).

Pendick, D. "Debate May Resume over Volcano-Climate link." *Science News*, vol. 142 (14 November 1992): p. 324.

Raloff, J. "Tough Carbon Budget Could Slow Warming." *Science News* (2 December 1989): p. 359.

Scheuer, James H. "Bush's 'Whitewash Effect' on Warming." *The New York Times* (3 March 1990): op-ed section.

Schneider, Steven H. *Global Warming*. San Francisco: Sierra Club Books, 1989.

Sedjo, Roger A. "Forests: A Tool to Moderate Global Warming?" *Environment*, vol. 31, no. 1 (Jan./Feb. 1989): p. 14.

Shabecoff, Philip. "Temperature for the World Rises Sharply in the 1980s." *The New York Times* (29 March 1988): p. C1.

———. "Team of Scientists Sees Substantial Warming of Earth." *The New York Times* (16 April 1990): p. B7.

Simons, Marlise. "Scientists Urging Gas Emission Cuts." *The New York Times* (5 November 1990): p. A5.

Stevens, William K. "Study Supports Global Warming Prediction." *The New York Times* (14 December 1989): p. A36.

———. "In the Ebb and Flow of Ancient Glaciers, Clues to a New Ice Age." *The New York Times* (16 January 1990): p. C1.

———. "Clouds are Yielding Clues to Changes in Climate." *The New York Times* (24 April 1990): p. C1.

———. "Global Climate Changes Seen as Force in Human Evolution." *The New York Times (16 October 1990): p. C1.*

———. "Separate Studies Rank '90 as World's Warmest Year." *The New York Times* (10 January 1991): p. A1.

———. "In a Warming World, Who Comes Out Ahead?" *The New York Times* (5 February 1991): p. C1.

———. "Warming of the Globe Could Build on Itself, Some Scientists Say." *The New York Times* (19 February 1991): p. C4.

———. "Volcano's Eruption in Philippines May Counteract Global Warming." *The New York Times* (19 June 1991): p. A1.

———. "Estimates of Warming Gain More Precision and Warn of Disaster." *The New York Times* (15 December 1992): pp. C1 & C9.

World Resources Institute Report, 1987.

Wright, Karen. "Heating the Global Warming Debate." *The New York Times* magazine (3 February 1991): p. 24.

Chapter 9 North Against South: The UNCED Summit at Rio de Janeiro

Berke, Richard L. "Clinton Supports Two Major Steps for Environment," *The New York Times* (22 April 1993): p. A1.

Bethell, Tom. "Rio: What Happened." *Friends of the Earth* (August 1992): p. 8.

Bronstein, Scott. "Is Bush Trashing Earth Summit? Critics Say Yes." *Atlanta Journal* (3 April 1992).

Brooke, Elizabeth Heilman. "As Forests Fall, Environmental Movement Rises in Brazil." *The New York Times* (2 June 1992): p. C4.

Brooke, James. "For the Environmentalists, Hurdles on the Road to Rio." *The New York Times* (27 March 1992): p. A6.

———. "Cleaning the Environment for Environmentalists." *The New York Times* (14 May 1992): p. A4.

———. "Homesteaders Gnaw at Brazil Rain Forest." *The New York Times* (22 May 1992): p. A1.

———. "U.S. Has Starring Role at Rio Summit as Villain." *The New York Times* (2 June 1992): p. 10.

———. "Britain and Japan Split with U.S. on Species Pact." *The New York Times* (6 June 1992): p. A1.

———. "To Protect Bush, U.N. Will Limit Access to Talks." *The New York Times* (8 June 1992): p. A5.

———. "Earth Summit Races Clock to Resolve Differences on Forest Treaty." *The New York Times* (10 June 1992): p. A8.

———. "U.N. Chief Closes Summit with an Appeal for Action." *The New York Times* (15 June 1992): p. A8.

Carey, John. "Will Saving People Save Our Planet?" *International Wildlife* (May/June 1992): p. 14.

Collett, Stephen. "PrepCom 3: Preparing for UNCED." *Environment*, vol. 34, no. 1 (January 1992): p. 3.

Davis, Bob. "The Outlook—in Rio They're Eyeing Greenhouse Two-Step." *The Wall Street Journal* (20 April 1992).

Dillingham, Catherine et al. "Environmental Studies: a Noncosmetic Approach." *The American Biology Teacher*, vol. 37, no. 2 (February 1975).

Greenhouse, Steven. "Ecology, the Economy and Bush." *The New York Times* (14 June 1992): p. A1.

Haas, Peter M. "Climate Change Negotiations." *Environment* (Jan./Feb. 1992): p. 2.

Havel, Vaclav. "Rio and the New Millenium." *The New York Times* (3 June 1992) op.-ed. section.

Hazarika, Sonjoy. "India Dam Plan: Environmental Symbol." *The New York Times* (2 June 1992): p. A10.

Hertsgaard, Mark. "A View from El Centro del Mundo." *Amicus Journal* (Fall 1992): p. 12.

Kildow, Judith T. "The Earth Summit: We Need More Than a Message." *Environment, Science and Technology*, vol. 26, no. 6 (June 1992): p. 1077.

Lewis, Paul. "Rio Planner: A Magnate Who Meditates." *The New York Times* (4 June 1992): p. A10.

———. "Delegates at Earth Summit Plan a Watchdog Agency." *The New York Times* (7 June 1992): p. A20.

———. "U.S. at the Earth Summit: Isolated and Challenged." *The New York Times* (10 June 1992): p. A1.

———. "Negotiators in Rio Agree to Increase Aid to Third World." *The New York Times* (14 June 1992): p. A1.

———. "Storm in Rio: Morning After." *The New York Times* (15 June 1992): p. A1.

———. "Island Nations Fear a Rise in the Sea." *The New York Times* (17 February 1992).

Linden, Eugene. "Rio's Legacy: Despite the Squabbles, the Earth Summit Could Go Down in History as a Landmark Beginning of a Serious Drive to Preserve the Planet." *TIME* (22 June 1992): pp. 44–45.

Newhouse, John. "The Diplomatic Round Earth Summit." *The New Yorker* (1 June 1992): p. 64.

Nixon, Will. "Can Talking Heads Save an Ailing Planet?" *E Magazine*, vol. 3, no. 3 (May/June 1992): p. 37.

Schneider, Keith. "Bush Plans to Join Other Leaders at Earth Summit in Brazil in June." *The New York Times* (13 May 1992): p. A8.

Simons, Marlise. "North-South Divide Is Marring Environmental Talks." *The New York Times* (17 March 1992): p. A8.

Speth, James Gustave. "On the Road to Sustainability." *Environment, Science and Technology*, vol. 26, no. 6 (June 1992): 1075.

Stevens, William K. "Washington Odd Man out, May Shift on Climate." *The New York Times* (18 February 1992): p. C1.

———. "White House Vows Action to Cut U.S. Global Warming Gases." *The New York Times* (28 February 1992): p. A6.

———. "Striving for Balance." *The New York Times* (24 May 1992).

———. "Rio: A Start on Managing What's Left of this Place." *The New York Times* (31 May 1992): p. A1.

———. "U.N. Chief Charts Defense of Nature." *The New York Times* (4 June 1992): p. A10.

————. "To U.S., Treaty's Flaws Outweigh Its Benefits." *The New York Times* (6 June 1992).

————. "U.S., Trying to Buff Its Image, Defends the Forests." *The New York Times* (7 June 1992).

————. "Bush Plan to Save Forests Is Blocked by Poor Countries." *The New York Times* (9 June 1992): p. A1.

————. "Earth Summit Finds the Years of Optimism Are a Fading Memory." *The New York Times* (9 June 1992): p. C4.

————. "Lessons of Rio: a New Prominence and an Effective Blandness." *The New York Times* (14 June 1992).

————. "U.S. Cracks Door to World Forest Agreement." *The New York Times* (13 April 1993): p. C4.

Wines, Michael. "Bush Leaves Rio with Shots at Critics, Foreign and Domestic." *The New York Times* (14 June 1992).

Editorials and unsigned columns

"Viewpoint: USC Tackles Global Problems." *Nucleus,* vol. 14, no. 2 (Summer 1992).

"The Talk of the Town." *The New Yorker* (4 May 1992): p. 28.

"The Talk of the Town." *The New Yorker* (29 June 1992): p. 25.

"U.S. Strikes Back at Its Critics." *The New York Times* (10 June 1992): p. A8.

Editorial. "The Courage to Bend in Rio." *The New York Times* (12 June 1992).

"U.S. Rejects Limits on Pollution." (wire services) *Philadelphia Inquirer* (25 March 1992).